"Those who consider Hans Loewald to have been one of the icons of the contemporary psychoanalytic world will be eager to get their hands on each of these thoughtful new books. The editors have put together rich and nuanced contributions by many of our most cherished contemporary psychoanalytic writers. This volume covers a multitude of perspectives, such as the intellectual history and evolution of Loewald's work, writers with whom he exchanged bold and far-reaching conversations, his well-known philosophical depth, and ardent approach to clinical and developmental issues."

Gerald Fogel, M.D., *Founding Member and Former Director of the Oregon Psychoanalytic Institute; Author,* The Work of Hans Loewald: An Introduction and Commentary

"This volume is explicitly intended to correct a surprising lack of emphasis on Hans Loewald's groundbreaking contributions to psychoanalytic practice and theory. Given how much ground ego psychology has lost to relational, British object relations, and intersubjective theories in our literature and professional conferences, many who trained or worked in New Haven are startled at what little credit is given to Loewald's contributions. It is as though Loewald's emphasis on internalization as well as the relational aspects of therapeutic action were not major steps in this evolution.

This book seeks to redress this gap while expanding on Loewald's ideas. Each chapter is written by an experienced analyst with clear familiarity and appreciation for Loewald's attempt at what a more self-promoting individual would have proclaimed a paradigmatic revolution.

Those interested in the history of psychoanalysis in the United States will find the early chapters fascinating. Carlson's description of Loewald's entry into the Western New England Psychoanalytic Institute and interaction with David Rapaport is illuminating, in particular, his contribution to Roy Schafer evolving beyond the ideas of Rapaport, his mentor.

Equally important was Loewald's interest in children and human development. The chapters on developmental issues and phenomena bring this often-unappreciated dimension of Loewald into view.

Finally, Loewald's longstanding interest in philosophy and the work of Heidegger highlight his impressive intellect and wish to keep psychoanalysis situated in the humanities and its focus on mind.

This book is a must read for anyone interested in the development of psychoanalytic thought as well as those whose interest lies more narrowly with therapeutic action. Several of its chapters should be included in any course on the historical evolution of psychoanalysis."

Alan Sugarman, Ph.D., *Training and Supervising Child, Adolescent, and Adult Psychoanalyst; Former and Inaugural Head, San Diego Psychoanalytic Center, Department of Psychoanalytic Education, APsA*

"These books show why so many people see Hans Loewald as the unmatched innovator in Freudian psychoanalysis and the most profound extender of its possibilities. Loewald brings out a whole new dimension of the Freudian mind. If you are disappointed that the Freudian discovery seems to miss the hopeful vibrance of human life, you will be amazed to see what Loewald draws from the tradition.

If you're a clinician whose old terms seem a little stiff and mechanical, your professional adventure will be refreshed when you see those terms spring to life. Loewald worked quietly without proselytizing, but his writing and teaching have kindled wide enthusiasm, and a Hans W. Loewald Center has formed, from which scholars and practitioners will explore applications of Loewald's outlook to the nature of mind and mankind, the workings of treatment and the more expansive use of theory.

Experts here discuss the philosophical grounding that silently underlies Loewald's thinking about, for example, the mental scrambling of past, present, and future and the role of 'futurity' in all present experience. Other topics include the history of his reception in the U.S.A., and the impact on clinical work, adolescence, a Loewaldian approach to gender, mourning, and finally, an obituary by a close colleague and friend.

This book, together with its companion, *The Emerging Tradition of Hans Loewald*, is a treasure trove for Loewaldians, and a prospectus for those who have wondered what all the fuss is about. It announces a new era of innovation that might, indeed, go far to secure a future for psychoanalysis."

Lawrence Friedman, M.D., *Clinical Professor of Psychiatry, Weill-Cornell College of Medicine; Psychoanalytic Association of New York*

"Loewald writes poetically: 'We would say that the patient instead of having a past, is his past. He does not distinguish himself as a rememberer from the content of his memory.'

This wonderful book conveys how the language of Loewald speaks to us profoundly, enlightens us, helps us clinically and theoretically, and conveys also that psychoanalysis may be approached in many different ways. Loewald has engaged Freud in such a complex fashion that we too become deeply involved with his investigation. I believe that everyone in the psychoanalytic field is looking towards the future and can benefit from this exciting, new encounter with Loewald."

Haydee Faimberg, M.D., *Training and Supervising Analyst, Paris Psychoanalytical Society (SPP); Author of* The Telescoping of Generations *(2005); winner of the Sigourney Award for Outstanding Achievement (2013)*

The Legacy and Promise of Hans Loewald

Alongside its continuing volume, *The Emerging Tradition of Hans Loewald,* this rich collection of essays addresses the current lack of familiarity with the ideas and life of the eminent psychoanalytic teacher and scholar, Hans Loewald (1906–1993), by presenting the most comprehensive account of his work ever produced.

Its chapters present Loewald's intellectual history and his reception in the North American psychoanalytic scene, as well as clinical developments from his thinking and their importance for the future. An obituary, written by a close friend, also provides a summary of Loewald's personal and professional life. With the benefit of authors being able to detect the functions and place of Heidegger's teaching in Loewald's thought, this book will newly enlighten readers to Heidegger's place in Loewald's expansive, open-system vision of the psyche.

Featuring contributions from those who worked directly with Loewald, and those inspired by his ideas, this book will be essential reading for any psychoanalyst or psychotherapist working today.

Rosemary H. Balsam, F.R.C.Psych., M.R.C.P., is Associate Clinical Professor of Psychiatry, Yale School of Medicine; Staff Psychiatrist, Yale Department of Student Mental Health and Counseling; and Training and Supervising Psychoanalyst, Western New England Institute for Psychoanalysis.

Elizabeth A. Brett, Ph.D., is in private practice in New Haven, Connecticut, and a training and supervising analyst at the Western New England Institute for Psychoanalysis.

Lawrence Levenson, M.D., is Training and Supervising Psychoanalyst and former Chair of the Education Committee at the Western New England Institute for Psychoanalysis.

The Lines of Development

Evolution of Theory and Practice over the Decades Series
Series Editors: Joan Raphael-Leff, Aleksandar Dimitrijević and Norka T. Malberg

The Anna Freud Tradition
Lines of Development - Evolution of Theory and PrWactice over the Decades
Edited By Norka T. Malberg, Joan Raphael-Leff

Fairbairn and the Object Relations Tradition
Edited By Graham S. Clarke, David E. Scharff

The Winnicott Tradition
Lines of Development-Evolution of Theory and Practice over the Decades
Edited By Margaret Boyle Spelman, Frances Thomson-Salo

The W.R. Bion Tradition
Edited By Howard B. Levine, Giuseppe Civitarese

The Lacan Tradition
Edited By Lionel Bailly, David Lichtenstein, Sharmini Bailly

The Klein Tradition
Lines of Development—Evolution of Theory and Practice over the Decades
Edited By Kay Long, Penelope Garvey

Ferenczi's Influence on Contemporary Psychoanalytic Traditions
Lines of Development—Evolution of Theory and Practice over the Decades
Edited By Aleksandar Dimitrijević, Gabriele Cassullo, Jay Frankel

The Marion Milner Tradition: Lines of Development
Evolution of Theory and Practice over the Decades
Edited By Margaret Boyle Spelman and Joan Raphael-Leff

The Legacy and Promise of Hans Loewald
Edited By Rosemary Balsam, Elizabeth A. Brett and Lawrence Levenson

The Emerging Tradition of Hans Loewald
Edited By Rosemary Balsam, Elizabeth A. Brett and Lawrence Levenson

The Legacy and Promise
of Hans Loewald

Edited by
Rosemary H. Balsam, Elizabeth A. Brett,
and Lawrence Levenson

Routledge
Taylor & Francis Group

LONDON AND NEW YORK

Designed cover image: Main image: Hans Loewald in his 20s, in Berlin; Left column: HL and sister Anna, with rocking horse; HL, aged 6 or 7, with sister Anna and his mother, on vacation, beside the Baltic Sea; HL hiking in the Black Forest; HL in Baltimore, 1948; HL on vacation at Monhegan Island, early 1980. All by permission of the Loewald Family.

First published 2025
by Routledge
4 Park Square, Milton Park, Abingdon, Oxon OX14 4RN

and by Routledge
605 Third Avenue, New York, NY 10158

Routledge is an imprint of the Taylor & Francis Group, an informa business

British Library Cataloguing-in-Publication Data
A catalogue record for this book is available from the British Library

ISBN: 9781032357348 (hbk)
ISBN: 9781032357331 (pbk)
ISBN: 9781003328230 (ebk)

DOI: 10.4324/9781003328230

Typeset in Times New Roman
by codeMantra

Contents

Acknowledgements   ix
About the Editors and Contributors   xi
Series Editors' Foreword   xv
Preface by Warren S. Poland   xvii
Introduction   xix

PART I
Intellectual History and Evolution of the Work   1

1 Hans Loewald and American Psychoanalysis: Notes on the Reception
   of His Work   3
   THEODORE JACOBS

2 Hans Loewald and New Haven   12
   DAVID CARLSON

3 Hans Loewald's "On the Therapeutic Action of Psychoanalysis": Initial
   Reception and Later Influence   25
   SEYMOUR MOSCOVITZ

4 The How of Hans Loewald and the Possibility of a Hans W. Loewald Center   38
   JONATHAN LEAR

PART II
Philosophical Underpinnings   51

5 Philosophy, Heidegger, and Hans W. Loewald's Early Papers   53
   ELIZABETH A. BRETT

6 Loewald, Heidegger, and Freud: A Dialogue   65
   ROBERT S. WHITE

7 Future Tense and the Unthought New: The Not Yet—Something
   More—and the Horizons of Time   96
   ALFRED MARGULIES

8 On Being Grown-Up: Loewald's Concept of Maturity   108
   JOEL WHITEBOOK

PART III
Clinical Loewald   127

 9 Gender Formation: Building from Hans Loewald   129
    ROSEMARY H. BALSAM

10 Why Mourn?   145
    LAWRENCE LEVENSON

11 When the World Looms Large: The Drive to Develop in
    Adolescence and Analysis   158
    MATTHEW SHAW

12 Loewald and Winnicott   170
    NATASHA BLACK AND GIL KATZ

13 Obituary: Hans W. Loewald M.D. (1906–1993)   184
    T. WAYNE DOWNEY

    Index   189

Acknowledgements

I, RB, have been honored, blest, and companioned to have as my co-editors my loved colleagues Betsy Brett and Larry Levenson. They were and remain a delight on this journey on behalf of Hans. Anne Rodems, our friend and WNE administrator, was invaluably knowledgeable in helping us organize and transport our efforts across the interspace pond to Routledge.

We thank Paul Schwaber, my husband, for his loving support at all times and his deft and helpful editing skills. We all want to thank our families and close friends for their emotional encouragement. Our colleagues at WNE have uniformly been supportive and excited for us and the new Loewald Center, and some have expressed their vast admiration for Hans through their brilliant essays in this volume. From the bottom of our hearts, we thank our magnificent contributors – Warren Poland for this Preface, our supportive colleagues who provided promotional statements, and all of our dear friends who so willingly poured their passions, ideas, and scholarship into these chapters; Nancy Chodorow (our adopted WNEnglander) and Jonathan Lear (our own WNEnglander) for loyally allowing us to publish their plenary talks from the Inaugural Conference of LC in April 2022. We thank Margery Kalb too, whose enthusiasm and creativity in building the Loewald Center are recorded here, and whom we applaud.

And now we together would like to thank, first among our issue editors, Joan Raphael-Leff, who was responsive to the idea of including Hans Loewald in their issue series within their noble array of psychoanalytic ancestors whose work is still seminal. The seeds of this book happened in 2017, during her visit to WNE. She was a long-admired heroine of RB for her work on women, and they finally met. The idea for this book was born. Norka Mahlberg, her issue co-editor at that time was a member of WNE and fully aware of our pride in Loewald. Her support has been and is much valued, as has that of Aleksandar Dimitrijevic. Their affirmation has been crucial to this publication.

We would also like to thank Routledge's Kate Hawes, and her team who came on board for the actual publication. We have appreciated their helpful interchanges along the way.

Next, we want to express our deep appreciation and ongoing pleasures in our colleagueship with the Loewald Center: Margery, Seymour, Gil, Chris, Doris, Matthew, Masha, Natasha, Barbara, Angela and Guy.

Most importantly, we would like to thank the Loewald family for everything they have helped us with, especially Liz and Caroline, who, in consultation with their other family members, have so generously been enthusiastic in supporting our requests and sharing information. As you will appreciate from reading these books, Hans was not the only gifted author with this last name! We are deeply grateful to them for their personal essays on these pages.

About the Editors and Contributors

The Editors

Rosemary H. Balsam, F.R.C.Psych., M.R.C.P., is a British medical doctor and an American psychoanalyst. She grew up in Northern Ireland, graduated Medical School at Queen's University Belfast, studied psychiatry, and moved to join the faculty of the Yale School of Medicine. She is Associate Clinical Professor of Psychiatry, Staff Psychiatrist in the Yale Department of Student Mental Health and Counseling, and a training and supervising analyst at the Western New England Institute for Psychoanalysis, New Haven, Connecticut. Her special interests are female gender developments, young adulthood and the body in psychic life, psychoanalytic education, and Hans Loewald's work. She was a member of the founding Board of Directors of the Hans W. Loewald Center. She has written award-winning papers and books and lectured nationally and internationally. On the editorial boards of the *Psychoanalytic Quarterly* and *Imago*, she is a former book review editor of the *Journal of the American Psychoanalytic Associatio*n. Her books are: *Becoming a Psychotherapist: A Clinical Primer; Psychodynamic Psychotherapy: The Supervisory Process; Sons of Passionate Mothering; and Women's Bodies in Psychoanalysis*, and her latest papers have been on Misogyny and the female body and Abortion. In 2018, she was a recipient of the Sigourney Award for Outstanding Psychoanalytic Achievement.

Elizabeth A. Brett, Ph.D., is in private practice in New Haven, Connecticut, and a training and supervising analyst at the Western New England Institute for Psychoanalysis. She is currently a lecturer in the Department of Psychiatry, Yale University School of Medicine and, for many years prior, an Associate Clinical Professor of Psychiatry (Psychology) and a recipient of the Outstanding Clinical Faculty Award. She conducted empirical research on combat trauma and has written research papers as well as articles about psychoanalytic perspectives on trauma. Related to this work, she served as President of the International Society for Traumatic Stress Studies. Her current scholarly interests include psychoanalytic theories of therapeutic action and technique. She was a member of the founding Board of Directors of the Hans W. Loewald Center.

Lawrence Levenson, M.D., is Training and Supervising Analyst and former Chair of the Education Committee at the Western New England Institute for Psychoanalysis. He teaches individual psychotherapy and group psychotherapy at Yale

University Health Services. He is a past recipient of the Menninger Prize from the American Psychoanalytic Association, and has been a Kohut Visiting Scholar at the University of Chicago and Visiting Scholar for the annual Paul Gray visiting scholar weekend. He currently is Treasurer and Board Member for the American Board of Psychoanalysis. He was a member of the founding Board of Directors of the Hans W. Loewald Center.

Preface

Warren Poland, M.D., is a psychoanalyst living in Washington, DC. He is the author of *Intimacy and Separateness in Psychoanalysis*, Routledge, 2017; and *Melting the Darkness: The Dyad and Principles of Clinical Practice*, Jason Aronson, Inc., 1996. He is a recipient of the Sigourney Award for Outstanding Psychoanalytic Achievement in 2009 and former Book Review Editor of the *Journal of the American Psychoanalytic Association*.

Contributors

Natasha Black, Ph.D., is an advanced candidate at the New York University Postdoctoral Program in Psychotherapy and Psychoanalysis. She is in private practice in New York City, and she teaches in the Pace University psychology doctoral program. She is a program chair at the Hans W. Loewald Center.

David Carlson, M.D., is a retired training and supervising analyst at the Western New England Institute for Psychoanalysis, an ex-chair of its Education Committee, and Clinical Professor of Psychiatry at the Yale University School of Medicine. In the American Psychoanalytic Association, he chaired the Committee on New Training Facilities, among others. He has written many articles, including, in 2003, A History of the Western New England Institute for Psychoanalysis: The First 50 Years. There is a lecture given in his name annually at the Western New England Institute for Psychoanalysis. He was a student, supervisee, mentee, and later long-term colleague and friend of Hans Loewald.

T. Wayne Downey, M.D. (1934–2021), was a training and supervising adult and child analyst at the Western New England Institute for Psychoanalysis, Chairman of the Education Committee and also of the Child Psychoanalytic Program for many years, Emeritus Clinical Professor of Psychiatry at the Yale University School of Medicine, and a major figure in the Yale Child Study Center. He was a talented clinician and teacher, and he had been in private practice for more than 50 years. His writing about child analysis, in particular, was compelling and creative.

Theodore Jacobs, M.D., is a Clinical Professor of Psychiatry (emeritus) at Albert Einstein College of Medicine and a training and supervising analyst at the New York and PANY Psychoanalytic Institutes. He is the author of two professional books: *The Use of The Self: Countertransference and Communication in the Analytic Situation* and *The Possible Profession: The Analytic Process of Change;* two novels, *The Year of Durocher* and *The Way it Ends,* and 65 papers on a wide variety of analytic topics.

Gil Katz, Ph.D., is a faculty and Training and Supervising Psychoanalyst at the Institute for Psychoanalytic Training and Research (IPTAR) and the New York University Postdoctoral Program in Psychotherapy and Psychoanalysis. He has written widely on enactment and is the author of *The Play within the Play: The Enacted Dimension of Psychoanalytic Process (2014).*

Jonathan Lear, Ph.D., is a Distinguished Service Professor at the Committee on Social Thought and Department of Philosophy at the University of Chicago. He trained as a psychoanalyst at the Western New England Institute for Psychoanalysis and serves on the faculty there and at the Chicago Institute for Psychoanalysis. His books include *Imagining the End: Mourning and Ethical Life; Radical Hope: Ethics in the Face of Cultural Devastation; Freud; Therapeutic Action: An Earnest Plea for Irony; Open-Minded: Working Out the Logic of the Soul; Aristotle: The Desire to Understand; A Case for Irony;* and *Wisdom Won from Illness.* They have been translated into 12 languages. He is a Fellow of the American Academy of Arts and Sciences.

Alfred Margulies, M.D., is a Training and Supervising Psychoanalyst at the Boston Psychoanalytic Institute. At the Cambridge Health Alliance, Harvard Medical School, he served as Director, Out-Patient Services; Director, Medical Student Education; Co-founder, the Program for Psychotherapy; and Associate Chair. He is a recipient of the Harvard Medical Prize for Excellence in Teaching, the Outstanding Clinical Psychiatry Award from the Massachusetts Psychiatric Society, and the American Psychoanalytic Sabshin Teaching Award. He serves on the editorial boards of the *International Journal of Psychoanalysis* and the *Journal of the American Psychoanalytic Association.*

Seymour Moscovitz, Ph.D., is a faculty member of the New York University Postdoctoral Program and the Institute for Psychoanalytic Training and Research, where he has taught courses in psychodiagnostics and contemporary psychoanalytic theory. He is a co-founder of the Hans W. Loewald Center. Since 1979, Dr. Moscovitz has occupied administrative, clinical, and supervisory roles in psychiatric and forensic settings. He is currently Director of Education and Training for the Health + Hospitals Family Court Mental Health Service in New York City. Dr. Moscovitz is a member of the Rapaport-Klein Study Group, and he has served on the board of the Psychoanalytic Research Consortium and the Association of Family and Conciliation Courts of New York.

Matthew Shaw, Ph.D., is a psychoanalyst for children, adolescents, and adults, teaches at the Yale School of Medicine, and is a Training and Supervising Psychoanalyst at the Western New England Institute for Psychoanalysis. He chairs the child and adolescent training program and has published a book and numerous articles. Dr. Shaw gave the Saltz Grand Rounds at Children's National Hospital, the plenary at the Association for Child Psychoanalysis, 2022, and the Beata Rank Lecture at the Boston Psychoanalytic Institute, 2022.

Robert White, M.D., is a faculty member of the Western New England Institute for Psychoanalysis. He chairs the program for psychotherapy training at the Western New England Psychoanalytic Society. He is a member of the International

Psychoanalytic Committee on Clinical Observation and Working Parties. He has written on the subjects of enactments, relational issues, and clinical observation, and he has a special interest in the study of fairy tales. A 2021 paper on Peter Pan, published in the *Journal of the American Psychoanalytic Association*, won the Deanna Holtzman Award from the Michigan Psychoanalytic Society. For many years, he was a member of an interdisciplinary study group of psychiatry and philosophy, with an emphasis on Continental Philosophy.

Joel Whitebook, philosopher and a psychoanalyst, is on the faculty of the Columbia University Center for Psychoanalytic Training and Research and was the founding Director of the University's Psychoanalytic Studies Program. In addition to many articles on psychoanalysis, critical theory and philosophy, he is also the author of *Perversion and Utopia: A Study in Psychoanalysis and Critical Theory* and *Freud: An Intellectual Biography.*

Series Editors' Foreword

The history of psychoanalysis is one of re-visiting, rewriting, and re-integration. Hans Loewald's life and work are an example of such processes at an individual level, as he navigated the spiral of a tumultuous, at times persecutory, yet also reparative external world. These volumes demonstrate the legacy of a highly creative yet disciplined theoretical writer and clinician. Loewald's writing is poetic yet well-structured and clear in delivery, both relational and developmental in a way that was ahead of its time. As illustrated by these volumes, his writing and life's work have inspired many analysts to explore beyond the corseted bounds of ego psychology while respecting and conserving its value both theoretically and clinically.

Furthermore, as many psychoanalysts know, making a difference in the lives of colleagues and patients' lives does not require too much fanfare. What matters is the capacity not only to connect with ideas but also to approach discourse and exploration with respect, dedication, and generosity. The chapters in these volumes illustrate the multiple applications of Loewald's work to interdisciplinary thinking while still maintaining a focus on the ever-evolving interaction between primary relationships and the many iterations of the self. Such is the case for many writers in this book whose professional and personal trajectories were impacted by what seems to be Loewald's kind and collegial manner, which remains a staple of the Western New England Psychoanalytic Society and Institute to this day.

These two volumes are the last in our series 'Lines of Development' – the evolution of tradition, theory, and practice over the decades, celebrating the lives of psychoanalytic 'giants' and their legacy.

Generally, chapters are commissioned rather than reprinted and drawn from an international pool of experts in this field, rather than just those 'close to home.' Series editors Norka Malberg, Aleksandar Dimitrijevic, and Joan Raphael-Leff helped each volume in the series to follow a similar basic presentation adjusted to the needs of any specific tradition. This included a **Historical Frame** giving an overview of the tradition, its origins, historical milestones, influences, viewpoints, and inspirations for contemporary development. **Clinical Applications:** to illustrate the evolution of theory and the expansion of original concepts and applications to clinical work with children, adolescents, adults, families, and/or groups (in different parts of the world). **Outreach:** how this particular school of thought has informed the work of allied professionals and thinking in other academic disciplines and social systems outside the consulting room. Finally, **Personal Reflections:** pertinent historical recollections from active participants in the process of growth and development of its ideas.

These two volumes on Loewald differ from the overall format of other books in this series. The three co-editors are situated in one location in New Haven, CT, rather than different countries or transcontinental locations which we advocated for other volumes, to ensure a wide variety of contributors from around the world. Nonetheless, the chapters in these two books are organized with the overall philosophy of this series, bringing to the reader a survey of the author's main contributions while exploring how they emerged in the context of his personal and professional life. The reader will take a journey through the landscape of the relational, the mystical, and the divine, the creative therapeutic dyad, Loewald's life, and his voice as it resonates in the work and lives of former supervisees, training analysands, and newcomers who find their voice in the writings of a quiet yet revolutionary mind.

Lastly, this series began as a way of preserving Anna Freud's work and legacy, a quiet yet productive force in the world of psychoanalysis. For instance, although Anna Freud's thinking about 'the best interest of the child' was influential in psychoanalytic and legal circles in the United States. However, like Loewald, their unassuming and humble manner restricted wider recognition of their ideas in our contemporary world. We trust that, as with Anna Freud's volume in this series, these two books will serve to illustrate the robustness of Loewald's theoretical ideas and their clinical application, lending themselves to discovery, revisiting, creative rewriting, and re-integration.

Norka Malberg, Barcelona, Spain
Joan Raphael Leff, London, UK
Aleksandar Dimitrijevic, Vienna, Austria

Preface

Why Loewald? Why Now?

Why Loewald *now*? We live in a world on fire, flames erupting everywhere. Society, civilization, war, and threats of more, the very survival of human life, even of our planet, are unsure. Great actions are called for. It is reality, not alarmism, that says the urgency is existential.

The danger is so great that apathetic global officialdoms and even slow-moving organizational psychoanalysis are now turning attention to such crises of burning need. Yet our efforts will *not* succeed and will turn to naught if we move forward, forgetting the individual.

And Loewald? In Loewald's concern for both the engagement with *and* the separateness of people at the very same time, he showed us that neither the individual nor the group can be helped if the other is ignored.

For me, Loewald always brings to mind the very first moment I met his thinking. My institute class was assigned his paper on therapeutic action (Loewald 1960). Reading him in that era, I was amazed that others seemed to slide over what felt to me stunning. His regard for the patient's *potential*, the patient's *own* possibilities, felt revolutionary, an attention to otherness not addressed at a time when depth and ego psychology were the focus. Loewald certainly did not minimize unconscious forces, as evidenced in his felicitous phrase of turning ghosts into ancestors, a goal tuned to what was hidden in the *patient's* own self.

Many years after I read Loewald's paper, I had an out-of-the-office experience that brought to life Loewaldian recognition of the other. In Florence for the first time, I came upon Donatello's incredibly realistic, life-sized wooden sculpture of Mary Magdalene, a figure so bereft as to seem real, frozen in horror and grief. Mesmerized by its power, and despite knowing it was a 500-year-old sculpture, I had a strong impulse to scream, '*There's a real person in there!*'

Loewald's statement about the patient's potential was *his* screaming, '**There is a real person in there**!' Not only a case to be treated, but a person to be understood. Helping *another's* self-inquiry and growth is Loewald's fundamental approach.

So why now? The world is in flames, or potentially so. Hatred and violence run amuck as people feeling threatened react by threatening others. Science has a hand in this. Scientific and intellectual advances now replace much of the need for human labor, possibly creating a world to which we humans cannot adapt. We have come from stone-age hunting societies, to settled agrarian cultures, and more recently, to the Dickensian horrors of the industrial revolution, with human lives often debased to commercial assets or victims.

Today, in our scientific society, we face a rush into the new realities of a strange world of artificial intelligence and virtual reality. Workers find their jobs obsolete. Those newly redundant turn their rage on others, turning blame on immigrants rather than robots. People need to be needed. People may not be able to live in a world where they feel themselves not needed.

Analysts may wonder whether the freedom to kill in computer games interferes with children taming aggression. Philosophers wonder whether virtual reality interferes with developing intimate friendships. Can humans adapt to what the human mind has wrought?

People fall back to what had been safe before the new dangers. They draw new lines between inside and outside, between good selves and bad others. *Tribalism* flourishes. Desperation for the survival of both self and group is the adaptive root of tribalism. The world can feel one of self *or* other.

And Loewald, now? Some problems can be *overcome* by power, but if power alone is involved, that progress is temporary at best. On the other hand, problems can be *resolved* only when understanding based on regard for the other is included, regard *even for the enemy other* as well as for oneself. Clearly, the monsters of self-glory who ruthlessly grab power will not respond to kindness, and their relentlessness demands the full force of our opposition. But those who support and empower them as the best way of getting along in the world, as they themselves see it, they require as well as deserve respectful thought.

The relevance of Loewald is therefore mighty. He calls us to insistent regard for the other. Loewald never lost sight of the other, even clinically working not to change the other but to be in the other's service, helping liberate the other to be the most possible of the *other's* own self. Once experienced, such regard in the face of difference spreads. *Respectful regard spreads, opening – not closing – new possibilities.*

The disintegrating fabric of society will not be saved if we forget that humanity is a tapestry woven of endless individuals, each alive in unique personal particularity. Even though respect alone is never enough, mutuality and kind governance cannot be achieved without an approach that includes such understanding.

Mindless power can win domination, but without respectful understanding, it perpetuates conflict. Loewald teaches us that the way to vanquish tribalism must include attentive regard for each unique other's self, whether individual or group, knowing that *only* such an attitude has both immediate and spreading effects. *Respectful* regard spreads. Thank you, Hans Loewald.

Warren S. Poland, Washington D.C.

Introduction

All of us influenced personally by this great scholar of psychoanalysis, we three editors want to present a comprehensive set of essays based on the work of our distinguished late colleague, the psychoanalyst, Hans W. Loewald (1906–1993).

We present two books that hopefully could be read together, or can stand alone. They will have the same introduction as they were created at the same time, except for the details of the content of each. This volume is called *The Legacy and Promise of Hans Loewald*. The other is called *The Emerging Tradition of Hans Loewald*.

"The Legacy" tells about Loewald's work, the history of its reception in North American psychoanalysis, its foundational philosophical influences, and its clinical dimension. His obituary concludes this work. The "Emerging Tradition" locates his oeuvre as forming a tradition that stands among those of other major figures of our field, represented in the volumes of Routledge's "Lines of Development" series. "The Emerging Tradition" shows Loewald's interdisciplinary application and potential contribution to sociology, anthropology, comparative theories such as Bionian, LaPlanchian and Italian field theories, language theory, music, religion, art, creativity, culture, feminism, and gender studies; to the latest neurobiology and psychodelic treatments; and to ideas of the origins of life. The man himself is animated at the conclusion of the two books by his students, analysands, colleagues, and family.

We want to showcase his thinking about psychoanalysis, as reflected by all these contributors who are significant authors in our field and who have found different aspects of his work vital to their own understandings of analysis. We passionately want to demonstrate the value of Loewald's thinking as a contribution to the contemporary field of psychoanalysis. Hans Loewald's efforts to re-interpret Freud always sought for even more complexity and subtlety within the initial expansive framework already provided. We want to show elaborations of Loewald's work that allow one to see how quietly influential he has actually become, although somewhat vaguely, implicitly, and disparately focused within the general literature at the present time. We would like his explicit influence on our field to become more recognized and familiar to readers. With these rich essays, we therefore hope to encourage and invite the field to focus more intensely on his work, to search its depths for guidance, inspiration, and help in grasping what may well be at stake for a newer world of the present century, with its huge changes in global communication, baffling uncertainties and instabilities, and more questions than answers in every walk of life.

These essays demonstrate Loewald's thrust in opening aspects of a theory of mind that readily can include processes that are founded on psychic development through every phase of the life cycle; a theory of mind that concerns itself with origins, love, aggression, and nature; with living, imagination, and culture; that shows psychoanalysis as a clinical therapy, enriches and is enriched by philosophy, science, religion, and the arts. His open analytic thinking transcends and does not exclude any particular school of psychoanalysis. Loewald currently, we believe, offers many useful conceptual tools for the consolidation and advancement of analytic thinking further into the twenty-first century and the future.

The significant books by Loewald and on Loewald are few and listed below. The last book was published over 20 years ago – a collection of his work published in 2000, by Norman Quist, with a brilliant and helpful introduction about the essence of his thought, written by Jonathan Lear. That book was based on his collected works that had been published by Yale Press in 1979, together with two of his monographs: *Psychoanalysis and the History of the Individual: The Freud Lectures at Yale University (1978),* and *Sublimation: Inquiries into Theoretical Psychoanalysis* (1988). In 1991, Gerald Fogel published a book that contains some key commentaries on Loewald's work. Here is a list of the few books:

Loewald, H (1979) *Papers on Psychoanalysis* New Haven: London Yale University Press.
Fogel, G (ed.) (1991) *The Work of Hans Loewald: Introduction and Commentary* Hillsdale NJ: Jason Aronson.
Loewald, H (2000) *The Essential Loewald: Collected Papers and Monographs.* 2000 (with an Introduction by Jonathan Lear) ed. N. Quist. Hagerstown. MD: University Publishing Group.

There have been some panels in the national analytic scene over the years. For example, one occurred at the Western New England Institute for Psychoanalysis, where Hans was present, to celebrate his birthday. It was published by the *Psychoanalytic Study of the Child* in 1989, Vol 44; A panel at the American Psychoanalytic Association was published in the *Journal of the American Psychoanalytic Association,* 1996, Vol 44; and another one was published in the same journal in 2008, Vol 56. The last one, again by the Western New England Institute, was published in the *Psychoanalytic Study of the Child* in 2018, Vol 71. Each panel noted that he was a major creative thinker who had, up to that point, been undervalued and predicted the field's major future appreciation for his contributions.

There is specific evidence about a gap between the awe that his stature inspires (in the abstract), if mentioned at conferences, and yet a notable lack of teaching and reading his actual work. Looking at the statistics on the PEP web archive, Donald Winnicott, for example, the most popular writer, has many thousands of all his papers downloaded per year. Thomas Ogden, as an example of a contemporary influential writer and thinker, has statistics also in the thousands for several papers. Loewald's "On the Therapeutic Action of Psychoanalysis" (1960), the paper by far the best known and read, is comparable in downloads to Ogden's third- or fourth-tier papers. His other papers fall off precipitously. We assume that these downloads reflect, especially, the papers that analytic teachers assign for classes rather than necessarily for personal research. We worry that a lack of exposure to his work may leave too many analysts uninformed about his interesting approaches and exciting ideas that they may actually find groundbreaking.

We believe there are many reasons for the enthusiasm that his name inspires, yet, it co-exists with a neglect of his oeuvre. The usual suspects are that he gives exceptionally few clinical examples; his technical language is too close to Freud's; and he is dense and overly intellectual to read. We agree only that he gave few case examples. There are other factors as well. Loewald had a long-standing antipathy for fostering any "school" of followers devoted to him alone. Unlike Melanie Klein, Heinz Kohut, or Jacques Lacan, say, he shied away from such promulgations on his own behalf. He did not travel to promote his ideas and teach his point of view, like Anna Freud, Wilfred Bion, or the contemporary Kleinians. Winnicott was often on radio broadcasts in the United Kingdom, which may have contributed to his household name recognition. Mitchell, the relationists, Ogden, and others are modern users of the internet, where their work is helpfully disseminated. Not so, Loewald. Consequently, he has remained "local," is best known within the United States, and likely more on the East Coast, where he made his home. The time has come to launch efforts to draw attention to the attractiveness and usefulness of his ideas and approach, despite his self-limiting activity during his lifetime.

In 2021, just before the Covid pandemic, some colleagues from the Institute for Psychoanalytic Training and Research called us at the Western New England Institute for Psychoanalysis with a thrilling invitation – to join with them in founding and creating a "Loewald Center" (the LC). Margery Kalb, Gil Katz, and Seymour Moskovitz and we three from WNEIP, with Doris Silverman, Matthew Von Unwerth, and Christopher Christian from IPTAR, formed the founding Board of Directors of the new LC. After multiple delays due to trying to conduct it *in vivo* but finally deciding on a Zoom event, we had our Inaugural Conference in April 2022. We were delighted with the enthusiasm of the presenters and also our responsive national and international audience. The organizational structure of this virtual center, beyond its foundation now, is a work in progress. It is dedicated to promoting the style of open thinking that Loewald brought to our field and that is generative toward innovations that are based on past substantial thinking. Some series of successful presentations have occurred in the past year. We encourage readers to look at the website, loewaldcenter.org, to find out what is going on.

For those who already know his writings, we hope you join in future discussions of the chapters of both of these books that we have edited simultaneously and feel encouraged to use and build upon his work. And for those readers who have not encountered him before, we wish you joy in the discovery of a great mind and a creative master of psychoanalysis.

The Content of "The Legacy"

The book is divided into three sections. Part I is called *Intellectual History and Evolution of the Work*. Part II covers *Philosophical Influences*. Part III is *Clinical Loewald*. An obituary ends the book.

We are aware that one approach would be to begin with biographical material about Hans Loewald, consistent with our claim that he may not be well known to readers. However, as his theory and its development in our field are not well known, we decided to focus on his intellectual history, from the beginnings in pre-war Europe through the presentation of his work and its reception in the United States up to the present. We have chosen to share something personal about who he was by closing this book with his obituary. "The Emerging Tradition" closes with a longer section on "Personal Loewald."

Warren Poland, for this Preface, calls Hans Loewald's theoretical contributions "mighty" (echoes of Johnson writing about Shakespeare). He has been an early enthusiast of Loewald's radical creativity and an admirer of the reach and human wisdom of Loewald for many years. We are honored to place his piece at the entry gates of "The Legacy." We hope that the essays in this book will show the reader why we agree wholeheartedly with him.

Part I, on "Intellectual History," opens with Theodore Jacobs, who gives an account of the beginnings of psychoanalysis in the United States and puts into context the 1960s and the cool reception of Loewald's vision. His emphasis on a two-person drive and hermeneutic interpretation of Freud's theory contrasted starkly with the more objective science of mind preferred by the "powers that were" in the New York Psychoanalytic Institute, where Jacobs was trained. Next, David Carlson, a close colleague of Loewald beginning in 1961, talks with deep knowledge of the impact that interactions with the major figures in psychoanalysis at Yale University and Western New England Institute – among them David Rapaport – had on Loewald's philosophical bent and clinical thinking. Carlson also describes Loewald's great, if subtle, influence on countless colleagues and students in New Haven. In discussing Loewald's profound influence on Jonathan Lear, Carlson writes that Loewald envisioned for his students – and this observation could well serve as an epigraph for this volume – "one not an epigone of one's teachers or predecessors but continually refreshed, enlivened, and broadened by fresh reencounters with, and recreation of, their thoughts." Seymour Moscovitz illuminates the initial as well as later psychoanalytic reception of Loewald's "On the Therapeutic Action of Psychoanalysis." Moscovitz traces the development of Loewald's paper from early, unpublished drafts and presentations (c. 1956–1959) to its eventual publication in the International Journal of Psychoanalysis in 1960. Significantly, and with the use of archival material, he documents the difficulty grasping the novelty, originality, and clinical implications of Loewald's ideas. Citation analysis illustrates the article's growing influence and broad cross-over appeal to analysts of various orientations. Jonathan Lear's chapter, "The How of Hans Loewald and the Possibility of the Hans W. Loewald Center," was the afternoon plenary of the Inaugural Conference of the Hans W. Loewald Center on April 30, 2022. In this essay, Lear brilliantly examines three much-admired passages in Loewald's writings to show how these passages work to produce a deep psychoanalytic intimacy between Loewald and his readers. Passages such as these, Lear suggests, provide the reader with the very psychic integration that the passage is talking about. The text becomes an occasion for therapeutic action. Loewald's writings, Lear concludes, restore psychoanalysis in our souls, inviting us to join him in a spirit of inquiry, engagement, and renewal.

Part II, "Philosophical Influences" in Hans Loewald's oeuvre, opens with Elizabeth Brett's careful detection of, in Loewald's earliest published work, the pervading influences of Martin Heidegger's thinking. Her teaching of Loewald's purposes and theory of development are profound, and she shows that even the few psychoanalysts who accepted his re-examination of Freud and his soaring proposals were puzzled over or minimized their origin. Stanley Leavy was the exception, recognizing the depth of Hans's absorption of his beloved continental philosophy as later applied to Freud. The formulaic generalization that "he was influenced by Heidegger" continues to be examined thoroughly and in depth by Robert White. In greater detail than in previous Loewald scholarship, White paints the continental philosophical context in which

Freud, Heidegger, and Loewald were working. He proposes that many of Loewald's ideas were formed in a three-way dialogue between Freud (acknowledged) and Heidegger (unacknowledged). The multi-faceted and challenging concepts of Heidegger are made accessible and visible as sources of influence on Loewald's vision, most centrally on his view of the psyche embedded in the world. Alfred Marguiles also takes up Heidegger's influence on Loewald, an influence that Loewald left largely unstated because of Heidegger's betrayal in supporting Nazism. Loewald's famous and important idea of "something more" for the patient, which Loewald understood in terms of the future and the superego, is, Margulies argues, "part of our existential background, a reminder, a call to us, of our transience, our finitude: we must not waste time, which is, after all, our very being: as in Heidegger's Being is time." Margulies builds on Loewald's existential insights about time and the human situation by bringing those insights into dialogue with contemporary psychoanalytic concepts that relate to time, specifically, après coup and transference-countertransference enactment, which he demonstrates with a compelling clinical example. To round out this section, Joel Whitebook tackles the almost passé concept of "maturity" in contemporary mental health and shows how Loewald fearlessly re-invigorates this concept for us, linking it to individuality and a moral responsibility for oneself as the culmination of progressive development – a state to be gained, lost, and painstakingly re-gained.

In Part III, "Clinical Loewald," Rosemary Balsam notes that Loewald never mentions "sex and gender" in those terms. But she expands on four places in his work relevant to the formation of an individual's gender portrait. The first is the mother-infant matrix, in which archaic gendered and sexed interactions between mother and child are created. She illustrates the intensity and enduring power of these interchanges in a passion-filled clinical example. The second and third areas are Loewald's account of the Oedipus Complex and superego formation. Balsam objects to the primarily male perspective on these two subjects. Arguing against the notion of parricide as the formative event in the development of the female superego, she cites the earliest encoded emotional and bodily interactions and the importance of the mother during female biological maturity – as the woman becomes a mother herself. She shows how this direction can be used to underpin a theory based on two different natal bodies out of our control that branch into myriad flexible gender formations that become our own. Loewald's "sublimation" informs the fourth and sexed universe of the human body and the processes of conception, embedded growth and creativity, and the powerful ferocity of birthing and violence of separation that, for Balsam, make the fecund female body central to these galaxies of a lived universe. Lawrence Levenson examines Loewald's profound insights into mourning through a close reading of Helen Macdonald's memoir about the death of her father. Mourning was, for Loewald, a driving force in psychic development. Macdonald's poignant story serves as biographical material for Levenson to illustrate Loewald's thesis that mourning, the healthy alternative to melancholy, leads to higher differentiation and organization of the self and object relations. Matthew Shaw compellingly presents the analysis of a teenager who comes of age during the pandemic and the social strife over the 2020 election. Shaw, a child and adult psychoanalyst, uses Loewald's thought to help him make sense of his patient and her analysis, thereby demonstrating the dynamism of Loewald's developmental theory of mind, especially in connection with adolescence. "Loewald and Winnicott," written by Natasha Black and Gil Katz, highlights areas of theoretical overlap in the writings of Loewald and Winnicott. Black presents rich clinical material from the opening phase of an analysis that she conceptualizes in Winnicottian terms. Katz, in commenting on Black's case, discusses how Loewald, like Winnicott, contributed to our understanding of the importance of holding, play, and interpsychic/transitional space in the earliest stages of psychic life and continuing throughout the course of life.

The best and most informative obituary telling the life of Hans was written by Thomas Wayne Downey, one of the psychoanalysts closest to him in New Haven. Wayne, a wise and creative child and adult analytic colleague, intended to contribute to this book but, alas, died in 2021.

Rosemary H. Balsam M.D., FRCP (London); M.R.C.P. (Edinboro).
Elizabeth A. Brett Ph.D.
Lawrence Levenson, M.D.

Western New England Institute for Psychoanalysis,
255, Bradley St., New Haven, CT 06510. USA.

Part I

Intellectual History and Evolution of the Work

Hans Loewald and American Psychoanalysis

Notes on the Reception of His Work

Theodore Jacobs

To understand the reception accorded Loewald's work by his American colleagues when it first appeared in the 1950s and 1960s, it is necessary to have both an appreciation of the analytic scene in America at that time and some acquaintance with the history of psychoanalysis here. In what follows, I will provide a brief sketch of the psychoanalytic situation in the mid-twentieth century in the U.S. and its development to that point.

A Brief History, by Decade, of How Psychoanalysis Expanded in the United States

It was in the early years of the twentieth century that analysis first appeared on our shores, carried here on the broad shoulders of Abraham Arden Brill (1874–1948). Brill was one of Freud's most devoted and articulate followers, and he made it his mission to disseminate Freud's great discoveries into the New World. Brill was born in Austria and came to the U.S. in 1889 as a youth of 15. Penniless and without a word of English, for several years he survived by virtue of determination, grit, and a capacity for hard work. Taking whatever odd jobs he could find, he managed to keep himself together while he learned the language and educated himself through dedicated reading. Curious about the world, he read pretty much everything he could get his hands on. Through this disciplined commitment to self-education, Brill was able to qualify to enter the City College of New York in 1901, when he was in his mid-20s. After studying science and math, he entered medical school at the College of Physicians and Surgeons of Columbia University and graduated in 1903 at the age of 29. Being interested in the mind and mental disturbances, Brill took a position at Central Islip State Hospital on Long Island, where, for the next 4 years, he devoted himself to the study and treatment of psychoses and other forms of serious mental illness.

In 1908, on the recommendation of a colleague, Frederick Peterson, Brill sought out further training at the famous Burgholzli Clinic in Switzerland. There he met Eugen Bleuler, Carl Jung, and Ernest Jones, as well as Freud, and he immersed himself in Freud's writings. Returning to the U.S. in 1909, he married and entered private practice. On Jung's recommendation, Freud invited Brill to translate many of his major papers into English. These translations were instrumental in introducing psychoanalysis to a

DOI: 10.4324/9781003328230-2

wider world of academics, professionals, and individuals in the creative arts. His first translation of Freud appeared in 1909 as *Some Papers on Hysteria*.

Along with Clarence Oberndorf, on returning to the U.S., Brill formed a study group of interested psychiatrists who met monthly at his New York apartment or the nearby Medical Alliance building to study and debate Freud's ideas. Most of the group consisted of colleagues who worked at Manhattan State Hospital. Fascinated by the revolutionary theories of the doctor from Vienna, the group members engaged in spirited discussions that often continued until well past midnight.

Learning about psychoanalysis, however, was one thing; attempting to apply Freud's theories, quite another. The first naïve efforts of these state hospital psychiatrists to do so were not notable for their success. One pundit[1] characterized these attempts by Brill's colleagues as a process of targeting a patient—perhaps an agitated one, pacing the floor of an inpatient ward, sneaking up behind him, and "analyzing" his complexes. Despite these awkward beginnings, interest in the new "depth psychology" grew in America. In 1911, Brill, along with several colleagues, formed the New York Psychoanalytic Society, the first such organization in the country.

This initial formation of an analytic society was followed soon after by the establishment of societies in Boston and Chicago. Local study groups also sprung up in various parts of the country. An interesting footnote to this development is that one of the first of these new groups was the Coney Island Psychoanalytic Society, an in-gathering of Brooklyn-based psychiatrists, social workers, and other interested mental health professionals who met to read Freud, just yards from the Coney Island boardwalk and in the shadow of the famed Cyclone rollercoaster (Beloff, Klein, Herzog, 2016). Brill was an industrious and dedicated proselytizer for psychoanalysis, and it was through his almost single-handed efforts that the new psychology gained a foothold in America. He lectured widely and took every opportunity to acquaint the uninitiated with Freud's theories.

While Brill's efforts and those of his colleagues led to increased interest in the new science, psychoanalysis also aroused much opposition. The same reactions of fear and hostility that Freud encountered in Austria confronted Brill and the early analysts in this country. In the early years of the twentieth century, psychiatry in America was under the domination and control of the medical establishment. Conservative and resistant to change, American medicine viewed the radical, unproven ideas and treatment methods of the little-known Viennese physician with much suspicion. And when it became known that Freud endorsed the idea that analytic practitioners need not necessarily be medical doctors, the opposition intensified. This led, ultimately, to the American Psychoanalytic Association restricting membership to physicians as the only professional group licensed to practice psychoanalysis. This decision had profound consequences for the development of psychoanalysis in this country, as many highly capable and creative individuals were barred from training at institutes affiliated with APsaA because their professional degree was not in the field of medicine. Despite the formidable problems he faced, Brill continued his educational activities with dogged determination, and he found receptive audiences to the wider view of the clinical practice of psychoanalysis in several psychiatric societies throughout the country.

Interest in Freud's work was enhanced by his visit to Clark University in 1909. Here, Freud met Brill and G. Stanley Hall, President of Clark University, and a leading psychologist trained by William James (rather than being a medical doctor), who subsequently gave important support to the study and practice of psychoanalysis in the U.S.

1920s

In the 1920s, increasing numbers of psychiatrists became interested in analysis. Several of them, eager to experience a personal analysis, traveled to Vienna and undertook treatment with Freud, typically for a period of between 6 and 12 months. On their return to the U.S., these pioneering analysands became leaders of the new psychoanalytic movement and were instrumental in teaching Freud's ideas and methods to younger colleagues. They also were active in giving talks to lay audiences, and because of their personal experiences with Freud, they were convincing when they spoke of the unique value of psychoanalysis.

1930s

In the decade of the 1930s, psychoanalysis was the subject of numerous newspaper and magazine articles and was taken up and popularized by other media as well. Plays and films about the unconscious mind and the psychoanalytic cure intrigued audiences, and the idea of the unconscious was also amply represented in works of art as well as in modern dance. Analysis was depicted as enhancing creativity, for example, by the Surrealist movement artists. A number of artists, writers, and performers thus sought analytic treatment. This interest in treatment spread to academics and the intelligentsia in general, and for the first time, Freud's works became required reading in college literature and psychology courses. While not expensive by modern standards, analytic treatment was still too costly for many young people to afford. In Hollywood, where analysis had become something of a fad, a group of young performers came up with an inventive solution to the issue of cost. They hit upon the idea of hiring listeners, individuals who, for a fee of two or three dollars a session, agreed to play the analyst. The listener's role was to sit behind the client and remain absolutely silent as the "patient," reclining on a couch, attempted to free associate. This treatment became quite popular, and a number of participants claimed that they had made great progress in this form of self-analysis.

One young actor reported that he was progressing quite well in his analysis and gaining a good deal of insight until a sudden disruption took place. Having listened for hours to what he viewed as repeated acts of foolhardy and self-destructive behavior on the part of his client, the listener could no longer contain himself. "Why in the world did you do that?" he suddenly burst out. At that moment, the analysis effectively ended. The spell was broken. The actor became self-conscious, could no longer free associate, and the treatment foundered. An early warning about the perils of not maintaining neutrality![2]

Although increasingly recognized as a fascinating, if mysterious, explanation of the mind and a therapy particularly suited to neurotic problems, until the early 1940s, analysis remained a limited and elitist treatment. Analytic patients came primarily from the wealthy class and from the artistic and entertainment communities.

1940s

After WWII, in the mid-1940s, all of this changed. Almost overnight, psychoanalysis became "the cure" America had been waiting for. Its popularity grew enormously, and potential patients vied for places on analysts' couches. This era, up to the 1960s, has commonly been known as "The Golden Age" of psychoanalysis in the U.S.

Two factors were chiefly responsible for this remarkable shift in public opinion. The first was the successful use of brief dynamic therapy—treatment based on analytic principles—that was introduced by the Army to treat soldiers who suffered from shell shock and other war neuroses. This important innovation in treatment was spearheaded by William Menninger, MD, who, with his brother Karl, was keenly interested in psychoanalysis. Together, they founded the first analytically oriented psychiatric hospital in the U.S. Remarkable organizers, the Menningers developed a program that taught analytic principles and their use in brief psychotherapy to Army psychiatrists tasked with treating soldiers who developed acute anxiety and other disabling symptoms on the front lines. This approach proved highly effective, and word of its success spread widely. This development greatly enhanced the reputation and growth of analytically oriented treatment as late as the 1980s.

WWII Immigration of European Analysts to the U.S.

The second growth factor for American psychoanalysis was also the result of the war. Starting in the late 1930s and continuing for 5 or 6 years, a large number of experienced analysts from Europe emigrated to the U.S. These analysts, many of whom were close to Freud and his original group of followers in Austria and Germany, changed the face of analysis in this country. Being far more experienced than their American counterparts, the émigré analysts soon became the dominant force in the major training centers in America (Kuriloff, 2013). These had been established several years earlier in New York, Boston, and a few other metropolitan areas in an effort to create formal, regulated, high-quality psychoanalytic training. Prior to their establishment, physicians who wanted to become psychoanalysts sought out mentors who served as tutors and supervisors, providing what education they could in theory and practice. Those Americans who had been in treatment with Freud and those who had worked with Brill became leaders in these training centers, but their qualifications as teachers could not match those of their European colleagues who had been immersed in psychoanalytic study and practice for many more years. As a result, the Europeans took over the institutes in the major centers, and from then on, their close adherence to Freud's theories and principles of technique became the model for generations of American analysts. What from the beginning stood out about the Europeans was, in fact, their fierce loyalty to Freud. He was "the Professor," their leader and hero, who had given the world the precious gift of depth psychology.

Freud disliked America, which he viewed as espousing modern pragmatic attitudes and superficial values and lacking a rich cultural heritage. He feared that his life's work would be diluted by American psychiatry and that the psychoanalysis he created would no longer exist. It would, instead, be converted into a superficial and practically oriented psychotherapy. This fear was shared by the émigré analysts, and they sought to protect psychoanalysis from this threatening Americanization of their leader's work. In their effort to do so, they rejected any analytic theory or way of working that differed in any substantial way from Freud's teachings. In practice, this meant the rejection and dismissal of the American Interpersonal School of Harry Stack Sullivan in Washington, DC, and of those Freudians who challenged any aspect of Freud's thinking. As is well known, this meant not only criticism of, but open attacks on, Karen Horney, Franz Alexander, Sandor Rado, and Sandor Ferenczi, among others. In Horney's case, the New York Psychoanalytic Institute attempted to exert censorship over her teaching, an effort that led to her walking out of the Institute in 1941 with a few supporters while singing the equivalent at the time of "We Shall Overcome."[3] Alexander became the bête noir of the Freudians, and his idea of the "Corrective-Emotional Experience" was lambasted as manipulative and anti-analytic. When it came to Melanie Klein, the American Freudians totally backed her rival Anna Freud and her group of loyalists in London and viewed Klein's work as speculative and unsupported by evidence, if not constituting outright wild analysis.

Winnicott's approach was also severely criticized as not truly analytic in nature, as his theories failed to emphasize some of Freud's fundamental ideas, in particular the importance of infantile sexuality and the power of the drives. When he presented a paper at the New York Institute, he was savagely attacked.[4] Perhaps not totally coincidentally, he suffered a heart attack a few days later and had to be hospitalized.

Students' assigned readings in most APsa Institutes were limited to approved texts, almost exclusively those of Freud and his followers, with exposure to no other points of view than a strictly drive-conflict model with an ego psychological emphasis based on Freud's 1923 work. An atmosphere of intimidation, subtle in some cases but less so in others, prevailed, leading to a stifling of critical thinking, freedom of expression, and creativity. It is important to say that the atmospherics of this era in U.S. psychoanalysis were less recorded in written texts as transparent theoretical disagreements. Rather, the history remains alive still in 2024, in the memory of those who remember the insistence of their teachers of that time and the insistent "rightness" of their personal analysts in their attitude toward their own interpretations.

The result of this chauvinistic and restrictive educational approach, passed on from one generation to another through institutes' teaching programs, training analyses, and widespread identification with the attitude of superiority and contempt for other perspectives that characterized the views of many of the traditional Freudian analysts, was to limit and retard the growth and development of American psychoanalysis for over three decades.

Enter Hans Loewald

This was the situation that prevailed when, in the mid-century, Hans Loewald published his innovative ideas.

Born and raised in Alsace-Lorraine and trained in Germany as a philosopher as well as in medicine and psychiatry in Italy, Hans Loewald was known for his scholarship and was highly respected by his peers. He came to the U.S. in 1939 and trained in analysis subsequently in this country. Unlike his fellow émigré analysts, however, who circled the wagons around Freud to protect his legacy and reputation, Loewald felt free in his work and writing to differ with "the Professor" while, in many respects, remaining a traditional Freudian analyst. The opening lines of his famous paper, "On the

Therapeutic Action of Psychoanalysis" (Loewald, 1960), made clear both his critique of traditional Freudian theory and his own broader and more inclusive view. In this seminal contribution, one that was to have a profound effect on American psychoanalysis, Loewald called for recognition of the importance of the environment, both in human development and in the analytic situation. By "the environment," he meant the human environment. In the field of development, this meant the crucial importance of the mothering person's influence on the psychological growth of her infant; in psychoanalysis, it meant the crucial importance of the analyst as a potential new object in the psychological growth of his or her patient. Although based on extensive experience and apparent to any objective observer of the analytic situation, what this paper said about the analyst's role in treatment and the therapeutic action of analysis had long been rejected by classical analysts. For these traditionalists, there was no question about the correctness of Freud's view that analysis worked by making the unconscious conscious and that the analyst's role was to make that happen by means of interpretation and interpretation alone. They contended that this fact is what distinguishes psychoanalysis from other therapies, which, they argued, primarily utilize suggestion and influence to achieve therapeutic results.[5] For Freudians to accept the idea that, in addition to his role as interpreter of the unconscious, the analyst functions as a new, influential object who makes an essential contribution to the effectiveness of analysis and the psychological growth of the patient, was to challenge Freud's conception of the therapeutic action of analysis and to acknowledge that when it comes to how it operates, analysis is not unique among the therapies. In 1960, they were not prepared to do, at least in their published writings on theory and practice (Brenner personal communication, 1985).

In reality, the situation was quite different. A number of Freudians, including some of the most distinguished names in psychoanalysis, made a point of using their personalities quite freely in treatment and deliberately creating an atmosphere of warmth, acceptance, and caring. As clinicians, they were highly disciplined and, in all other respects, close followers of Freud. But they saw no contradiction between being warm, human, and responsive to their patients and conducting a rigorous and effective analysis. In fact, they contended that in the way they worked, they were closer to Freud, the clinician, than to Freud, whose writings on technique (Freud, 1912) contradicted the way he actually practiced. And they deplored the approach of those fellow Freudians who, in the name of neutrality, maintained a cool, removed, unresponsive attitude in their work. Those colleagues, they maintained, were, in fact, creating an anti-therapeutic atmosphere (Kris, E.1956). In recent years, the late Anton Kris, son of Ernst and Marianne Kris, clarified and amplified this perspective (Kris, 1990). In doing so, he championed the changing view of technique that had begun to transform traditional Freudian analysis.

Loewald's contribution was in another sphere. Although those who were in treatment with him describe him as a kind, gentle, and caring individual who transmitted a quiet, low-key warmth (Stern, 2009), Loewald did not call for changes in well-established technique and always worked as a traditional analyst. Where he differed from his Freudian colleagues was not in the way the analyst works but in his conceptualization of the effect he has on the psychological growth and development of the analysand. Loewald was a developmentalist and believed that, in varying degrees, neurotic conflict—or psychosis—has the effect of impairing or disrupting normal development. This results in limitations and distortions in the affected person's thinking and perception that, in turn, impact her object relations and idea of self. Although he agreed with the central importance of insight, Loewald contended that "making the unconscious conscious" (the Freudian mantra of the "classical" analyst) and working through previously concealed conflicts, although key steps in the analytic process, were not, by themselves, solely responsible for the therapeutic action of analysis.

Disagreeing, then, with his strict Freudian colleagues who championed the traditional view of change, Loewald held that change requires that the patient gradually form a relationship with the analyst as a new, psychologically more mature object. The work together entails distinguishing this person from the familiar old, internalized objects in the transference. Ultimately, the patient can identify and use the new object through the positive traits he internalizes. Reconnections to the old objects also become available through the new objects. This growth-enhancing relationship was modeled on mother–infant interactions and, specifically, on the role that the mothering person plays in the psychological development of her child. Loewald's training in child psychiatry, as well as his experience as an analyst, had shown him that for patients to overcome the psychological arrests brought on by neurosis, a kind of neo-developmental process has to take place in treatment, with the analyst, akin to a mother with her infant, lending the patient her more advanced ways of thinking and being.

For this to happen, Loewald made it clear that sustained interpretation of the transference had to take place. Early in treatment, due to transference, the patient is bound to experience the analyst as an old and familiar object. The analyst as a new object can only emerge in time, as repeated interpretations of transference distortions made it possible for the patient to distinguish the new from the old. To accomplish this, the analyst has to work painstakingly in the traditional mode. For the new object to appear, he does not have to change his way of working. What changes is the patient's perception of the analyst, followed by processes of internalization and incorporation that gradually promote the addition and eventual replacement of pathological internal objects with new and healthier ones.

Unlike many Freudians, Loewald was not hostile to the relationalist group. He did not view relational theory as a threat to Freud's work. He saw it as adding a dimension to traditional thinking that was needed to bring it up to date with contemporary understanding of human development.

By the mid-twentieth century, significant studies of mother-infant interaction were underway in America, several led by analysts (Mahler, 1958). Their work, as well as ordinary observation, made clear the central importance, throughout life, of this primary relationship. This was not in dispute among Freudians. What was resisted was the application of this understanding to the analyst-patient relationship. For many traditionalists, to take this step was to alter Freud's view of the analytic situation and the therapeutic action of analysis, a step that, to them, was heretical.

Perhaps it was Loewald's prior contact with relationally oriented analysts that, in part, accounted for his appreciation of the contributions they were making to psychoanalysis? For several years after emigrating from Germany, Loewald lived and worked in Washington, D.C., at the time a Center for the Interpersonal Analysis of Harry Stack Sullivan. There he encountered Sullivan and read his work along with that of a number of his followers, including Frieda Fromm-Reichman, Thomas French, and Clara Thompson. Recognizing the validity and importance of much of their thinking, he developed a view of the analytic process that synthesized aspects of these relational theoretical interests with his essentially traditional perspective.

The Challenge

The fact, however, that Loewald's thinking departed from and challenged Freudian doctrine did not sit well with the traditionalists. They could not accept his interactional view of the analytic process, and some regarded his approach as inviting potentially dangerous engagement with patients (Moscovitz, 2014, p.582). Out of respect for his standing in the field as a prominent scholar and leading thinker, Loewald was not openly attacked in the way that Horney, Alexander, and Winnicott were. Privately, he was criticized as not being a "true Freudian" and having undermined the position of Freudian analysis in America (Brenner personal communication, 1998). Publicly, this view of Loewald's work was expressed not so much in words as by comparative neglect. Loewald's initial presentation of his ideas at meetings at Austen Riggs and the Western New England Psychoanalytic Society were met with mixed reviews. There was some recognition of its originality, but considerable criticism of his perspective as well. Rappaport also contended that there was nothing really new in his approach (Moscovitz, 2014). Later presentations at panels at APsaA and at a meeting of the International Psychoanalytic Association fared no better. They were paired with papers quite irrelevant to Loewald's ideas, and his presentation evoked little enthusiasm. This was also true of Loewald's paper on therapeutic action when it appeared in 1960.

American psychoanalysis, it seems, was not yet ready for Loewald's original and transformational ideas. That appreciation did come, however, over the next three decades. As the influence of the émigré analysts and their disciples waned in American Psychoanalysis and younger analysts read more widely in the Object Relations, Kleinian, and Relational literature as well as in the new American Independent tradition (Chodorow, 2019) featuring contributions of such authors as Poland (1988), McLaughlin (1958), Ogden (1997), and Balsam (1997), there also occurred increasing recognition of the way that Loewald's work has transformed our field, Fogel (1991) and Mitchell (1988).

Although equal appreciation of Loewald has not yet taken place to the same degree in other parts of the world (Zorzi personal communication, 2022), it is only a matter of time before this happens. For there is no doubt that through his originality, his vision, his deep appreciation of human development and its relation to the analytic situation, and his undoubted courage, Hans Loewald brought psychoanalysis into a new era—one that, building on his groundbreaking—and liberating—contributions, has opened the way to the continued growth and development of our field.

Notes

1 An informal past professional contact.
2 A story told to me (about 1980) by Norman Ryder, an analyst from San Francisco.
3 Karen Horney subsequently successfully founded, in 1941, The American Institute of Psychoanalysis and the Karen Horney Clinic in New York.
4 This claim supports both rumor in the U.S. and an account of Brett Kahr (1996), a London analyst, whereas a more recent account by an American from the NY Institute, Francis Baudry (2009), soft-pedals the issue. Winnicott's paper presentation in 1968 was "The Use

of the Object," which many NY analysts at the time claimed that they did not understand. One young and subsequently important child analyst present at that event was Samuel Ritvo. In later years, when asked about the event, he said, "Winnicott was a 'poet,'" which, however, was implied as condescension (personal experience). Old biases were not so easy to shift! (ed.RHB).

5 One of the Western New England Institute teachers from the 1960s and 1970s, Cryrus Friedman, MD, a training analyst taught by David Rapaport, regularly asserted strongly both of these ideas in his clinical teaching to my own class of candidates circa 1974–1978 (ed.RHB).

References

Balsam, R. (1997). Active Neutrality and Loewald's Metaphor of Theatre. *The Psychoanalytic Study of the Child*, 5:3–16.

Baudry, F. (2009). Winnicott's 1968 Visit to the New York Psychoanalytic Society and Institute: A Contextual View. *The Psychoanalytic Quarterly*, 78(4):1059–1090.

Beloff, Z., Klein, N., Herzog, A. (2016). *The Coney Island Amateur Psychoanalytic Society and Its Circle*. New York: Christine Burgin.

Chodorow, N.C. (2019). *The Psychoanalytic Ear and the Sociological Eye: Toward an American Independent Tradition*. New York and London: Routledge.

Fogel, G. (1991). *The Work of Hans Loewald: An Introduction and Commentary*. Northvale, NJ: Jason Aronson.

Freud, S. (1912). Recommendations to physicians practising psycho-analysis. Standard Edition 12:109–120.

Kahr, B. (1996). *D.W. Winnicott: A Biographical Portrait*. Madison, CT: International Universities Press.

Kris, E. (1956) On Some Vicissitudes of Insight in Psycho-Analysis. *International Journal of Psychoanalysis* 37:445–455.

Kris, A. (1990). Helping Patients by Analyzing Self-Criticism. *Journal of the American Psychoanalytic Association*, 38(3):605–636.

Kris, M. (1985). Personal Communication.

Kuriloff, E. (2013). *Contemporary Psychoanalysis and the Legacy of the Third Reich: History, Memory, Tradition (Psychoanalysis in a New Key)*. London: Routledge.

Loewald, H.W. (1960). On the Therapeutic Action of Psychoanalysis. *The International Journal of Psychoanalysis*, 41:221–256.

Mahler, M. S. (1958) Autism and Symbiosis, Two Extreme Disturbances of Identity. *International Journal of Psychoanalysis* 39:77–82.

Mahler, M., Pine, F., Bergman, A. (1975). *The Psychological Birth of the Human Infant*. New York: Basic Books.

McLaughlin, J. (1958). The Analyst's Insights. *Psychoanalytic Quarterly*, 57:370–388.

Mitchell, S.J. (1988). From Ghosts to Ancestors; The Psychoanalytic Vision of Hans Loewald. *Psychoanalytic Dialogues*, 8(6):825–855.

Moscovitz, S. (2014). Hans Loewald's "On the Therapeutic Action of Psychoanalysis": Initial Reception and Later Influence. *Psychoanalytic Psychology*, 31(4):575–587.

Ogden, T.H. (1977). *Subjects of Analysis*. London: Karnac.

Poland, W. (1988). Insight and the Analytic Dyad. *Psychoanalytic Quarterly*, 57:341–369.

Stern, S. (2009). My Experience of Analysis with Loewald. *Psychoanalytic Quarterly*, 78:1013–1031.

Chapter 2

Hans Loewald and New Haven

David Carlson

It was 1955 when Hans Loewald decided to leave Baltimore for an unusual psychoanalytic institute and psychiatry department in New Haven.

He had been born in Alsace Lorraine in 1906, 2 months before his father, a dermatologist, died of tuberculosis, then grew up in Berlin with his mother and an aunt until university first in Marburg, then in Freiburg, to study philosophy under Heidegger. As Hitler rose to power, Heidegger became a Nazi, prompting Loewald to turn from philosophy to the study of medicine and psychiatry in Italy, where he practiced in Padua until 1939, when the status of Jews in Fascist Italy became precarious, migrating to the United States for a residency at Rhode Island State Hospital to qualify for a medical license, then in 1941 moving to Baltimore for an intense 15 years. His first wife developed some kind of paranoid psychosis, and he was distressed, entered analysis with Lewis Hill and divorced his wife, taking custody and care of their two young boys. Analysis coincided with analytic training, and he graduated from the Baltimore-Washington Institute in 1946, having in the meantime finished a child psychiatry fellowship at the University of Maryland in 1941–1943.

His professional activities show a side not apparent in later years. He worked in a Baltimore mental hygiene clinic and gave a series of public lectures for parents on "Show Offs" and "When Children Feel Inferior" – and a lecture on Christianity and psychoanalysis that was published (Loewald, 1953) but was never mentioned in his bibliographies: he gave me a copy in the 1970s when I inquired about possible religious implications in something else he had written. The paper on Christianity and Psychoanalysis is a remarkably accessible, more direct version of the argument he soon afterward developed in Ego and Reality, that through an obsessional perspective, Freud saw the world and reality as intrinsically hostile and thus had a limited view of the potentials in development, that religious feelings can develop throughout the maturation process just as scientific thinking can.

His analytic papers employ a much subtler, more demanding style, as though to enlist the reader in an effortful exercise, like the experience of analytic listening or contemplation of poetry and its ways of engaging the reader; he was a great admirer of the French poet Paul Valery.

Baltimore-Washington was one of the oldest psychoanalytic groups in the country, and its members varied a great deal in their psychoanalytic educations, analytic

DOI: 10.4324/9781003328230-3

immersion, and orientations. Harry Stack Sullivan and many of his followers were prominent members. Most of the Baltimore-Washington group were American born anglophones, and consistent interpretations of Freud's work were not yet available, and Hans immediately, on graduation, became the teacher of the institute's Freud courses, reading Freud in German and discussing him in English. The immersion in German texts while he worked, lived his private life, and taught in English reinforced his previous Heidegger-derived sense that nothing can be definitively captured in words, that what matters is a never-ending process of seeking meaning. From those years came some of his perceptive revisions of, e.g., the Strachey translation, such as his saying, instead of "Where id was, there ego shall be" with "there ego shall come into being."

Jenny Waelder-Hall moved to Baltimore in 1946, just as Hans began to teach his Freud courses. She immediately clashed with Sullivan and organized a group dedicated to the views of Anna Freud and to strict observance of that version of theory and technique. Ongoing debates and intense battles between the two resulting groups ultimately led to a split into the Baltimore, more Freudian, and Washington, more Sullivanian groups, with Hans and his friends the Lidzes joining the Baltimore group.

In those Baltimore years, Hans developed and introduced the themes he would burnish and elaborate on over the rest of his life (Loewald, 1951, 1952, 1955).

In 1954, he remarried Elizabeth Longshore, a 15-year-younger woman who had endured repeated hospitalizations for tuberculosis. Several factors made New Haven attractive to the Loewalds and made them attractive to the psychoanalytic establishment in western New England. They had friends in New Haven; they had known both Ruth and Ted Lidz in Baltimore, where Ruth and Hans shared a waiting room until, in 1951, Ted accepted an appointment as Professor of Psychiatry in the newly reformed department at Yale. Ted Lidz urged the newlyweds to come to New Haven and set up meetings with several local analysts. As Loewald later recounted, he had also met Norman and Eugenia Cameron at a meeting in New York and had been deeply impressed and drawn to them (Loewald, 1976). Cameron, then the chair of psychiatry at Wisconsin, had just been recruited by Yale psychiatry chair Fritz Redlich for a position in which Cameron would do some teaching but otherwise be free to write and do research; so, he was another New Haven attraction. Interestingly, Cameron's move from a professorship in psychology then through a medical education and psychoanalytic training had come about when, bedridden with tuberculosis, he first read Freud's *The Interpretation of Dreams*. Tuberculosis again was the background of what became one of Hans's closest relationships. By the mid-1950s, effective antibiotic treatment was available, but Liz recounts that she suffered intense fears of relapse through her first 10 years in New Haven (Loewald, 2022, p. 222).

The Korean War had been underway since 1950, and the country was still shadowed by McCarthyite persecution of anyone sympathetic to the left. Loewald knew of the stance Eric Erikson, then a professor at Berkeley, had taken when the state legislature required the loyalty oath of all faculty in the University of California system. Failing to get California law changed, Erikson resigned and was recruited by Robert Knight to join the Austin Riggs Center in Stockbridge, Massachusetts, thus becoming the fourth training analyst from another center in the Western New England area, the others being Knight, and in New Haven, Alfred Gross and William Pious. Erikson's work in looking beyond biologically based factors in childhood development was already very well-known and, in some ways, paralleled that of Loewald, who also knew the work of Knight, a central figure in the American Psychoanalytic Association, and of David Rapaport, then the country's leading authority on meta-psychology. The Western New England senior analysts all had some experience in treating borderline and psychotic patients at Menningers and/or at Riggs; this was a time of "widening scope", and Hans's ego and reality formulations lent support and a fresh background to that work.

Having known the suppression of academic freedom first in Germany, then in Italy, and with McCarthyism rampant in America, Loewald found the unusual structure of Western New England, an institute designed to be completely independent of a psychoanalytic society and hence of non-academic pressures, appealing. All educational matters, promotions, appointments, etc., were done by the education committee. More importantly, Western New England from the outset was designed to stress research and theory much more than practice and was even organized at first into three divisions: metapsychology, research, and clinical issues. For years to come, almost all candidates at the institute held half- or full-time academic appointments. The new institute had fought successfully with the American Psychoanalytic Association for its right to train non-MDs. Psychologists were valued for research skills physicians often lacked, and over the next few decades, the institute's atmosphere was colored and enriched by research candidates from English literature, French studies, history, law, philosophy, and social work.

As for Yale's medical school, it was then more closely tied in with the rest of the university than was true in other places, and interdisciplinary work was very much encouraged.

Hans was actively recruited, greeted in New Haven with an introductory banquet in his honor and tours of the Yale campus and of available real estate, where his enthusiasm was tempered by learning that his first choice of a neighborhood was not available to Jews (Loewald, 2022, p. 216). The introduction continued with an invitation to the most dramatic, potentially most confrontational event of his career. He was invited to launch the 1956–1957 series of society meetings in September by presenting the paper he had been preparing – On The Therapeutic Action of Psychoanalysis – at a meeting in Stockbridge, where David Rapaport would surely be present. The Loewald-Rapaport confrontation frames Loewald's work in ways that persisted after Rapaport's death five years later, and the drama of it had much to do with Rapaport's character.

Karl Menninger had recruited Rapaport from the Osawatomie State Hospital after the psychologist administered Rorschach and Szondi tests to Menninger and astonished him with a lengthy and sophisticated report on the results. Rapaport had learned of psychoanalysis as a boy in Hungary from an older relative, a psychoanalyst who found it hard to write. The young Rapaport wrote two psychoanalytic books for that relative, both published before Rapaport's 21st birthday. He left for 2 years in Palestine, then returned to Hungary at the behest of a Zionist organization to promote youth recruitment. Four years ago in Hungary, he earned degrees in mathematics and experimental physics, a doctorate in psychology and philosophy, and a Montessori teaching certificate while undertaking two or three years of personal analysis. He is said to have learned testing "almost entirely on his own". He hoped psychoanalysis would produce a unified theory of thinking and learning, confirming the validity of Kant's view of knowledge as codetermined by experience and inherent mental tendencies (Rapaport, 1942).

He was intense and restless, worked endless hours, and expected others to do the same. His badly damaged, rheumatic heart led him to feel that his days were numbered, and he carried on as if life were a race against time. An insomniac, he read half the night and taught himself to take notes in the dark while tossing in bed.

Robert Knight claimed that in his first years in America, Rapaport had sat up most of each night reading the entire back issues of all the English language psychoanalytic literature, having already learned all of the German and Hungarian literature (Knight, 1961).

He worked incessantly and had almost no social life. Margaret Brenman noted that when he made a major point, he "pronounced it in a loud, evangelical, and absolutely authoritarian tone that hardly promoted discussion", and Merton Gill noted that "He discussed abstract metapsychology with the fervor of a political orator and the thunder of a Hebrew prophet" (Gill, 1967).

He criticized loose thinking and even in casual conversation required all assertions to be supported by precise and abundant references, demanding that associates and students recall not only exact passages but their page numbers. Transcripts of his famous series of Western New England metapsychology courses bear out the picture of an extremely intelligent, endlessly demanding, and severely formal seminar leader. One early candidate, the chief of Yale's psychiatric consultation-liaison service, took off a whole day a week to prepare for each Rapaport seminar, having found nights and weekends insufficient for the task (Pilot personal communication, 1961). By 1955, David Rapaport's special place in the institute was formally acknowledged when he was appointed Chair of the Department of Psychoanalytic Theory and faculty consultant. Preserved correspondence between Pious and Rapaport shows the latter acting as a de facto dean of faculty.

The therapeutic action paper Loewald presented in Stockbridge is an almost final version of the first three of the four parts that were published in 1960. He said in Stockbridge that a necessary part of his thesis would be a treatment of transference, which would require that fourth section. When that section did appear in the 1960 paper, its tone was more abstract than that of the first three parts and stressed the derivation of his view of transference from Freud's Chapter 7 discussion of Ucs-Pcs transference, as though to emphasize the scholarly, systematic quality of the work (Loewald, 1960). According to those who were at the Stockbridge presentation, he was cordially received, and the discussion was mostly positive, with the usual mix of those asking for explanations, etc. Seymour Moscovitz (2014), who carefully examined archival materials in the Loewald archive at Yale, has described some of the written responses to this work, letters Hans received in the days after his presentation, and concluded the reception had been muted; but that is not the impression of those who were there and is, I think, a natural conclusion to draw from written materials whose authors one doesn't know. And very few papers then or now draw so much written comment.

We have copies of Rapaport's underlinings and marginalia on a copy of the paper and of subsequent correspondence between the two men. In some ways, their interaction follows the pattern of the children's game: rock, paper, scissors. Each tries to show that his own point of view is more general and encompasses the other's formulation and only after the other fails to acknowledge defeat cuts into the other's statements. In the first letter, Rapaport draws Loewald's attention to local sources, including his own extensive writings, and tries to assimilate the paper's content into the earlier Hartmann, Kris, and Loewenstein (Hartmann, 1958). He also says he finds the emphasis on object relations in ego development too broad. Loewald challengingly writes back that he finds the traditional view of object relations too narrow and criticizes the tendency to view the ego as a defensive shield and the organism as a closed system whose drives are only secondarily related to the environment.[1]

Similarly, when Hans presented the fourth part of therapeutic action at a Western New England meeting a year later, Rapaport commented that it clarified genetic but not adaptive, economic, structural, and dynamic points of view – the framework he and Gill developed and described as necessary metapsychological points of view (Rapaport, 1950; Rapaport and Gill, 1959). This time Loewald responded that his paper hadn't been primarily from a genetic point of view but was more broadly theoretical, implicitly ignoring Rapaport's schema of points of view and stressing rather a view of secondary processes tied closely to primary processes (Moscovitz, 2014). Continuing to ignore some of Rapaport's comments, Loewald states in the published paper that a full discussion of pertinent literature was "a task which I have found it impossible to assume at this time".

The correspondence is of note for several reasons, especially as it highlights Hans's tendency to keep intensely held views expressed and debated off stage, as though to minimize public conflict.

After that exchange of views with Rapaport and 5 years after the latter's death, there was a new edition of the debate when the Knight Foundation underwrote a graduate seminar on internalization in the 1965–1966 academic year led by Hans and Roy Schafer. Roy was a lot like his mentor Rapaport: his was a clear, forceful manner with an impressive, instant recollection of references and a readiness to demolish an opponent's argument. He insisted that, for clarity, terms should retain fixed meanings, while Hans felt terms should not be frozen. A number of leading analysts from around the country were brought to New Haven and presented at meetings of the group, and from that time on, one began to see some opening in Schafer's views, which went on to diverge widely from Rapaport's. Schafer's *Aspects of Internalization* (1968) is clearly inspired by working with Hans but strikes out along Schafer's own path.

> One more adaptational vantage point was deliberately chosen by Hartmann; it is not the only possible vantage point for psychoanalytic theorizing. Indeed, the natural-science model itself is a theoretical option: rather than its flowing from 'the data', it is an *a priori* that determines the definition, selection and arrangement of data. Other *a priori* models, such as the historical and existential, though their adequacy for dealing with the full range of phenomena defined in Freud's psychoanalysis has not yet been established, are available as options for the psychoanalytic investigator and remain to be worked out and evaluated comparatively.
>
> (Schafer, 1970)

Much later, in a retrospective account of his career, Schafer (2000) describes the work on internalization as having begun his liberation from a kind of Rapaportian world view.

As for the rest of Western New England, Loewald either ignored opposing views if he couldn't subsume them under his own formulations or dismissed them with glancing acknowledgement, as he did in 1973 in *On Internalization*, where he noted that Roy Schafer had discussed the paper at its presentation in New Haven and said, "Nor can I consider here Roy Schafer's important contribution to the subject (1968) and his critique of my conceptions referring to an earlier version of the present paper" (Loewald, 1973).

For a few years, the institute's few senior analysts were stretched to fill one committee role or another; later, Hans generally was spared everything other than the one-day-a-month Education committee, and even there, he was later granted a year's leave of absence to work on some papers.

For Hans, New Haven provided an ideal place to expand on his thought while encountering in his daily work of teaching, supervision, and training analyses intelligent holders of other views in an institute held together in a kind of tolerance not found everywhere: students in the medical school, psychiatry residents, analytic candidates, and graduate analysts all came with considerable backgrounds in other psychoanalytic viewpoints. A description of the Yale and Western New England communities will convey something of New Haven's influence on Hans and of the climate he in turn helped shape.

Those who had been Yale medical students in the 1950s were exposed at least weekly to psychoanalytic thinking in a first-year course on human development through the life cycle, to physiology lectures and demonstrations by Karl Pribram, who was attempting to test out parts of Freud's *Project for a Scientific Psychology*, and to Harry Saxton Burr, who offered an elective course on "Philosophy of the Organism" based largely on work he had conducted in collaboration with the Canadian literary critic Northrop Fry (Burr and Fry, 1935). In their second year, students took a course on psychopathology taught by Loewald's friend Norman Cameron, and in the third and fourth years, weekly lecture demonstrations of psychopathology were given by an analyst, followed by a six-week full-time rotation through a VA psychiatric ward whose chief was always an analyst or analytic candidate. Even on medical rotations, students attended weekly rounds with Ted Lidz, who spoke of psychosomatic illness and, more generally, of the psychiatric and psychodynamic aspects of patients on each ward. All these courses, plus a number of electives and study groups, stressed the centrality of conflict and an emphasis on research: several professors told each class that private practice, as opposed to a life of teaching and research, would be a betrayal of their Yale educations.

Yale psychiatry residents in the 1950s and early 1960s were similarly immersed in psychoanalytic thinking, an emphasis on research, and the attempt to learn psychotherapy. Beginning residents were advised to buy Rapaport's *Organization and Pathology of Thought* and Charles Brenner's *An Elementary Textbook of Psychoanalysis*. On Saturday mornings, Brenner commuted from New York to lead weekly seminars for them based on his book, part of whose emphasis is suggested by the titles of two of his much later works, *Psychoanalytic Technique and Psychic Conflict* and *The Mind in Conflict*, as well as by a book of essays in his honor, *Psychoanalysis: The Science of Mental Conflict*. Rapaport's book was used not only for some of his metapsychology but also for his translations of otherwise inaccessible early psychoanalytically informed research, and several hours a week were spent in academic conferences led by analysts who had trained mostly at the New York Institute. Except for the section on student health, every service chief and every ward chief during Loewald's first few years here was an analyst or advanced candidate, and the emphasis on every service was on learning interview skills and psychotherapy, both for treatment purposes and as a necessary tool for research. More often than not, residents who later sought analytic instruction had spent a year at the Yale Psychiatric Institute, where Lidz's Baltimore origins held more sway, with seminars based not only on relevant Freudian texts but also on Sullivan and his followers and Kleinians.

There were sharply contrasting views: a few doors away from Hans's office, a Reichian analyst was practicing, and for a few years, two Reichians were instructors in the Yale department of psychiatry. Helmuth Kaiser, who had been a training and supervising analyst in Berlin and then in Topeka, came to Connecticut confident of being, like Hans, greeted and appointed a training analyst:, and the Western New England's education committee expected to appoint him. He had published in the German Imago and the International Zeitschrift in the early 30s, spending some years in what was then Palestine before heading to Menningers. Like Hans, he saw therapeutic change as a function of the patient-analyst relationship that in some ways inherited aspects of maternal relationships: unlike Hans, when he presented material, he stressed a face-to-face encounter and sought what he styled an egalitarian exchange, sharing his thoughts step by step, statement by statement, with the patient. His stance was thought, like Reich's, to have diverged too radically from what the WNE felt was psychoanalytic[2]: after participating in some society work and meetings, he resigned from the society and settled into private psychotherapy practice. Loewald in those times seems to have been mindful of hazards in being deemed "not psychoanalytic", avoided reference to Sullivan, etc.

So, the candidates Loewald encountered were often strongly influenced by other psychoanalytic thinkers, and he was exposed every working day to other points of view from psychiatry residents, candidates, and colleagues of every age. Their years of struggling to learn psychoanalytic theory and apply it to their work also left their mark, as it does on analysts of every age: the work of learning and of doing dynamic psychotherapy or psychoanalysis involves years of intense, difficult, and often painful focus on conflict in both the patient and oneself. To candidates and graduate analysts, any formulation minimizing the role of conflict was suspect. Loewald himself would have agreed, but his writing style – less insistent and always evocative of the maternal field – seemed to some students and faculty to dilute rather than enhance analytic theory.

Alongside admiring accounts of his clinical work was the complaint from the Baltimore years of an analysand who was to become well known – Heinz Lichtenberg – who complained that in his analysis Hans was lacking in empathy and unable to tolerate expression of feelings, apparently intent on analyzing him as a candidate who was expected to maintain an adult perspective at all times (Friedman, 2016; Khan, 2020). Lichtenberg blamed his analysis with Hans for his not becoming a training analyst, left to found his own institute, and published extensively, eventually writing on the history of therapeutic action and omitting any mention of either James Strachey or Hans (Lichtenberg, 2012).

What Hans wrote of his friend Norman Cameron could also have been said of Hans in his practice and in his attitude toward some students. He was "most endearing.

But he also could be quite intolerant and contemptuous of signs of artifice and duplicity in others" (Loewald, 1976). A young psychiatric colleague who had just stormed out of Loewald's office complained to me that "I don't think anyone has the right to challenge a devotion to teaching" (Fleming personal communication, 1963). A few weeks later, that colleague began to organize the Psychiatric Institutes of America, a large profit-making enterprise based in Washington. In a New Haven practice, one encountered patients and the occasional supervisee who had found Hans intolerant, to whom he referred, and whom most analysts would find quite appropriate, sometimes unusually interesting. Those who came or that he referred to me had in common a high social status, and in initial interviews, they spoke highly and defensively of their fathers and probably seemed pretentious.

Some candidates, if pressed, would dismiss his work, as they would other important psychoanalytic thinking, perhaps because of American optimism and passion for solutions with a reluctance to face a tragic sense of life. Then too, he stressed psychoanalysis and psychotherapy as ways to unlock potential, while mental health professionals felt pressed to focus on symptom reduction and, ideally, resolution. One graduate analyst, when pressed on his thoughts about Hans's 1951 Ego and Reality paper, claimed it was anti-Freudian, that everything worthwhile in psychoanalysis had been written before 1920 (Armstrong personal communication, 1976). In general, though, awareness of Loewald's value increased with the experience of the student or colleague, as though to illustrate that part of his work that captures the possibility of a lifelong enrichment of meaning.

In general, Loewald as a supervisor stressed reconstruction and overt transference interpretation less than most other supervisors, even though he clearly saw the universality of transference at a time that was not universally accepted among analysts.

Rosemary Balsam vividly describes the Loewald most students encountered:

> He was a slightly built man, a quiet presence who often sat crunched up as he listened to case material, his hand on his forehead like Rodin's *Le Penseur*; a man given to receptive, reactive listening, with an economical but incisive flow of words, a capacity to be blunt and not waste time beating about the bush. He frightened some with his air of austerity, but he also had a naughty twinkle and a great readiness to see humor.
>
> (Balsam, 2008)

Two of Loewald's analysands described his analytic manner: Hurwitz (1986) and Stern (2009).

Loewald's influence, in its broadest reach among candidates, was often a subtle one. He was known to those who had spent a year at the Yale Psychiatric Institute, where, together with other senior analysts in the community, he spent several hours a week supervising the psychotherapy of schizophrenic patients. His approach usually was most appreciated there, where his comfort in dealing with primitive thought and behavior and with rapid regressions and progressions gave courage to young therapists, and some of them continued to gain from his example as they went on to analytic work and to supervision with him. Most generally, students witnessed a psychoanalyst who expressed his thoughts clearly but almost gently; his presence contributed to the more "civilized" and tolerant atmosphere of Western New England.

Candidates were familiar with most of his papers, but his writings seldom lent themselves to the concerns of beginners, as he was not so obviously concerned with rigor and clarity but with keeping many perspectives open at once. To the neophyte, his writing sometimes evoked a sense of mystery. He opposed fixities of all sorts: ranging from Kant's inborn tendencies that Rapaport worked to develop, to developmental views involving resolution, as in his paper on the waning of the Oedipus Complex (Loewald, 1979).

The potential fault line in the Western England community's theoretical perspectives lay between the ego psychological explanations definitively expressed by David Rapaport on the one hand and, on the other, the more inclusive views of Loewald and of William Pious. Pious in his description of the nadir event in schizophrenia and the rapid or slow recovery of representational function – a phenomenon he considered universal but in most of us so rapid as to be unnoticeable while much slowed down to take minutes, days, or years in some schizophrenics – shared Loewald's more fluid, process – based view of psychic organization, and candidates responded to that view in both men. A few years later, Stanley Leavy's work also diverged sharply from the Rapaport and ego psychological orientations, with a beginning in linguistic theory progressing through French analytic literature and Lacan. Partly because of disillusionment when Lacan lectured at Yale and partly because of a shared interest in continental philosophy, in their later years, Stan and Hans met to discuss philosophical readings. Stan referred often to Hans and wrote appreciatively of his work, e.g. (Leavy, 1989).

Tensions along the Loewald-Rapaport fault line increased when Sam Ritvo became a training and supervising analyst a year after Hans. Sam was deeply immersed in ego psychological views of therapeutic action and development. He, like Al Solnit and Seymour Lustman, who joined in the next few years, were all involved in The Yale Child Study Center's longitudinal study designed and launched by Ernst Kris, and Ritvo and Solnit remained deeply engaged with the work of Hartmann, Kris, and Lowenstein, as well as with Anna Freud herself. Sam nevertheless attended thoughtfully to Hans's work, partly by appreciating Hans's child psychiatry knowledge, citing him repeatedly, and finally recruiting him for a panel on reconstruction at the Spring 1977 American Psychoanalytic Association meetings, where Sam's introduction to the panel frames its task in terms of Hans's paper on therapeutic action (Ritvo and Scharfman, 1979). Through many meetings that involved both men, I remained impressed by their mutual respect and modus vivendi, even though their approaches clearly differed, and Sam later devoted himself to the views of Paul Gray, who decried internalization as a form of suggestion and hence something to be minimized, if not avoided altogether, in analytic technique.

Recently, Chodorow (2004, 2020) has spoken of an American Independent Tradition, starting with Erikson and Loewald. The two men certainly did lead the way toward dealing theoretically and technically with the developmental influences of the external world, and both skimmed over any organic underpinnings of development. In his therapeutic action paper, Loewald cited Erikson's concept of the identity crisis as illustrating the way challenges and opportunities throughout life can reactivate earlier stages with a consequent reformation and enrichment. Erikson references Loewald once (albeit quite generously) in his 1962 plenary at the American (Erikson, 1962). This was indeed not a school with a web of interactions but a tradition that formed over the years. And it's of interest that both men originally German trained in U.S. institutes: Erikson in Boston and Loewald in Baltimore-Washington.

No chapter – perhaps no one volume – can do justice to the impact of Loewald's thinking on Western New England analysts. More than 40 graduates of our small institute cite him in publications, and his influence is apparent in many more papers, books, and presentations than bibliographies indicate. To mention only a few:

Rosemary Balsam has written often and in detail about both her experience of supervision with Loewald and some implications of his thought that open the way to many of her contributions. His view of development's enriching life through its whole course is just one example, in its having inspired her views on mother – daughter relations and development and, less remarked, the implications she finds for male development as well. Her openness to the body both extends and contrasts with Loewald's usually scant attention to the somatic (Balsam, 2015).

Donald Cohen, who went on to chair the Yale Child Study Center and to contribute heavily to the child analytic literature, was analyzed by Loewald and based many of his discussions of analytic work on Loewald's writings (Downey, 2003). Among other things, Cohen saw Loewald's view of drives as internalizations as a necessary theoretical step Anna Freud approached but just failed to see (Mayes and Cohen, 1996).

Sidney Blatt, whose 16 books and over 200 papers established new fields in the understanding and treatment of depression (Blatt, 1974) and in art and who mentored many of the world's leading clinical psychology researchers, was drawn to New Haven by the openness of the institute to psychologist trainees and the prospect of being able to work with David Rapaport. Rapaport's early death frustrated that plan, but Blatt worked closely with Roy Schafer, who was as much an authority on Rapaport as anyone. Loewald clearly inspired Blatt's seminal 1985 paper with Rebecca Behrends on internalization (Behrends and Blatt, 1985). Sid attributed the distinctive turn of his work to Loewald's influence, which is acknowledged in a number of his papers but that he said underlies all of them (Blatt personal communication, 1982).

Wayne Downey, another of Loewald's analysands, engaged in ongoing dialogue with him for decades and provided a creative combination of the views of Hartmann and Loewald on sublimation (Downey, 2000).

The poetic aspect of Loewald's thought is captured by another Western New England graduate in a remarkable paper that conveys a sense of Loewald's thought through a contemplation of Wallace Stevens's "Rage to Order" (Wexler, 2002), and yet another graduate related Loewald's view of the fantasy character of the psychoanalytic situation (Loewald, 1975) as a parallel to poet Stephen Dobyn's account of the actions of poetry (Brett, 2018; Dobyns, 1996).

Although Hans seldom wrote directly about technique and in fact worried that if he did, his words would be mistaken for advocating a warm, cuddly approach to the patient, a later version of the Rapaport-Loewald split years later involved leaders of the WNE. In two remarkably well-argued papers, Lawrence Levenson urged the importance of Gray's recommendations on technique (Levenson, 1998), and then Sidney Philips cited Levenson's work in using, among other sources, Loewald's views to put Gray's in another perspective (Phillips, 2006), a friendly version of the earlier rock-paper-scissors exchange.

Loewald's life ended miserably in several years of depression and organic mental decline, but before that, his intellectual life had come to a most rewarding full circle with Jonathan Lear, then Professor of Philosophy at Yale, seeking him out for a series of weekly meetings that extended over six years, during which Lear undertook psycho-analytic training at Western New England. Loewald thus came back to his first love of philosophy while facilitating Lear's entry into psychoanalysis, and conversation with the philosopher in turn stimulated Loewald's thought.

Since that Lear-Loewald time, Lear has so far published 12 books and innumer-able articles in both the psychoanalytic and philosophical literatures. He has expli-cated, extended, and put in widely ranging contexts lines of thought that trace back first through Loewald to Greek philosophers and to Freud, sometimes forward from the ancients through Loewald, then further into Lear's own, sometimes broader, ever-freshly, vibrantly expressed formulations. He exemplifies what Loewald began to en-vision: one not an epigone of one's teachers or predecessors but continually refreshed, enlivened, and broadened by fresh reencounters with and recreations of their thoughts.

It is likely that Hans's final, most abstract publication in turn reflects the influ-ence of his weekly talks with the younger philosopher. In "Psychoanalysis in search of nature: Thoughts on metapsychology, 'metaphysics,' projection" (Loewald, 1988). Loewald returns to the basis of his work: "With the psychoanalytic conception of the unconscious and of psychic reality psychoanalysis is stepping outside the bounds of nineteenth-century natural science and its interpretation (a hermeneutic construction) of nature as objective material reality". Fittingly, this last paper is still often said to be obscure and is only gradually coming into its own.

Notes

1 I earlier mentioned Rapaport's explicit commitment to an elaboration of Kant. Lear, in a remarkable footnote (1996), has described Loewald's development of a more fluid, lively extrapolation from the Kantian formulation.
2 For a description of Kaiser's point of view, see Fierman (1965).

References

Balsam, R. (2008) The essence of Hans Loewald. *The Journal of the American Psychoanalytic Association*, 56:1117–1128.

Balsam, R. (2015) Oedipus Rex: where are we going, especially with females? *The Psychoana-lytic Quarterly*, LXXXIV:555–588.

Behrends, R.S. and Blatt, S.J. (1985) Internalization and psychological development through-out the life cycle. *Psychoanalytic Study of the Child*, 40:11–39.

Blatt, S.J. (1974) Levels of object representation in anaclytic and introjective depression. *Psychoanalytic Study of the Child*, 29:107–157.

Brett, E.A. (2018) The play's the thing: Loewald's metaphors of the theater and the force-field. *The Psychoanalytic Study of the Child*, 71:217–223.

Burr, H.S. and Northrop, F.S.C. (1935) The electro-dynamic theory of life. *Quarterly Review of Biology*, 10:322–333.

Chodorow, N. (2004) The American independent tradition: Loewald, Erikson, and the (possi-ble) rise of intersubjective ego psychology. *Psychoanalytic Dialogues*, 14:207–232.

Chodorow, N. (2020) *The Psychoanalytic Ear and the Sociological Eye: Toward an American Independent Tradition*. London: Routledge.

Dobyns, S. (1996) *Best Words, Best Order: Essays on Poetry*. New York: St. Martin's.

Downey, T.W. (2000) Little Orphan Anastasia: the analysis of and adopted Russian girl. *Psychoanalytic Study of the Child*, 55:145–179.

Downey, T.W. (2003) Donald and his coat of many colors: an appreciation. *Psychoanalytic Study of the Child*, 58:291–306.

Erikson, E. (1962) Reality and actuality. *The Journal of the American Psychoanalytic Association*, X:451–474.

Fierman, L., ed. (1965) *Effective Psychotherapy: The Contribution of Helmuth Kaiser*. New York: Free Press.

Friedman, H.J. (2016) *Psychoanalytic Theory, Research, and Clinical Practice: Reading Joseph D. Lichtenberg*. Edited by L. Gunsberg and S. Hershberg. New York: Routledge. *The Journal of the American Psychoanalytic Association*, 64:1283–1287.

Gill, M.M. (1967) *Foreword to The Collected Papers of David Rapaport*. New York: Basic Books, p. 3.

Hans, W. (1988) *Loewald Papers. Manuscripts and Archives*. New Haven, CT: Yale University Library.

Hartmann, H. (1958) *Ego Psychology and the Problem of Adaptation*. New York: International Universities Press.

Hurwitz, M. (1986) The analyst, his theory, and the psychoanalytic process. *Psychoanalytic Study of the Child*, 41:439–466.

Khan, S. (2020) Joseph D. Lichtenberg: A doer doing. Book essay. *Journal of the American Psychoanalytic Association*, 68:267–281.

Knight, R.P. (1961) David Rapaport—1911–1960. *Psychoanalytic Quarterly*, 30:262–264.

Lear, J. (1996) The introduction of Eros: reflections on the work of Hans Loewald. *Journal of the American Psychoanalytic Association*, 44:673–698.

Leavy, S.A. (1989) Time and World in the Thought of Hans W. Loewald. *Psychoanalytic Study of the Child*, 44:231–240.

Levenson, L.N. (1998) Superego defense analysis in the termination phase. *Journal of the American Psychoanalytic Association*, 46:847–866.

Lichtenberg, H. (2012) Therapeutic action: old and new explanations of therapeutic leverage. *Psychoanalytic Inquiry*, 32:50–59.

Loewald, E. (2022) *The Tree Grows Standing Still: A Memoir*. Thomaston, ME: Maine Authors Publishing.

Loewald, H.W. (1951) Ego and reality. *International Journal of Psychoanalysis*, 32:10–18.

Loewald, H.W. (1952) The problem of defence and the neurotic interpretation of reality. *International Journal of Psychoanalysis*, 33:444–449.

Loewald, H.W. (1953) Psychoanalysis and modern view on human existence and religious experience. *The Journal of Pastoral Care*, VII:1–15.

Loewald, H.W. (1955) Hypnoid state, repression, abreaction and recollection. *Journal of the American Psychoanalytic Association*, 3:201–210.

Loewald, H.W. (1960) On the therapeutic action of psychoanalysis. *The International Journal of Psychoanalysis*, 41:16–33.

Loewald, H.W. (1973) On internalization. *The International Journal of Psychoanalysis*, 54:9–17.

Loewald, H.W. (1975) Psychoanalysis and the fantasy character of the psychoanalytic situation. *Journal of the American Psychoanalytic Association*, 23:277–299.

Loewald, H.W. (1976) Norman A. Cameron, M.D. – 1896–1975. *The Psychoanalytic Quarterly*, 45:614–617.

Loewald, H.W. (1978) *Psychoanalysis and the Individual: The Freud Lectures at Yale*. New Haven, CT: Yale University Press.

Loewald, H.W. (1979) The waning of the Oedipus complex. *Journal of the American Psychoanalytic Association*, 27:751–775.

Loewald, H. (1988) Psychoanalysis in search of nature: thoughts on metapsychology, 'metaphysics,' projection. *Annual of Psychoanalysis*, 6:49–54.

Mayes, L.C. and Cohen, D.J. (1996) Anna Freud and developmental psychoanalytic psychology. *Psychoanalytic Study of the Child*, 51:117–141.

Moscovitz, S. (2014) Hans Loewald's "On the therapeutic action of psychoanalysis": initial reception and later influence. *Psychoanalytic Psychology*, 31:575–587.

Phillips, S.H. (2006) Paul Gray's narrowing scope: a "developmental lag" in his theory and technique. *Journal of the American Psychoanalytic Association*, 54:137–170.

Rapaport, D. (1950) On the psycho-analytic theory of thinking. *The International Journal of Psychoanalysis*, 31:161–170.

Rapaport, D. (1967) The History of the Awakening of Insight [June 10, 1942 presentation at the Menninger Clinic]. In M.M. Gill (ed.), *The Collected Papers of David Rapaport*. Basic Books.

Rapaport, D. and Gill, M. (1959) The point of view and assumptions of metapsychology. *The International Journal of Psychoanalysis*, 40:153–162.

Ritvo, S. and Scharfman, M.A. (1979) Conceptualizing the nature of the therapeutic action of psychoanalysis. *Journal of the American Psychoanalytic Association*, 27:627–642.

Schafer, R. (1968) *Aspects of Internalization*. New York: International Universities Press.

Schafer, R. (1970) An overview of Heinz Hartmann's contributions to psychoanalysis. *International Journal of Psychoanalysis*, 51:425–446.

Schafer, R. (2000) The development of my ideas about psychoanalysis. In P. Fonagy, R. Michels, & J. Sandler (eds.), *A Changing World: The Revolution in Psychoanalysis: Essays in Honour of Arnold Cooper*. New York: Karnac, pp. 33–40.

Stern, S. (2009) My experience of analysis with Loewald. *Psychoanalytic Quarterly*, 78:1013–1031.

Wexler, J. (2002) "Rage to Order": Wallace Stevens and Hans Loewald. *Psychoanalytic Study of the Child*, 57:458–476.

Chapter 3

Hans Loewald's "On the Therapeutic Action of Psychoanalysis"

Initial Reception and Later Influence

Seymour Moscovitz

Hans Loewald's "On the Therapeutic Action of Psychoanalysis" (Loewald, 1960) is unquestionably regarded as a modern classic, one of the "most important papers of the second half of the 20th century" (Chodorow, 2008, p. 1089).[1] It has been hailed by analysts of various theoretical persuasions (Arlow & Brenner, 1990; Chodorow, 2003, 2008; Cooper, 1997; Fogel, 1989; Fosshage, 2007; Friedman, 1996; Hoffman, 1983; Stolorow, Atwood, & Ross, 1978) for its seminal contributions. In an appreciation of Loewald's work as a whole and "Therapeutic Action" in particular, Stephen Mitchell (1988) wrote: "In his quiet, undramatic fashion, Loewald ... transformed the basic values guiding the analytic process, substituting meaning for rationality, imagination for objectivity, vitalization for control" (p. 850). Loewald's "Therapeutic Action" has also been the subject of major panels and symposia. The papers presented at the 1993 Winter meeting of the American Psychoanalytic Association were published in their entirety "[a]s a tribute to Loewald's lifetime of achievement, and in belated recognition of his preeminent position in the field of psychoanalysis" (Fogel et al., 1996, p. 863).

And yet, praise and acceptance have not always accompanied Loewald's views of therapeutic action. The "belated recognition" referenced by Fogel is the subject of this article, which will examine the evolution of "Therapeutic Action" from early drafts and prepublication presentations to its postpublication influence. Both archival material and citation analysis will be used to illustrate how Loewald's novel ideas about therapeutic action evolved, how they were initially received, and how their influence broadened over time. Discussion of the possible significance of this piece of intellectual history concludes the essay.

Early Stages and Initial Reception

When Hans Loewald was invited to join the faculty at Yale Medical School and the Western New England Psychoanalytic Institute,[2] his move from Baltimore to New Haven in 1955 was both geographic and ideological.

After emigrating to the United States from Germany in 1933,[3] Loewald pursued a residency in psychiatry at Rhode Island State Hospital (1939–1941), became a fellow in child psychiatry at the University of Maryland Medical School (1941–1943), and completed psychoanalytic training at the Washington-Baltimore institute (1943–1946), where his teachers and supervisors included the leading interpersonal analysts of the day: notably, Harry Stack Sullivan, Thomas French, and Frieda Fromm Reichmann; his training analyst, Lewis B. Hill, was himself analyzed by Fromm Reichmann.

DOI: 10.4324/9781003328230-4

Loewald began his independent practice in Baltimore after he completed analytic training and was appointed training and supervising analyst at the Washington-Baltimore Psychoanalytic Institute in 1951. He was an associate professor in the psychiatry departments of two medical schools (Johns Hopkins and the University of Maryland). At the time he was asked to join the faculties of Yale and the Western New England Institute, Loewald had become an established figure in the Baltimore analytic community for over a decade.

Loewald's exposure to interpersonal and humanistic thought and his training in child psychiatry may well have primed him to study the role of early development and interaction in the psychoanalytic situation (Chodorow, 2009; Downey, 1994). We may also surmise that Loewald was disenchanted with the interpersonal approach. In one of his few direct references to his former training (Loewald, 1970), Loewald criticized the "tendency of Sullivan's interpersonal theory" for "doing away with intrapsychic conflict and structure" (p. 60).

Loewald's move from Baltimore to New Haven is also significant for bypassing New York City, where many other European analysts had relocated,[4] making the New York Psychoanalytic Institute the epicenter of American ego psychology (Richards & Lynch, 1998). Loewald found the ego psychology dominated by the work of Hartmann "reductionistic and mechanistic" (Fogel et al., 1996, p. 865). The recently founded Western New England Institute[5] likely presented a more receptive ground for the development of Loewald's vision of an ego psychology that took interactions with others (and their internalization) as its theoretical core. Recently remarried (Downey, 1994) and about to turn fifty at the time of his move to New Haven, Loewald seemed poised for a major statement of his ideas.

Preliminary Drafts and Sketches

An early draft of what would become the "Therapeutic Action" article focuses on technical issues, an aspect of therapeutic action Loewald later ignored. In a brief unpublished "Essay on Psychoanalytic Technique," Loewald (1956a) takes issue with the emphasis on interpretation of transference and resistance as the only legitimate forms of psychoanalytic technique. He objects to relegating all noninterpretive interventions to the "outer darkness" of auxiliary or educational measures, and he questions whether we fully understand the mechanism of interpretation of transference and resistance. In a developmental formulation that would become central to his later article, Loewald describes the psychoanalytic process as "a restaging and reactivation of childhood interaction between the patient and his environment" (Loewald, 1956a, p. 2). Loewald posits that early ego development has to be resumed in treatment and that development, rather than being a self-contained process, is an interactive one. Interactions occur continually in analysis and, even if they are not an object of scrutiny, serve as "integrative experiences."

Loewald presents an idea in this essay that will later become a central thesis of "Therapeutic Action": that there is a bias against theorizing about interaction stemming from the view that the analyst "is supposed to be not a coactor on the analytic stage, but simply a reflector, a mirror, albeit a mirror of the unconscious as well as of consciousness" (Loewald, 1956a, p. 2).

In another brief (three-page) unpublished abstract and summary, Loewald (1956b) provides an early statement of several other key ideas evolving into the "Therapeutic Action" paper. He asserts that a theory of technique and therapeutic action has to start with the role of object relations in psychic development; that "remnants" of an "intact ego" are critical for successful treatment (cf. Freud's "normal ego;" Freud, 1937); and that the resolution of *infantile* transferences is an analytic goal, not the elimination of transference in general, which he views as enriching experience. Loewald seems to retreat from his earlier position that noninterpretive interventions may have a legitimate place in fostering analytic process, along the lines then being advanced as contributing to a therapeutic alliance (Zetzel, 1956). Rather than new technical procedures, Loewald now asserts that what is needed is a deeper understanding of our present technique.

Prepublication Presentations

With these early sketches serving as a model, Loewald presented the "Therapeutic Action" paper in various parts and stages of completion from 1956 until its submission to the *International Journal of Psychoanalysis* in 1959 and eventual publication in 1960.

Western New England Psychoanalytic Institute, September 1956

An early version of "Therapeutic Action" was rejected for a panel presentation at the American Psychoanalytic Association annual meeting in May 1956. In a note written to Charles Brenner, the program chair for the APsaA meetings, Loewald (1956c) offered a twofold apology: first, for having sent merely an abstract of the article for consideration at the 1956 meeting (surmising this may have been partly the reason for its rejection) and next for submitting the current, more complete draft[6] after the deadline for proposals. Despite the tardiness, Brenner apparently accepted the presentation for the 1957 annual meeting.

The next day (September 29, 1956), Loewald presented the first three parts of the "Therapeutic Action" article at a meeting of the Western New England Psychoanalytic Society at the Austen Riggs Center.[7] Judging from the correspondence Loewald received, the presentation met with mixed reviews. Several letters offered point-by-point summaries, as if asking, "Did I really hear you to be saying this?" Norman Cameron, in a generally appreciative note,[8] gave only a "two-star rating" to one of Loewald's most lyrical statements, that interpretations are "like poetry, a new language for contexts, connections and phenomena not previously expressible."

Henry Wexler offered some candid impressions of the meeting. In a letter to Loewald on September 30, 1956, Wexler complained, "That old bibliograf(ter) David R. [Rapaport] contributed little (when he could have a great deal) beyond the raising of 'questions' and appealing to the next generation to answer them."[9] Wexler adds that Helmuth Kaiser critiqued "the presumed ... dichotomy" between analysts subscribing to the "Mirror concept"—the analyst as opaque reflecting screen—versus the "interaction" model. "By keeping the lines of these two concepts sharply delimited," Wexler opined, "he [Kaiser] rode one of his favorite war horses against the old ideas of the functions of resistance, transference, and so forth in the analytic situation." Kaiser, echoing Rapaport, reportedly offered the faint praise that Loewald raised interesting issues without "settling" them. Wexler appreciated Loewald's application of the mother–child relationship to the analytic situation (as the mother aids the child's "struggle for integration at increasingly higher levels," so does the analyst) as a formulation bridging the dichotomy between "Mirror and Interaction Concepts." He commiserated with Loewald's "acquiescence" to the criticisms of some members of the audience as a "formality" of "time and circumstance."

Samuel Hunt, another attendee, wrote[10] that he later presented Loewald's ideas at a discussion group, where the reaction was that "[i]t's dangerous to be human with your patient," as it will "prevent the development of the negative transference ...." "[T]hese mirror analysts," Hunt complained, "don't realize they are mirrors until you bring up some clinical examples and compare what they would do to what an interacter might do, and then they're not on your side anymore."

After reviewing a prepublication copy of the paper, David Rapaport[11] wrote Loewald a detailed critique in a letter dated November 1, 1956. He acknowledged that Loewald "came independently to many problems and tentative solutions, closely related to those Hartmann, Erikson, Gill, I and others have arrived at" (Rapaport, 1956, p. 1). Rapaport's comment appears both to credit Loewald's original thinking while assimilating his ideas with received knowledge and practice. At the end of the letter, he assures Loewald that he was not "nagging" him to make these "connections" explicit. Rapaport also appreciated that Loewald's stress on the crucial role of interaction and his criticism of analytic neutrality as a form of cool detached scientific objectivity tapped a "widely felt uneasiness with the 'remote' role of the analyst" (Rapaport, 1956, p. 2). The therapist's availability as a "new object," however, merely reiterated what Rapaport and others working with borderline patients "already knew," namely, that the "therapist is always, besides being a transference object, also a *real* object" (Rapaport, 1956, p. 3; Rapaport's emphasis). (Loewald does not use the term "real object" in the article.) Although Rapaport also recognized Loewald's emphasis on the role of object relations in ego development as a crucial component of his theory of therapeutic action, he believed Loewald let the concept become "too broad."

In response to Rapaport's criticism, Loewald countered (letter of November 11, 1956) that the object relations concept in traditional theory was too *narrow* because it did not encompass all the relations to the environment. Loewald maintained that objects have been taken for granted as finished products and praised Winnicott's idea of transitional objects as a step in the right direction toward a more nuanced understanding of part object relations. Loewald further objected to the traditional view of the organism as a closed system moved by instinctual drives with no primary relation to the environment; as a result, in this traditional view, the organism is forced into contact with objects and has to evolve an "ego" as a defensive shield.[12] The implication is that the ego is the agency of adaptation and that instinctual drives are not involved with the environment. Loewald goes on to say that this notion has led to a misguided and ill-conceived concept of neutrality.

Loewald was leery of potential misinterpretations of his idea about therapeutic action as a resumption of ego development. In his response to Samuel Hunt (Loewald, 1956e), he remarked that he had planned to offer a "postscript" at the meeting at Riggs to address a potential misreading of his developmental analogy: His "word of caution" went as follows:

The mother– child relationship is taken as a model not because the relationship between analyst and patient is considered similar to it. I believe these are two fundamentally different relationships . . . The mother–child relationship is taken as a model only because some essential features of the organization of the psychic apparatus through interaction can be seen more clearly in this primitive stage of development than in later stages. And I wish to clarify some aspects of the function of interaction in the therapeutic action of psychoanalysis. I am aware of the danger of confusing use of such model with a facile notion that the essence of the action of analysis is an emotional, "warm" relationship with the patient; that the analyst should be a mother figure or father figure to the patient. The uniqueness of the analytic relationship has not been touched upon in this paper. Elements of many different types of human relationships are fused into something new. This new type of relationship between two human beings is far from clear and is far from being unambiguous as any other human relationship.

> (Loewald, 1956e, unpaginated letter)

Loewald viewed his use of the mother–child analogy as a heuristic model for the analytic relationship, a way of seeing more clearly into "some essential features of . . . the psychic apparatus," not a prescription for modifying standard technique to become a good maternal or paternal figure for the analysand.

This is very emphatically not the way, as far as analysis is concerned. The analyst does not have to add anything to his analyzing, does not have to plan on interacting. There is interaction in his analyzing. This is the point I'm trying to make when I speak of interaction as against neutrality, namely, that analysis *is* interaction, *not* that analysis has to be given up ... in order to arrive at interaction with the patient.

> (Loewald, 1956e)

In sum, Loewald's initial presentation of this early but nearly complete version of "Therapeutic Action" encountered a spectrum of reactions: some recognizing its cogency and originality; others assimilating it into already received knowledge; and still others seeing it as a potentially "dangerous" departure from standard practice. Loewald himself was concerned that his ideas might lend themselves to oversimplification and misreading, but held back from issuing his private reservations in a public forum.

Annual Meeting of the American Psychoanalytic Association, May, 1957

After the presentation at the Western New England in 1956, Loewald presented Parts 1 and 3 of "Therapeutic Action" at a meeting of the American Psychoanalytic Association in 1957 (the proposal submitted to Brenner on the eve of his Riggs presentation). The discussant of the article was Emanuel Windholz from San Francisco, whose remarks are not recorded. Windholz does not cite Loewald in any of his own published work, making it difficult to discern whether he viewed the article favorably. There also did not appear to be a coherent theme to the panel. The other presentations were seemingly unrelated and obscure articles such as "Learning Theories and the Analytic Process" (Gerhart Piers) and "On the Relationship of Intellectual Achievement to the Process of Identification" (Alfredo Namnum). The abstract of Loewald's presentation emphasizes the resumption of development, the role of interaction, and the critique of analytic neutrality:

> The therapeutic action of psychoanalysis is viewed as a resumption of ego-development promoted and sustained by the interaction of analyst and patient. The specific nature of the psychoanalytic interaction is discussed and clarified by correlating it with the role of interaction in early ego-development and internalization. Discussion and refutation of the mirror model and of the ideal image of the analyst as a "neutral" scientific observer in the context of a reappraisal of the theory of the relations of instincts to objects.
>
> (Loewald, 1957, p. 13)

Loewald's early presentations of "Therapeutic Action" contained only the first three parts of the final article. Some of the responses to the presentations may have been muted by the absence of this culminating section on the role of transference in therapeutic action.

Congress of the International Psychoanalytic Association, July 1957

Loewald presented the final part of the "Therapeutic Action" article—on the role of transference in therapeutic action—at the International Psychoanalytic Association Congress on July 30, 1957. His paper, "Transference and the Therapeutic Action of Psychoanalysis: Metapsychological Considerations," was the fifth and last presentation at a panel under the chairmanship of Raymond DeSaussure.[13] In it, Loewald's broader conception of the object relational underpinnings of transference becomes clearer. He attempts to "regain the original richness" of the concept of transference by tracing connections among three traditional meanings of the term: as the transfer of libido to objects; as the transfer of infantile object-cathexes to contemporary objects, especially the analyst; and as a displacement. Loewald returns to Freud's earliest conception of transference as an interplay between the *Ucs.* and *Pcs.* systems for a fourth meaning. The analyst, as a "contemporary object," promotes regression to unconscious levels of organization to reestablish communication between the *Ucs.* and *Pcs.* systems. This connection, Loewald posits, can lead to the resumption of ego development and structural change. It is the basis for his metaphorical description of the analytic process of converting ghosts into ancestors. Loewald does not conceive transference as a pathological dynamism perpetuating infantile forms of relating to objects or distorting reality but as a way of giving present reality "meaning and depth" and as such a part of normal psychological growth.

Western New England Institute, November 1957

Loewald also presented what would become Part 4 of "Therapeutic Action" at a meeting of the Western New England Institute on November 9, 1957. Rapaport reviewed the paper before it was presented and responded positively, in a letter dated October 23, 1957, to Loewald's efforts at a metapsychological exposition of the subject, in contrast to those who, "like Sullivan," believe that "their rationalizations from the clinical realities were psychoanalytic theory." Rapaport credited the article with giving a "genetic" (metapsychological) perspective on transference, but only "touching on" the "economic, structural, dynamic, and adaptive issues."

In a letter dated October 30, 1957, Loewald replied that he did not think of his paper as primarily written from a genetic viewpoint but rather a more broadly theoretical one. He objected to Rapaport's description of the secondary process as "drive-restraining" rather than as intimately linked with the primary process.

Following this series of presentations in 1957, the four-part "Therapeutic Action" article was ready for submission for publication.

The Influence of "On the Therapeutic Action of Psychoanalysis"

It is unclear whether Loewald initially submitted "Therapeutic Action" to the *Journal of the American Psychoanalytic Association*, and no corroboration of receipt of this manuscript or an editorial decision to reject it could be obtained. Loewald eventually submitted the paper to the *International Journal of Psychoanalysis* on February 11, 1959, and it was published in 1960.

After its cautious and mixed introduction, Loewald's article became increasingly popular. The increase in its frequency of citation over the following fifty years (1960–2010) may best be illustrated graphically (see Figure 3.1).

This chart depicts a steady growth in citation frequency, reaching a plateau around the time of Loewald's death in 1993. Many of Loewald's contributions have been widely adopted: the analyst as a "new object," one of the most widely used and misused ideas, referring to new configurations in the organization of experience; the resumption of ego development as the central component of therapeutic action; the analyst's function of holding an image of the patient's yet-unrealized developmental potential, reflecting aspects of this core of "undistorted reality"; and the formulation that "development is facilitated when higher level organizations place their order upon more diffuse organizations and help them take shape" (Pine, 2006, p. 191).

Cumulative Journal Citations by Decade, 1960–2019

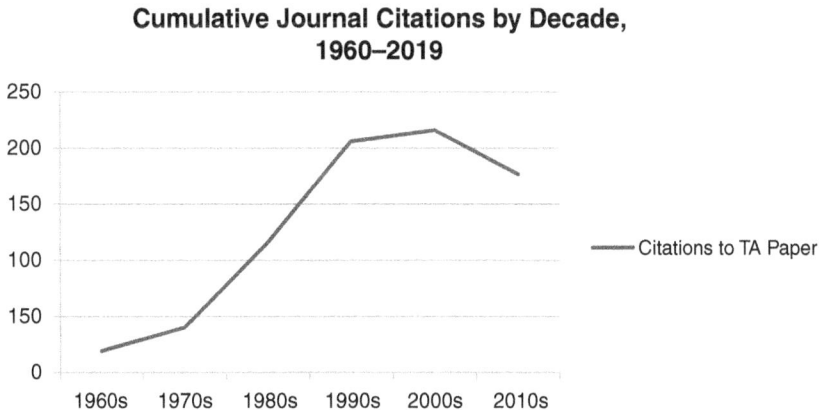

Figure 3.1 Cumulative journal citations by decade, 1960–2009.

Loewald's reformulation of neutrality and objectivity and his rejection of a "closed" (or one-person) model of the psychic apparatus in favor of a view of the analyst as a "coactor on the analytic stage" adumbrated the increased attention to countertransference, enactment, and two-person models of the analytic process. Loewald's view of drives as related to reality and objects, which Rapaport considered a misunderstanding of Freud and Hartmann, has provided a view of instinctual life as organizing, and organized by, reality, and as emerging within a relational matrix.

Loewald's developmental model and analogies between the mother-infant relationship and analyst-patient interaction, when understood as Loewald intended, have contributed to the recognition of processes such as mentalization and reflective function. The child internalizes the parent's image of the child and begins to experience himself "as a centered unit by being centered upon" (Loewald, 1960, p. 20). Loewald's understanding of the role of language in articulating inchoate experience has contributed to a broadened understanding of interpretation, not as simply providing knowledge of the unconscious but as a medium for the growth-facilitating interaction between patient and analyst.

Finally, from Part 4 of the article comes the idea of transference as the process by which "ghosts" (repressed and unintegrated aspects of experience) are converted into "ancestors" (fully metabolized and internalized experiences that become part of the self). This view of transference derives from Freud's topographic model. Loewald's idea of an open commerce between strata of the psyche has offered an enriched model of emotional health and the goals of analysis. Perhaps most central to Loewald's contribution has been his ability to integrate previously disparate models, the "mirror analyst" versus the "interacter," as this controversy was expressed in the 1960s, or the rivalry between insight and relationship, in contemporary discussions.

Loewald's formulations were increasingly taken up by Freudian, Relational, and interpersonal theorists, contributing to the frequency of citation, along with the increase in the number of psychoanalytic journals. This "cross-over" appeal of "Therapeutic Action" may be depicted by the following figure of citations by leading journals (see Figure 3.2).

The increased number of citations of the "Therapeutic Action" article also reflects a growing interest in "therapeutic action" as a concept. Following Strachey's introduction of the term (Strachey, 1934), there appeared to be little usage of "therapeutic action" as a specific theoretical term until after Loewald's "Therapeutic Action" paper. Loewald's formulations appear to have stimulated interest in explanations of therapeutic action, and in turn, the interest in therapeutic action has led to more citations of both Loewald and Strachey[14] (see Figure 3.3).

Discussion and Future Directions

The present study has addressed the seminal importance of Loewald's "On the Therapeutic Action of Psychoanalysis" and has examined its origins and later influence. The initial reception at the meeting of the New England Institute in September 1956 seems to have been a mixed and muted one. The atmosphere, as best as can be reconstructed, appeared tense, and Loewald is described as "acquiescing" to critical

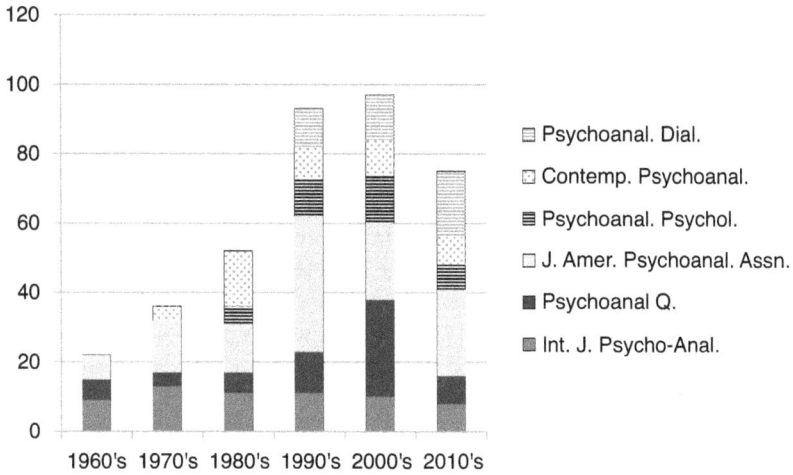

Figure 3.2 Citations of "Therapeutic Action" in major journals.

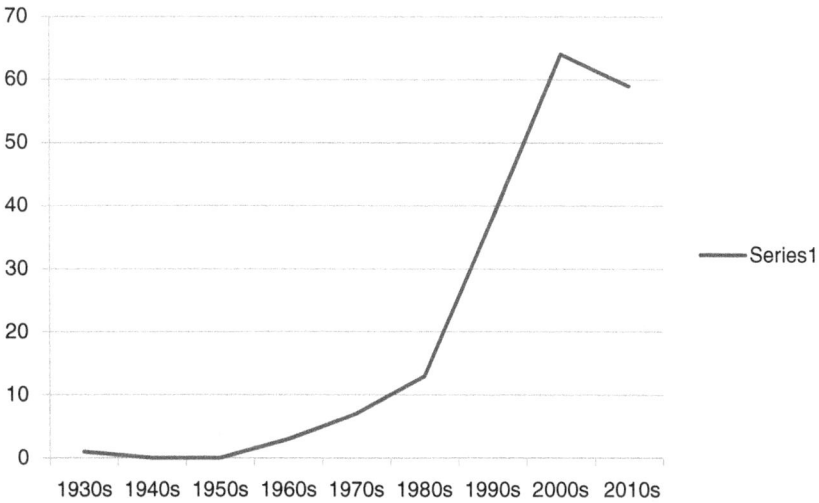

Figure 3.3 Usage of "Therapeutic Action" as a term of art, 1934–2010.

or condescending comments. Some (Henry Wexler, John Dollard, and Samuel Hunt) immediately recognized that they were hearing extraordinary and novel ideas, and registered their excitement in personal letters to Loewald. Some (David Rapaport and Norman Cameron) gave mixed reviews. Reports from outside the meeting spoke of the "danger" of being "so human," driving negative transference underground and opening the door to a potentially dangerous form of interaction with the patient. An early version of the paper was rejected for an APsaA conference and later placed alongside other seemingly unrelated and obscure papers at other conferences. The fallibility of contemporary appraisals of the significance of a work is abundantly evident in these reactions.[15]

There is an irony to using citation analysis as a method to study Loewald's influence. Loewald himself did not take pains to systematically cite a vast ego psychology literature, perhaps to free his own original thinking, and he was politely chided by Rapaport for his lack of attribution to the work of others. Citation, however, is a deliberate and conscious act, and as such may fail to register more latent and underlying sources of influence. This seems particularly true of Loewald's absence of citation not only of fellow ego psychologists but also of his earlier interpersonal colleagues and supervisors and of his former mentor in philosophy, Martin Heidegger.[16] It is as if Loewald's geographic moves (Germany to the United States, Baltimore to New Haven) also represented repudiations of a past that nonetheless continued to influence and move him, the "ghosts" in Loewald's theorizing.

A further irony in conducting this study is that Loewald began with an interest in a technical issue yet eschewed specific application of "Therapeutic Action" to technique. "Anything my paper can say as far as technique is concerned," he ultimately advised, "has to be worked out very carefully. I myself certainly am not ready to do this piece of work at this point" (Loewald, 1956d). We are left to infer that from Loewald's point of view, the traditional analytic stance—reserved, unobtrusive, and quietly listening—provided sufficient opportunities for new pathways to emerge from the patient's experience. Although Loewald recognized the importance of countertransference, his approach to its handling entailed a silent act of self-scrutiny on the analyst's part, so that the analyst's participation could be woven into the stream of free associations by the patient. Loewald was emphatic in his rejection of a technical approach of greater activity or deliberate demonstration of emotional warmth or other parental attitudes to foist the analyst as a new object onto the patient.

Loewald did not rule out the possibility that new technical procedures *could* be derived from his ideas, but simply demurred setting about that task himself. Loewald's deconstruction of analytic objectivity and neutrality, his description of the analyst as a coactor on the analytic stage, and his view of drives as emerging from the relational matrix between mother and child resonate with the work of Stephen Mitchell, who was strongly influenced by Loewald (Mitchell, 1998, 2000a, 2000b). Attachment research, too, has confirmed Loewald's description of the development of the child's sense of self by being centered upon as an intentional agent. Loewald here presages the work of Fonagy and others on mentalization (Fonagy et al., 2004).

If anything is consistent with Loewald's position it is the integration of polarities. Loewald insisted on the importance of maintaining the topographic model along with the structural model. His model of health is not one in which the conscious replaces the unconscious or the ego replaces the id but rather one in which there is a free and open exchange within and between systems. Interpretation is not exclusively a means to insight but is also a pathway to the formation of a new relationship; interactions with the analyst are not just a way of finding a new object but also contribute to understanding. Interaction and interpretation, relationship and insight, the "mirror" analyst and the "interacter" are complexly interwoven and mutually influencing roles and processes. Although citations to "Therapeutic Action" may have reached a plateau, after decades of steady increase, the influence of his integrative thinking is likely to endure.

Notes

1 As of August 24, 2014, PEP-WEB statistics indicate that "Therapeutic Action" had been cited 626 times. Only Melanie Klein's 1946 article, "Notes on Some Schizoid Mechanisms," has been cited more frequently, with a total of 669 citations. The Thomson-Reuters Web of Science Core Collection Citation Index, using different journal selection and search criteria, indicates that "Therapeutic Action" has been cited 543 times, placing it eighth in the most frequently cited articles in psychoanalysis.

2 Theodore Lidz, M.D., urged Loewald to consider moving sooner (in the Fall of 1954 rather than 1955) and encouraged meeting with Erik Erikson of the Western New England Institute to facilitate the transition (Letter dated January 28, 1954; Lidz, 1954).

3 Biographical material derives from Loewald's Curriculum Vitae (December 1953, July 1984), available in the Hans W. Loewald papers, Manuscripts and archives, Yale University Library. These papers include correspondence, writing, and notes documenting Loewald's influence as a writer, teacher, and clinician. They were donated to the Yale library by Loewald's widow, Elizabeth L. Loewald.

4 Among the leading European analysts were Heinz Hartmann, Rudolf Loewenstein, Ernst Kris, and Edith Jacobson.

5 Per its Web site (www.westernnewengland.org), the Institute was founded in 1952 and fully accredited by the American Psychoanalytic Association in 1956. Among its charter members, The New England Institute included Robert Knight, William Pious, Henry Wexler, and Erik Erikson.

6 The article submitted to Brenner and presented at Riggs excluded Part 4, the section on transference, which was written later. Perhaps because of time constraints, Loewald presented only Parts 1 and 3 at the APsaA meeting in 1957.

7 Loewald sent a draft of this article to David Rapaport, which was made available through the courtesy of the Austen Riggs library. Rapaport underlines key passages and places exclamation points or question marks alongside others. His full critique of the article was provided in a letter of November 1, 1956, as discussed in this article.

8 Undated correspondence to Loewald available in Hans W. Loewald papers, Manuscripts and Archives, Yale University Library.

9 Henry Wexler, letter dated September 30, 1956.

10 Probably in October 1956, but undated.

11 Letter dated November 1, 1956, available in Manuscripts and Archives.

12 This idea is further elaborated in Loewald's article "Ego and Reality" (Loewald, 1951).

13 This information, including an abstract of Loewald's presentation, was provided through the assistance of Mike Tilley of the International Psychoanalytic Association.

14 Strachey's article "The Nature of Therapeutic Action of Psycho-Analysis," according to PEP-WEB, has been cited 608 times, placing it third (after Loewald) in cumulative citation frequency; per the Web of Science, it has been cited 498 times, placing it tenth among psychoanalytic journal articles.

15 Loewald himself was not immune from this fallibility. In a review of Lacan's *Ecrits*, Loewald (1967) wrote the editor of the University of Chicago Press that in his opinion "there is no audience in this country for the Ecrits."

16 The absence of reference to Heidegger was a conscious repudiation of his mentor, whose joining of the Nazi Party was a profound betrayal (Loewald, 1980). Heidegger's influence is nonetheless considered prominent in Loewald's work (Whitebook, 2004).

References

Arlow, J. A., & Brenner, C. (1990). The psychoanalytic process. *The Psychoanalytic Quarterly, 59,* 678–692.

Cameron, N. (1956). *Letter to Hans Loewald. Hans W. Loewald papers. Manuscripts and archives.* New Haven, CT: Yale University Library.

Chodorow, N. J. (2003). The psychoanalytic vision of Hans Loewald. *The International Journal of Psychoanalysis, 84,* 897–913.

Chodorow, N. J. (2008). Introduction: The Loewaldian legacy. *Journal of the American Psychoanalytical Association, 56*, 1089–1096. doi:10.1177/0003065108325587

Chodorow, N. J. (2009). A different universe: Reading Loewald through "On the therapeutic action of psychoanalysis." *The Psychoanalytic Quarterly, 78*, 983–1011. doi:10.1002/j.2167-4086.2009.tb00424.x

Cooper, S. H. (1997). Interpretation and the psychic future. *The International Journal of Psychoanalysis, 78*, 667–681.

Downey, T. W. (1994). Hans W. Loewald, M. D. (1906–1993). *The International Journal of Psychoanalysis, 75*, 839–842.

Fogel, G. (1989). The authentic function of psychoanalytic theory: An overview of the contributions of Hans Loewald. *The Psychoanalytic Quarterly, 58*, 419–451.

Fogel, G. I., Tyson, P., Greenberg, J., McLaughlin, J. T., & Peyser, E. R. (1996). A classic revisited: Loewald on the therapeutic action of psychoanalysis. *Journal of the American Psychoanalytical Association, 44*, 863–924.

Fonagy, P., Gergely, G., Jurist, E., & Target, M. (2004). *Affect regulation, mentalization, and the development of the self.* New York, NY: Other Press.

Fosshage, J. L. (2007). Searching for love and expecting rejection: Implicit and explicit dimensions in cocreating analytic change. *Psychoanalytic Inquiry, 27*, 326–347. doi:10.1080/07351690701389544

Freud, S. (1937). Analysis terminable and interminable. *The International Journal of Psychoanalysis, 18*, 373–405.

Friedman, L. (1996). The Loewald phenomenon. *Journal of the American Psychoanalytical Association, 44*, 671–672.

Hoffman, I. Z. (1983). The patient as interpreter of the analyst's experience. *Contemporary Psychoanalysis, 19*, 389–422. doi:10.1080/00107530.1983.10746615

Hunt, S. (1956). *Letter to Hans Loewald. Hans W. Loewald papers. Manuscripts and archives.* New Haven, CT: Yale University Library.

Klein, M. (1946). Notes on some schizoid mechanisms. *International Journal of Psychoanalysis, 27*, 99–110.

Lidz, T. (1954). *Letter to Hans Loewald. Hans W. Loewald papers. Manuscripts and archives.* New Haven, CT: Yale University Library.

Loewald, H. W. (1951). Ego and reality. *The International Journal of Psychoanalysis, 32*, 10–18.

Loewald, H. W. (1956a). *Essay on psychoanalytic technique.* Unpublished manuscript.

Loewald, H. W. (1956b). *Contribution to the theory of therapeutic action and technique of psychoanalysis.* Unpublished manuscript.

Loewald, H. W. (1956c). *Letter to Charles Brenner. Hans W. Loewald papers. Manuscripts and archives.* New Haven, CT: Yale University Library.

Loewald, H. W. (1956d). *Letter to Henry Wexler. Hans W. Loewald papers. Manuscripts and archives.* New Haven, CT: Yale University Library.

Loewald, H. W. (1956e). *Letter to Samuel Hunt. Hans W. Loewald papers. Manuscripts and archives.* New Haven, CT: Yale University Library.

Loewald, H. W. (1957, May). *On the therapeutic action of psychoanalysis.* Abstract of paper presented at the American Psychoanalytic Association Annual Meeting, Chicago, IL.

Loewald, H. W. (1960). On the therapeutic action of psycho-analysis. *The International Journal of Psychoanalysis, 41*, 16–33.

Loewald, H. W. (1967). *Letter to Morris Philipson. Hans W. Loewald papers. Manuscripts and archives.* New Haven, CT: Yale University Library.

Loewald, H. W. (1970). Psychoanalytic theory and the psychoanalytic process. *Psychoanalytic Study of the Child, 25*, 45–68.

Loewald, H. W. (1980). *Dr. Hans L. Loewald testimony. Fortunoff video archive for Holocaust testimony.* New Haven, CT: Yale University Library.

Mitchell, S. A. (1988). The intrapsychic and the interpersonal: Different theories, different domains, or historical artifacts? *Psychoanalytic Inquiry, 8*, 472–496.

Mitchell, S. A. (1998). From ghosts to ancestors: The psychoanalytic vision of Hans Loewald. *Psychoanalytic Dialogues, 8*, 825–855. doi:10.1080/10481889809539297

Mitchell, S. A. (2000a). Chapter 1: Language and reality. In S. A. Mitchell (Ed.), *Relationality: From attachment to intersubjectivity*. Hillsdale, NJ: The Analytic Press, 3–29.

Mitchell, S. A. (2000b). Chapter 2: Drives and objects. In S. A. Mitchell (Ed.), *Relationality: From attachment to intersubjectivity*. Hillsdale, NJ: The Analytic Press, 31–53.

Pine, F. (2006). A note on some microprocesses of identification. *Psychoanalytic Study of the Child, 61*, 190–201.

Rapaport, D. (1956). *Letter to Hans Loewald. Hans W. Loewald papers. Manuscripts and archives*. New Haven, CT: Yale University Library.

Richards, A. D., & Lynch, A. A. (1998). From ego psychology to contemporary conflict theory: An historical overview. In C. S. Ellman, S. Grand, M. Silvan, & S. J. Ellman (Eds.), *The modern Freudians: Contemporary psychoanalytic technique* (pp. 3–23). Northvale, NJ: Jason Aronson Inc.

Stolorow, R. D., Atwood, G. E., & Ross, J. M. (1978). The representational world in psychoanalytic therapy. *International Review of Psycho-Analysis, 5*, 247–256.

Strachey, J. (1934). The nature of the therapeutic action of psycho-analysis. *The International Journal of Psychoanalysis, 15*, 127–159.

Wexler, H. (1956). *Letter to Hans Loewald. Hans W. Loewald papers. Manuscripts and archives*. New Haven, CT: Yale University Library.

Whitebook, J. (2004). Hans Loewald. *The International Journal of Psychoanalysis, 85*, 97–115. doi:10.1516/8YFC-382H-2XKQ-XHQ3

Zetzel, E. R. (1956). Current concepts of transference. *The International Journal of Psychoanalysis, 37*, 369–375.

Chapter 4

The How of Hans Loewald and the Possibility of a Hans W. Loewald Center

Jonathan Lear

We are here today to celebrate the opening of the Hans W. Loewald Center.[1] In one sense, that answers the question of why we are here; in another sense, the question is wide open. What brings us here to do that? To answer that question, it seems appropriate to invoke the concepts of *mourning* and *internalization*, which Loewald himself did so much to enrich. We want to acknowledge our loss while at the same time striving to re-connect with Loewald in meaningful ways. And we also express the hope of doing this by forming a community.[2] Perhaps the Hans W. Loewald Center will come to be that for us and for others.

Still, there is a question of why we tend in the direction of mourning and internalization when it comes to this very person, Hans Loewald. His ideas are of great depth, and he had an astonishing ability to bring the ideas of others, notably Sigmund Freud, to life. Indeed, Loewald's fidelity to Freud shows itself in the originality of his interpretation. All this would explain our attempts to remember – in the deep sense of re-animating – *the ideas themselves.* Whence comes the felt need to keep these ideas attached to a particular person – the need to remember *him*? After all, this center is not named the Eros Center, the Association for the Study of Differentiated Fields, or the Individuation Institute. Something more is going on here than an attempt to keep important ideas alive.

Of course, some of us knew Hans Loewald personally; we formed significant relations with him, and he remains a powerful presence in our hearts and minds. That is part of the explanation. But, in the bulk of this essay, I want to focus on an intimacy that is open to any reader of Loewald's work. It seems to me that one does not have to have met Hans Loewald in person to form a personal relation with him. This possibility may be ignored or passed over, but it is there. How does it come alive when it does? It is important to answer this question, because this is not a mere idiosyncrasy in the writing but a form of teaching that, of its own internal force, brings us back to the teacher. This essay is preliminary, but it aims to bring to conscious awareness *the how* of Hans Loewald's writing.[3] At the end of this paper, I shall share a few vignettes, in part to mourn but also to illustrate how, in certain forms of teaching, a relationship is formed with the very person who has helped us understand.

******

I have noticed that readers of Hans Loewald tend to have favorite passages: turns of phrase that they – or we – return to in memory, share with others, or quote in papers.

DOI: 10.4324/9781003328230-5

This observation is anecdotal, but its significance is not. Many thinkers have persuaded us with their thoughts, insights, and arguments, but their actual words do not remain memorable, nor do they provoke a desire to repeat them. Loewald is different in this way, and this difference matters. In this essay, I will take a look at three favorite passages and ask how they work. The reason for doing so is this: Loewald's writings are remarkable because they have the capacity to inform readers in two distinct ways. They inform in the familiar sense of providing valuable information – in Loewald's case, rich interpretations of the fundamental concepts of psychoanalysis. But they also "inform" in a less familiar sense of that term: namely, *to form or shape the mind or character* of a person.[4] Loewald's writings, I want to claim, have a capacity *to shape the psyches* of his psychoanalytic readers. When Loewald writes on the therapeutic action of psychoanalysis, the explicit focus is on the work that the analyst and patient do together. But in the very same writing, there is room for *therapeutic action between Loewald, the author, and his psychoanalyst readers.* We are largely unaware of how his writing works on us.

To begin, consider this passage:

> I say ***new discovery of objects, and not discovery of new objects***, because the essence of such new object-relationships is the opportunity they offer for rediscovery of the early paths of the development of objectrelations, leading to a new way of relating to objects as well as of being and relating to oneself.[5]

A new discovery of objects, not a discovery of new objects. It is like an infant's repetition of sounds – the same and yet different. The cadence, the rhythm. And the simple transposition of one word – "new" – opens a possibility of comprehending psychoanalysis afresh. On offer is a shift of attention – away from the familiar direction toward objects, whether old or new, and toward the mind's own activity. This shifting of attention is emphatically not onto a new object – "the mind's activity" – but is rather a development of self-consciousness itself: the mind's awareness of its activity in its activity. There is a double pleasure here: first, the pleasure of a dawning way of seeing things; and second, the pleasurable sense that it will take time for the meaning to unfold. The double pleasure of a good interpretation.

The fact that it is a catchy phrase matters. There are repetitions internal to the phrase – *new... new... discovery... discovery, objects... objects* – that invite repetitions of the phrase in its entirety. It is not just that this is a good thought to have; indeed, it is a fun thought to have. The material vehicle of the thought – the sounds, the musical beat, the gentle transpositions – makes it pleasurable to return to in imagination. And over time, one discovers an unfathomable depth. In my decades of clinical work, I have repeatedly returned to this phrase, and with experience, I have come to understand it better. Yet at each return, I have a sense that Loewald was already here. It is as though my deeper understanding of the phrase brings along with it a deeper understanding of the person who coined it: *so this is what he meant!* In this way, the teacher comes along with the teaching. And the teaching itself takes time. It is not as though, if only he had chosen different words, I could have understood what he was saying more quickly. My task was to come to understand better those very words.

Note that while the phrase is written in the present tense, its temporality is timeless. It's not that it is true now, but it was not true yesterday or may not be tomorrow. Freud tells us the unconscious is timeless; so is the wisdom expressed in this phrase. And in its timelessness, what might at first have looked like a categorical description of the psychoanalytic situation morphs into an ideal. The phrase is also capacious and inviting. Although it was specifically written for the psychoanalytic situation, are there any human encounters where it might not be useful to bring it to mind? So, this is a phrase that expresses a basic psychoanalytic ideal, has a musical beat, has timeless temporality, and extends out indefinitely in its meaning to encompass all sorts of human relationships. Of course, like any phrase, it can turn into a cliché and go dead. I shall talk about this later. Right now, I want to concentrate on how it works when it works.

It is one thing to write *about* the formation of an ego-ideal; it is another *directly to promote* the formation of a psychoanalytic ego-ideal in the psychoanalyst. In his writing, Loewald does both. We tend not to be explicitly aware of the latter, though a sign of it shows up in this phenomenon of having favorite passages. The turn of phrase can facilitate integration: the rhythm and sounds reach down to infantile pleasures found in experiences of order, yet the meaning opens out indefinitely in the direction of insight.[6] The phrase brings them both together. The point is this: it is not that I first deepen as a psychoanalyst and then return to the phrase with a deepened understanding; the rhythmic returning to the phrase is itself constitutive of the deepening process. This phenomenon helps to explain the persuasive power of Loewald's writing. With a normal empirical claim, say, about ego functioning, one can test it against the available empirical evidence. But Loewald's claims about differentiation, separation, internalization, and mourning are "tested" in part by the direct experience of those very phenomena by the people who are doing the "testing." This is what Kierkegaard called *essentially indirect* communication.[7] In a nutshell, no one else can do my internalizations for me, but Loewald provides verbal vehicles that invite me to use them as I go through my own process of psychic development. It is by going through this process myself that I come to understand what Loewald meant. This is a very special form of demonstration – a creative repetition.

There is also room for a moment of humorous recognition. When one first reads "a new discovery of objects, not a discovery of new objects," it is easy to assume that Loewald is recommending the first of two alternatives. The humor comes as one recognizes that nothing could possibly count for us as a "new object" unless we were already able to engage in new modes of discovery. For someone locked in neurotic repetition, there are no "new objects"; that is what the neurotic repetition is all about. So, Loewald is not recommending the better of two alternatives; he is inviting us to deepen our self-conscious understanding of the one truly viable alternative we have. It is the new discovery of objects that makes the discovery of new objects possible.[8]

******

In a conversation about their fathers, Bruce Springsteen gave Barak Obama this advice:

> The trick is you have to turn your ghosts into ancestors. Ghosts haunt you. Ancestors walk alongside you and provide you with comfort and a vision of life that's going to be your own. My father walks alongside me as my ancestor now. It took a long time for that to happen.[9]

It is clear that *these very words* matter to Springsteen, for he also uses them in his autobiography.

> In analysis you work to turn the ghosts that haunt you into ancestors who accompany you. That takes hard work and a lot of love, but it's the way we lessen the burdens our children have to carry. ... I work to be an ancestor.[10]

Springsteen is, of course, a world-famous lyricist, and there can be no doubt that he takes words seriously. In an important sense, these words come *from him*: they express a sincere, and I suspect deep and accurate, account of the hard-won accomplishments of a long and successful psychoanalysis. For him, a man of words, *these words work.* They are the words of a healthy ego and ego-ideal, expressing core commitments. And yet, it is unlikely that Springsteen put those words together completely out of the blue without any prior influence tending him in that direction. My hypothesis is that he heard these words from his analyst in the midst of an interpretation, a summing up of the good work they had done together, *and* that the analyst had been influenced by Loewald. There has been a transmission of sayings of which Springsteen may be unaware. For here is a second favorite passage from Loewald:

> This indestructibility of unconscious mental acts is compared by Freud to the **ghosts in the underworld of the Odyssey – "ghosts which awoke to new life as soon as they tasted blood"**... the blood of conscious preconscious life, the life of contemporary present-day objects. It is a short step from here to the view of transference as a manifestation of the repetition compulsion – a line of thought which we cannot pursue here.
>
> The transference neurosis, in the technical sense of the establishment and resolution of it in the analytic process, is due to **the blood of recognition, which the patient's unconscious is given to taste so that the old ghosts may reawaken to life.** Those who know ghosts tell us that **they long to be released from their ghost life and led to rest as ancestors. As ancestors they live forth in the present generation, while as ghosts they are compelled to haunt the present generation with their shadow life.** Transference is pathological insofar as **the unconscious is a crowd of ghosts, and this is the beginning of the transference neurosis in analysis: ghosts of the unconscious, imprisoned by defenses but haunting the patient in the dark of his defenses and symptoms, are allowed to taste blood, are let loose. In the daylight of analysis, the ghosts of the unconscious are laid and led to rest as ancestors whose power is taken over and transformed into the newer intensity of present life,** of the secondary process and contemporary objects.[11]

There is something contagious about this passage. I have read the secondary literature on Loewald, and this phrase – ghosts into ancestors – is the most frequently quoted. Why?
  First, feel the cadence of repetition:

> ghosts in the underworld ... ghosts ...awoke to new life ... tasted blood... blood of conscious... life ... blood of recognition... unconscious ... taste ... old ghosts ... reawaken to life. Those who know ghosts... ghost life ... led to rest as ancestors. As ancestors ... as ghosts ... compelled to haunt ... unconscious ... crowd of ghosts, ... ghosts of the unconscious, ... haunting ... allowed to taste blood, ... ghosts of the unconscious ... led to rest as ancestors.

In this short passage, the word "ghosts" is repeated six times; "blood" is repeated three times; "taste" three times; "ancestors" three times; "haunt" twice; "awoke – awake," twice; "live" or "life" eight times. "Led... to rest" twice. The more complex phrase "ghosts of the unconscious" twice. That is 31 repetitions in six sentences, and the count could go on. And there is a rhythm here, almost like the beat of one's heart. There is more going on here than the mere transmission of information.

Second, the repetitions go down chains of associations. So: *tasted blood, blood of conscious, blood of recognition, allowed to taste blood.* And, *ghosts which awoke, ghosts which tasted blood, ghosts of the unconscious, ghosts led to rest as ancestors.* It is as though Loewald is *performing* associations for the benefit of the reader.

This is important because the intended readers are psychoanalysts and psychoanalytic candidates. These are readers who, to some extent, are working through or have worked through their own transference neuroses in analysis and have participated in working through the transference neuroses in clinical work with analysands. So, when it comes to the intended audience, these are readers who can remember *for themselves, first personally,* what it is like to be in the midst of a transference neurosis. That is, *we readers.* This passage then can function as a goad to re-awaken memory and lead us along an interpretive path. For readers who have themselves had their own analyses, the phrase can function *as an interpretation* of what it was all about. There is a power in the prose that transcends a mere report of how things are when it comes to psychoanalysis. For some readers, this passage can provoke the very integration that it is talking about. This helps to explain its rhetorical power. This passage can persuade readers of its truth by inviting them to experience it for themselves firsthand in the very moment of reading it. Although in some sense this is a "scientific paper," originally published in the *International Journal of Psychoanalysis,* its method opens out beyond a straightforward reporting of empirical facts. (We shall see more about Loewald's attitude to science in the next section.)

Tasting blood, the blood of recognition, coming to life. Taste takes us back to our tongues. Taste is a sensory capacity that is much more difficult to put into words than sight or hearing. We can do it, but it is not easy, and our capacity for fine-grained discrimination is limited. Putting taste into words is a capacity that can be developed with practice and training, as some connoisseurs do when it comes to tasting wine. But notice how strange their vocabulary is. It is almost as though one has to learn to speak a new language of taste. Ghosts taste blood. By contrast, we humans normally taste food, and it takes digestion – the activity of our nutritive soul – to turn it into blood. Ghosts do not seem to need a digestive process. They are like us (they taste, even seem to feed) and unlike us (no digestion; do they have bodies?). Ghosts are uncanny. It is essentially unclear what categories they inhabit: alive? dead? embodied? unembodied? They have the capacity to haunt.

This passage reminds readers of early sensual experiences of taste and touch as well as superstitious and magical forms of thinking, and it invites us to integrate them with elemental recognitions of what they mean. It also suggests metamorphosis, a transformation of being from ghost to ancestor. This involves a transformation in temporality. Ghosts, like denizens of the unconscious, are timeless. They occur again and again in the mode of haunting. For a ghost to turn into an ancestor is for it to begin to occupy a place in the temporal order; the mind can now locate it in the passage of time. This is a transition from the uncanny to the comprehensible. This transition is enacted in the text. Accompanying the timeless rhythm of *ghosts... blood... ancestors ...* Loewald makes a conscious reference back to Freud, who makes a reference back to Homer and a classic origin text of western literature, the Odyssey. We are presented with a myth that has at once endured timelessly *and* has a history that can be recounted. Both can be experienced interwoven in Loewald's text, and in this way, the text can itself be an occasion for internalization and integration. It does not merely describe the phenomena.

******

Here is a third favorite:

> It also needs to be said that the love of truth is no less a passion because it desires truth rather than some less elevated end. In our field the love of truth cannot be isolated from the passion for truth to ourselves and truth in human relationships. In other fields, too, the love of truth cannot be isolated from the passion for truth to ourselves and truth in human relationships. In other fields too, the scientist is filled with love for his object precisely in his most creative and "dispassionate" moments. Scientific detachment in its genuine form, far from excluding love is based on it. In our work it can be truly said that in our best moments of dispassionate and objective analyzing we love our object, the patient, more than at any other time and are completely passionate with his whole being."[12]

Loewald says this *needs* to be said, but why? Because what he is saying does not seem immediately obvious – that dispassion can be passionate and passion dispassionate. Why is this not obvious? Is there trouble within the thought itself? Is it truly contradictory to try to think of passion and dispassion together? Or, by contrast, are there constrictions within our own familiar patterns of thinking that make it appear to us as though the constrictions were part of the very fabric of the world? That is, have we, unbeknownst to ourselves, been laboring with clichés of *detachment, dispassion, neutrality, science, and love* – and mistaken the cliché for the concept? For example, over the past decades, there has been widespread rejection of the image of the "detached" or "neutral" analyst – images that held sway in the mid-twentieth century.[13] But to reject a clichéd image of *detachment* or *neutrality* is only to get to the negation *of the cliché*. In this way, an intense debate over a clichéd image of the "dispassionate" analyst can take the place of serious thinking about passion or dispassion. The debate itself, purportedly covering all sides, serves as resistance. That is why this "needs to be said."

But how could saying this make a difference? Of course, it doesn't always happen. But let's consider what happens when it does. It helps to think of a single activity, *making a difference,* in two aspects. On the side of the author, Loewald is not merely stating (unusual) facts about the relations between love, truth, passion, and dispassion; *in the saying he is exemplifying the very things he says.* It is precisely his love of truth, his passion, and his dispassion that enable him to write these very sentences, and, in so writing, he puts them on display.[14] It is a very special demonstration: making a claim and establishing its truth in the very same act. On the side of the reader, we have the capacity to notice this even if we are not fully conscious of what is happening. We hear a ring of truth ourselves, and our own passion is stimulated.

We find ourselves *intrigued by* and *attracted to* the exemplar in his activity of exemplifying.

In this way, Loewald's writing is invitational. We are invited to join him in imaginative play with the very concepts with which we think. Somehow our most dispassionate moments become the moments of our greatest passion – and *not* by changing from dispassion to passion, but by dispassion itself expressing the passion. This is an example of Kierkegaardian irony – utterly earnest, playful thought.[15] The thought, I want to say, is right there in the thinking. If we just let ourselves hear the call of *dispassion*, we can ourselves experience the passion of living up to that commitment. To put it in psychoanalytic terms, dispassionate engagement is itself constitutive of a psychoanalytic ego ideal and, as such, can become a passionate commitment. Loewald's writing opens up an intermediate space in what had hitherto looked like an exhaustive dichotomy, for or against. Part of what it is to think seriously is to be creative with the concepts with which one thinks. As we saw earlier, Loewald encourages us to explore new forms of discovery (rather than the discovery of new objects). Here, we can see him doing just that. Concepts are not themselves objects; they are that in terms of which we encounter objects and comprehend them. And in any case, Loewald is not asking us *to look at* them; rather, he is inviting us to join in imaginative yet rigorous play with them. Concepts, when deployed well, are themselves modes of discovery, and if we can play with them, we enable ourselves to encounter objects anew. This is one way in which Loewald lives his love for truth.

The power of exemplarity needs to be studied more in psychoanalysis because it cannot all be understood in the familiar terms of erotic or positive transference. There is something about an exemplar that *strikes us, inspires admiration, and awakens a desire for more.* Here I am indebted to the philosopher Linda Zagzebski: we can be struck by an exemplar without quite knowing *what it is* about the exemplar that is commanding our attention.[16] So, positive or erotic transference up to a point. But it is internal to the experience of exemplarity that there is something new here, something we do not yet understand, something that may entice us to open ourselves up in ways we do not yet understand. It is partly this intriguing sense of not quite knowing that draws us along – perhaps along new paths. Exemplarity entices us beyond stuck repetitions. It may be erotic, but it is not entirely transference.

Loewald uses the first-person plural: "In *our field* the love of truth cannot be isolated...."; "In *our* work ...*we* love *our* object, the patient...." What makes this *our* field, *our* work, and *our* object? Who gets to count as "we"? If a sociologist were to do a systematic study of the membership of the American Psychoanalytic Association, for example, she would not discover that in their dispassion they loved their patients with their whole being. As an empirical generalization and as a social fact, Loewald's statement is simply not true. But that does not make his statement false; it makes it something other than a statement of social fact. *Our field*, as Loewald names it, cannot be identified with any professional organization. And yet, *our field* is the field of psychoanalysis. Loewald, in his exemplarity, is issuing a call. These are the ideals of psychoanalysis: and if you can recognize the truth of this, however dimly, you are hereby invited to make them your own. Loewald's writing promotes the internalization of the values it commends by enticing our erotic natures with his example.

What is it like to follow his example? Psychoanalytically speaking, we are dealing with the internalization of a psychoanalytic ego ideal. Obviously, content matters. But so too does the manner of the internalization: that it is not just the ideas but there is also getting the hang of *passion* and *dispassion, love, truth, mourning, separation, and individuation*; of living these ideals and living up to them; of making them one's own.

And *making them one's own* involves taking responsibility for the very concepts in terms of which one thinks and lives. We have seen Loewald do this in the distinctive turns he takes with the concepts he tries to pass on to us. Our inheritance is not merely picking up *what he said* but internalizing a manner of taking responsibility ourselves. This activity of internalization is, to use Freud's language, *interminable*. There is no point at which the project is completed, where one has reached bottom.

These internalizations promote individuation, and yet those very individuating acts enable us to come together. We come to hear the call and share the responsibilities of *our field*. This is not an easy process. For the love of truth essentially involves tolerating a certain amount of loneliness. Part of what it is to love truth is to experience some dissatisfaction with how things seem to be. There is something about the appearances, something about the current fashions, and the currently accepted trends of thought that don't add up. This includes how we appear to ourselves. But, given our erotic natures, we are also *attached* to appearances (Freud called it cathexis). And we are attached to other people who are themselves attached to appearances. This means that the love of truth does not show up as an uncomplicated romance. It requires separating from one's attachments, and that often requires separating from others. This is the *passion* of the love of truth; to some extent, we have to suffer it. Here is a consolation of Loewald's work: If one does pursue this separation for the sake of figuring out how things are, one finds Loewald there, along with others who have gone through their own individuating processes with whom to form a different kind of community.

****

At this point, I am going to share a few memories. A few days before he died, Hans told me that he hoped that there would never be any Loewaldians.[17] His statement is enigmatic, but it is clear that there are ways of going on in his name that he did not want. I think he shared with Socrates a concern that the human mind tends toward the cliché of using names as a substitute for thinking. This is especially true in social settings, for instance, in the discourse of professional organizations. So, when I received an invitation to give this lecture, my initial response was skeptical. In truth, it was more than that: I felt some revulsion at the very idea of a Loewald Center and wondered how I could politely refuse. Then I heard that some of my friends at the Western New England Institute were involved and that Hans's family supported the venture, so I tried to think again and look on the bright side. And, in any case, I am certain that Hans did not want me to turn that phrase into some strict superego injunction. My ambivalence has not disappeared, but it has been leavened by a humorous vignette from Kierkegaard: of the religious figure who wants no disciples but, by saying so, attracts disciples who preach that there should be no disciples.[18] I do not want to be one of them, either. Here, I imagine Hans with an impish smile.

Nothing in excess! That was the inscription at Delphi. Perhaps there should be a sign at the entrance to the Loewald Center: *Let no Loewaldian enter!* But what good would that do?

In my case, I have tried to address this challenge by writing this very paper. In focusing on how Loewald's writing works I have tried to offer, if you will allow me a turn-of-phrase, a new discovery of Loewald, not a discovery of a new Loewald. And I have allowed myself to tolerate the emotional disturbance this invitation has provoked.

The fact is, I had become comfortable with familiar routines of memory. I make a martini many evenings before dinner (shaken, not stirred as Hans made them), and as I take the cold glass to my lips, I often enjoy a memory of Hans enjoying his first sip. But, with this invitation, my routines are disturbed. I am now about the age Hans was when I met him. What did I not understand back then as a young man?

Hans Loewald and I met weekly for approximately six years. It almost didn't happen. I had just arrived at Yale as a professor of philosophy, but I had decided I wanted to train as a psychoanalyst, so I was at the same time an entering candidate at the Western New England Institute. I had begun to read Loewald's work, and I was immediately bowled over by its beauty.

Hans was scheduled to teach a seminar to advanced candidates, and it was supposed to be the last before he retired. So I wrote him to ask permission to attend, and in the kindest of responses, Hans refused. The advanced candidates, he thought, needed their own seminar. At the time, I did not have the vocabulary for "maintaining boundaries," but I liked what he was doing. In a way, I enjoyed the frustration. So I wrote back and asked if I could hire him as my tutor. I would pay him his regular hourly fee. He agreed, and we began reading his essays together, one by one. Then we read Melanie Klein, then Winnicott, and then Kierkegaard. Then he wanted to read my work on Aristotle, Plato, and Wittgenstein. At some point, he did not want me to pay him any longer. Even at the time, I had the sense of being in the presence of someone extraordinary, and that sense has not diminished.

In the Preface to *Papers on Psychoanalysis,* Hans writes:

> Philosophy has been my first love. I gladly affirm its influence on my way of thinking while being wary of the peculiar excesses a philosophical bent tends to entail. My teacher in this field was Martin Heidegger, and I am deeply grateful for what I learned from him despite his most hurtful betrayal in the Nazi era which alienated me from him permanently.[19]

When the paperback edition came out, Hans gave me a copy in which he wrote, "My first love, philosophy is revived through our friendship." I was glad to have an inscribed copy, but at the time, I did not focus on the words. I was full of gratitude, but being young and somewhat troubled, I did not think much about what it was like for him. Writing is wonderful because it can help one later remember what one was never in a position to forget in the first place. I now see that, although Hans inscribed the book to me, it was not about me. It was about our friendship. That is something we did together. Through reading and conversation, we created a small community that enabled him to overcome a break and facilitate a re-creation. This helps me understand why there might be a good reason to establish a Hans W. Loewald Center. It is as though we need a community, ever renewed, to participate in activities of soul that transcend us all.

I shall close with a memory that I had forgotten and that has only come back to me in the process of writing this lecture. After Hans retired, he gave me a small clay statue of a man on a horse. Pre-Columbian. I believe it is a replica of no monetary value. He had it in his office, and he told me that for him, it represented the ego trying to ride the id. It is not unlike the small ancient figures that Freud had on his desk. I put it on the desk in my analytic office, and over the years, I have stared at it as I listened to patients.

One day, about 10 years ago, a colleague came to see me and asked to meet in my analytic office. This was unusual because I have an adjacent room where I see students and colleagues. Perhaps he wanted to discuss something confidential. Once we entered, he, very surprisingly, went over to one of the curtains to draw them shut. The problem was that those curtains operate on a pulley chain that goes up and down, and the curtains themselves cannot be pulled sideways. It all happened in an instant. My Loewald statue was swept into the curtain and catapulted into the air. It dropped on the floor and smashed into countless pieces. My colleague said something like "Oh dear!" and, again to my surprise, I found myself reassuring him. He then left. I was stunned. I grabbed a box and gathered up every shard and speck; some were as small as a fingernail cutting, or smaller. The tiniest of flecks. I walked fast over to the Institute for the Study of Ancient Cultures, a block away, as though I were rushing to an emergency room, and asked whether anyone could help me with this. I met a restorer of the antique originals, and she allowed me to hire her to bring this statue back to life. I was again hiring someone to help me. The restoration had to be done in stages, and it took months. But she did bring the horse and rider back from the dead, and the statue rides again in my analytic office.

When this memory came back, I shared it with my friend, the poet Louise Glück, and she wrote back: "It's almost too wonderful to tell, meaning it's so perfect it runs the risk of seeming tidy." And, thanks to Louise, my mind has since been wandering around tidiness. I realize it is not just the statue-shattering event that matters, so does the fact that the memory of it has come back to me now, in the process of writing this paper. While the facts are accurate, the memory is tidy. There are so many aspects – about my colleague, why he came to see me, how he came to pull that curtain, how we have dealt with each other over decades, so many facts about the young woman restorer and all the interactions we had over the course of those months, how we entered and left each other's lives, and so on – all of this had been left out. It seems to me that the memory has come back to me as a residue that has already been worked over. Although it is centrally and consciously concerned with my enduring relationship with Hans and the role played by this linking figure, the statue, it is also true that the peripheral figures have been transformed into tidy figures, part objects imaginatively caricatured: the Clumsy Colleague and the Restorer of Ancient Things.

I now read the return of this memory as an existential choice. Who's it going to be: Clumsy Colleague or Restorer? The Clumsy Colleague, I take it, is the "Loewaldian" whom Loewald did not want – an impassioned defender of some hollowed-out dogma misleadingly associated with his name. The Restorer of Ancient Things – who is she? She has a feel for the first stirrings of the human soul to express ourselves in symbolic form. And she feels a call to preserve and restore it as an occasion for remembering, for repetition in the creative sense of that term. She responds to that call both by submitting herself to a master craft of restoration and by using her own activity to keep it alive. She engages enormous skill, a craft that took her years to acquire, to take shards and flecks and reassemble them so as to make available, shall we say, new discoveries of an object. My analysands and I can now do new psychoanalytic dances in its presence. Without the Restorer, there would just be scattered shards that might haunt us, but with few ways to metabolize them into an ancestral past or project them into an imaginative future. The Restorer turns ghosts into ancestors, and, with her help, our ancestors do not drop off the back cliff of memory.

Let me conclude this essay by returning to Hans Loewald's first love, philosophy. Philosophy, like psychoanalysis, emerges from conflicts and problems that arise in the midst of life. Here is a conflict that emerges right now: we cannot rest content with timeless ideal of the Restorer. There is no trans-historical conception of what

Figure 4.1 The Statue Gifted to the Author by Hans Loewald. Photo by author.

it is forever going to mean to restore the past. And, in some sense, we already understand that the activity of restoration can go dead on us. Our ears hear the word "antiquarian," and we are ready for a pejorative use, as though it is of *merely antiquarian* interest. We tacitly intuit that a living concern with the past has been taken over by a fetishistic preoccupation. So, who then takes responsibility for restoring *the very idea of restoration*?

Psychoanalysis is, among other things, an art of restoration. Hans Loewald, in his writing, took on the responsibility of restoring, refurbishing, and, above all, *reanimating* the art of psychoanalysis itself. Whether you agree with his interpretation or not, Loewald's writing brings Freud – that is, the entire corpus of his writing – back to life. Actually, Loewald's work has a broader sweep than that. Hans Loewald is taking responsibility for what psychoanalysis has been, what it has become, and how it might be in the future.[20] And he is sharing all that with us. We need this. For if we are to help our analysands turn their *personal* ghosts into ancestors, we need to turn the ghosts of *psychoanalytic theory and technique* into ancestors. This is not just a matter of fastidiousness or "getting theory straight"; it is an urgent need to restore psychoanalysis in our psyches. This we do best in community: in friendships, in small discussion groups, and sometimes, if we get very lucky, in larger organizations. Hans Loewald, in his writings, invites us to join him in a spirit of inquiry, engagement, and renewal. It is his *spirit* that is exemplary: it not only animates us, it gives us a reason to form a community that is worthy of the name Hans W. Loewald Center (Figure 4.1).

Notes

1 This paper was originally delivered to celebrate the inauguration of the Hans W. Loewald Center on April 30, 2022.
2 Loewald described sublimation as an *alienating differentiation being reversed*: "a fresh unity is created by an act of unity. In this reversal – a restoration of unity – there comes into being

a differentiated unity (a manifold) that captures separateness in the act of uniting and unity in the act of separating." Loewald, *Sublimation*, p. 24 (my emphasis).

3 For my previous writings on Loewald, see "Eros and Development" and "Mourning and Moral Psychology," both in *Wisdom Won from Illness*, pp. 175–205. See also *Therapeutic Action: An Earnest Plea for Irony* and the Introduction to Loewald (2000).

4 *Oxford English Dictionary* online.

5 "On the Therapeutic Action of Psychoanalysis," in Loewald (1980 and 2000), pp. 224–225. My emphasis.

6 For the importance of the experience of rhythm in childhood for the establishment and maintenance of a just society, see Plato, *Laws*, Books 1–2. For two fine translations, see Plato (2016) and Meyer (2015).

7 Søren Kierkegaard, *Concluding Unscientific Postscript to the Philosophical Fragments*.

8 Loewald says as much himself: "This new discovery of oneself and of objects, this re-organization of ego and objects, is made possible by the encounter with a 'new object' that has to possess certain qualifications in order to promote the process. Such a new object relationship for which the analyst holds himself available to the patient and to which the patient has to hold onto throughout the analysis is one meaning of the term positive transference ("On the Therapeutic Action of Psychoanalysis," Loewald [1980 and 2000], pp. 224–225).

9 "Springsteen and Obama on Friendship and Fathers: 'You have to turn your ghosts into ancestors,'" *The Guardian* (UK) online: October 23, 2021.

10 Bruce Springsteen, *Born to Run*, p. 503.

11 "Therapeutic Action," Loewald (1980 and 2000), pp. 248–249; my emphasis.

12 "Analytic Theory and Analytic Process," Loewald (1980 and 2000), p. 297.

13 See also: "The objectivity of the analyst in regard to the patient's transference distortions, his neutrality in this sense, should not be confused with the "neutral" attitude of the pure scientist towards his subject of study... While the relationship between analyst and patient does not possess the structure of a scientist-scientific subject and is not characterized by neutrality in that sense on the part of the analyst, the analyst may become a scientific observer to the extent to which he is able to observe objectively the patient and himself in interaction. The interaction itself, however, cannot be adequately represented by the model of scientific neutrality. It is unscientific, based on faulty observation, to use this model.... What I am attempting to do is disentangle the justified and necessary requirement of objectivity and neutrality from a model of neutrality which has its origin in propositions, which I believe to be untenable." "Therapeutic Action," (Loewald 1980 and 2000, pp. 226–227).

14 See David Finkelstein, *Expression and the Inner*.

15 "But it doesn't follow from irony being present that earnest is excluded. That is something only *privat-docents* [assistant professors] assume." Kierkegaard (2009, p. 232n). See also Lear (2014, 2018).

16 Zagzebski, *Exemplarist Moral Theory*.

17 I reported on this earlier in "Mourning and Moral Psychology" (Lear, 2017).

18 *Concluding Unscientific Postscript*, pp. 63–64.

19 Loewald (1980, pp. viii–ix).

20 Heidegger's work on (what has standardly been translated as) "authentic" (*eigentlich*) is crucial here. See *Being and Time* (1962), pp. 312–382. A better translation may be "owned." In a sense, Loewald was an authentic psychoanalyst; he *owned* it or *owned up* to it by taking responsibility for it.

References

Finkelstein, D. (2008). *Expression and the Inner*. Cambridge, MA: Harvard University Press.

Heidegger, M. (1962). *Being and Time*. J. Macquarrie and E. Robinson, trans. New York: Harper and Row.

Kierkegaard, S. (2009). *Concluding Unscientific Postscript to the Philosophical Fragments*. Cambridge: Cambridge University Press.

Lear, J. (2014). *A Case for Irony*. Cambridge, MA: Harvard University Press.

Lear, J. (2017). *Wisdom Won from Illness: Essays in Philosophy and Psychoanalysis*. Cambridge, MA: Harvard University Press.

Lear, J. (2018). *Therapeutic Action: An Earnest Plea for Irony*. New York: Routledge.

Loewald, H.W. (1980). *Papers on Psychoanalysis*. New Haven, CT: Yale University Press.

Loewald, H.W. (1984). *Sublimation: Inquiries into Theoretical Psychoanalysis*. New Haven, CT: Yale University Press.

Loewald, H.W. (2000). *The Essential Loewald: Collected Essays and Books of Hans Loewald*. Hagerstown, MD: University Publishing Group.

Meyer, S.S. (2015). *Plato, Laws 1&2*. Oxford: Oxford University Press.

Plato. (2016). *Plato's Laws*. M. Schofield, ed., T. Griffith, trans. Cambridge: Cambridge University Press.

Springsteen, B. (2016). *Born to Run*. New York: Simon and Schuster.

Zagzebski, L. (2019). *Exemplarist Moral Theory*. New York: Oxford University Press.

Part II

Philosophical Underpinnings

Chapter 5

Philosophy, Heidegger, and Hans W. Loewald's Early Papers

Elizabeth A. Brett

Hans Loewald began writing about psychoanalysis in the early 1950s.[1] Since that time, there has been a growing recognition that his work was underestimated or misunderstood. In response, a number of analysts, each eminent in his or her own right, have written lengthy explications of his work in order to enhance its accessibility and draw attention to its significance. They begin with Arnold Cooper's (1988) comparison of Lytton Strachey's "The Nature of the Therapeutic Action of Psycho-analysis" (1934) to Loewald's "On the Therapeutic Action of Psychoanalysis" (1960). This is followed by *The Work of Hans Loewald: An Introduction and Commentary*, edited by Gerald Fogel (1991a), which included a revision of Cooper's paper, Loewald's therapeutic action paper, two other articles of his added at his request, and commentary by Fogel, Lawrence Friedman, and Roy Schafer. A third discussion of "On the Therapeutic Action of Psychoanalysis" followed as part of the Journal of the American Psychoanalytic Association's A Classic Revisited series, with comments by Fogel, Phyllis Tyson, Jay Greenberg, James McLaughlin, and Ellen Peyser (1996).

Thereafter, a wider consideration of Loewald's work appeared in articles, chapters, and books by Lear (1996, 1998, 2000); Mitchell (1998, 2000); Teicholz (1999); Whitebook (2004, 2008); and Chodorow (2003, 2004, 2020). In addition, The Loewaldian Legacy, a collection of articles by Chodorow, Jacobs, Friedman, Balsam, and Pinsky, was published in 2008. There are many single papers taking up circumscribed aspects of Loewald's ideas, which are unfortunately too numerous to mention in this paper. All of the commentaries are extensive reviews, locating Loewald within the analytic controversies of his and the author's time (Cooper, Fogel, and Mitchell for earlier, and Teicholz, Whitebook, and Chodorow for more recent history). They provide perceptive and vivid summaries of his work and an appreciation of his unique and compelling vision. Despite this recognition, however, the sense remains for those interested in his writings that he still has not received the sustained attention his work deserves.

To the commentaries above, I would like to add what I believe is an underappreciated aspect of Loewald's contribution: how substantial and developed a point of view he presents from the outset. In order to demonstrate this, I will trace his method of scholarship and the content of his positions in the early papers which lead up to and include "On the Therapeutic Action of Psychoanalysis" (1960). This examination involves considering the influences on Loewald of his philosophic training and studies with Martin Heidegger. Finally, from our current perspective, I will argue that it is possible to see more clearly why it has been difficult to understand and recognize the strength and relevance of Loewald's writing. Factors contributing to the challenges

DOI: 10.4324/9781003328230-7

he presents to the reader include reconciling both his alignment with and oppositions to Freudian theory, following the density of his own theoretical argumentation, and relating this conceptual scaffolding to the emotional and expressive quality of his writing, which is always present but especially heightened in passages of bodily and sensory description.

Ego and Reality

I will concentrate on Loewald's style of exposition and the clarity, rigor, and substance of his proposals.[2] In "Ego and Reality," published in 1951, he presents a critique of widely accepted psychoanalytic explanations of the development of the psyche and its relation to reality. He objects to the predominantly defensive understanding of the ego and the hostile relationship between ego and reality contained in it. Loewald proceeds in the following manner: he begins with incisive and close readings of Freud, challenges certain of Freud's terms, agrees partially with others, and uses this examination as the platform for proposing his own theoretical constructions. This remains a characteristic method of his writing.

He points out that Freud held two incompatible views of the development of ego and reality. In the first, they are conceived as distinct entities (see Lear 1998 on Freud's concept of reality, pp. 316–317). The ego functions to restrict internal instinctual urges to meet the requirements of external realities. In the second, ego and reality are undifferentiated in the early stage of primary narcissism and separate out from each other as the ego acts to recover their original unity. The ego's action for, Freud, however, remains defensive.

Building on this second version, Loewald agrees that initially, ego and reality exist together in an undifferentiated state and that development must occur for the two to become distinct. Through the infant's repeated experiences that "a part of him, is not always available" (p. 5), separations, e.g., between mouth and breast, begin to form. These divisions stimulate the urge to restore the original connections. The urges created by differentiating elements are the earliest forms of libidinal movements and attachments, which operate in a mixture of primitive, action-dominated, introjective, and projective processes. At this stage, "inside and outside are still so rudimentary and fluid that the two terms signify different directions of the same process" (p. 17). As differentiating, boundary-setting processes begin to form, the ego connects and organizes these increasingly complex registrations of internal and external experience. At first, these registrations are experienced as magical and omnipotent. Only very gradually do they become organized on a more objective basis. Loewald emphasizes that the ego's synthetic function is broader than its defensive one: libidinal connections form relationships between elements of experience in addition to and intermingled with the connections instigated by defense. Development is a continuous process of ego/reality differentiations and integrations based on libidinal and defensive forces.

Loewald's new conception of "mother-infant unity" (p. 14) and of the nature of the earliest processes in psychic development led him to revise the dynamic understanding of the Oedipus Complex. Rather than viewing the paternal castration threat as the most prominent stimulus for its emergence, Loewald begins his account with the primary narcissistic unity with the mother. This positive relationship is associated with the fear of remaining in or returning to the undifferentiated state of unity. The positive identification with the father and the fear of merger with the mother support the ego's striving for a higher level of organization. Within this context, the oedipal castration threat acts as a further inducement to individuation and reorganization. Throughout these vicissitudes, the libidinal ties to both parents support the integrative forces. This reconceptualization of the Oedipus Complex, based on increasingly complex integrations of libidinal as well as defensive forces, replaces the one centered on antagonistic processes. Loewald is arguing that greater attention to early development as well as the libidinal contribution to psychic growth is necessary for adequate comprehension of later stages, in this case the Oedipal one.

I would like to emphasize the magnitude of the differences between Loewald's and Freud's positions. Loewald begins with the mother-infant unity, an interpersonal "tension system," as he describes it in "Ego and Reality," as the basis for understanding the formation of the psyche with its reconceived view of the emergence of the ego, the nature of reality, and the dynamics of development – all foundational concepts in psychoanalytic theory. Loewald directly opposes conceptualizing the psyche and its drives as an isolated unit, reality as a given, and development as propelled by antagonistic and defensive processes only. The new and revised metapsychological concepts are accompanied by detailed descriptions in his portrayal of the earliest, differentiating, and boundary-setting processes in psychic functioning and in his account of the dynamics in his reformulated Oedipal Complex.

Loewald is also aware of the consequences of his new formulations of psychoanalytic theory. The processes involved in early development aid in understanding infantile aggression, the loss of boundaries in psychotic phenomena, the erosion of integration in regression, and the positive attributes of oceanic and religious feelings. In discussing the latter, Loewald makes clear that Freud defensively avoids the earliest undifferentiated realms of merger (see also Lear 2000; Nields 2003). Loewald describes the nature of the early ego/reality experience, in which both ego and reality share concrete, magical, and omnipotent qualities for the child. The passion and intensity of early experience survive alongside later integrations as well as providing dynamic sources for the subsequent integrations. He ends with the statement that the ability to access multiple levels of organization gives a fuller picture of maturity than a narrow idea of moving beyond early experience.

In summary, "Ego and Reality" contains, in an early form, Loewald's model of the mother–infant matrix, which became the cornerstone of his work, as well as his recognition of its far-reaching theoretical and clinical implications, which he spent a lifetime explicating. It is an astonishing, bold, and trenchant achievement.

Influences on Loewald's Vision

"Ego and Reality" immediately raises the question of where this original, articulate, and robust point of view came from. As a teacher of Loewald's work, I became interested in the influences contributing to this perspective, which differed so significantly from Freud's. Cooper (1988), wondering too, writes, "One of the intellectual mysteries... is the source for Loewald's vision of the nature of psychic life and for the power of his conviction about his ideas" (p. 21). He notes that Loewald did not cite other analysts with similar views, e.g., Rado, Sullivan, Horney, or analysts from the British object relations tradition, and concludes that perhaps these ideas were "in the analytic air." Chodorow (2020), who quotes Cooper's puzzlement, suggests Loewald's analytic training in Baltimore with Sullivan as an influence. Fogel (1991b) initially considers whether Loewald's work with children or exposure to Sullivan and Fromm-Reichmann were factors but rejects the latter due to the interpersonal school's lack of intrapsychic focus. Fogel comes closer to an answer by describing Loewald's twentieth-century scientific and philosophical Weltanschauung: a post-Newtonian world of processes, interacting energy fields, and dynamic systems; a post-Cartesian world "in which there is no mind-body split, no simple 'objective' or 'external' reality"; one in which "observer and observed inevitably influence and alter each other" (p. 172). Fogel mentions Loewald's philosophic training and exposure to Heidegger as "probably relevant" but does not comment further (p. 173).

G. Stanley Leavy, M.D. (1989) was the first to elaborate Heidegger's profound influence on Loewald's thought. Leavy was a Training Analyst at the Western New England Institute and a colleague of Loewald's who had his own serious interest in philosophy. Leavy writes of Heidegger's *Being and Time* that it "is the whole impact of this massive work in its immense complexity relating many unfamiliar concepts to one another that we sense in following Loewald's application of them" (p. 235). Leavy observes that Heidegger's central concept, "being there, the *Dasein*, possesses his or her own future, as "project" to be fulfilled," and quotes Loewald (1988), indicating the similarity of such ideas regarding development to Freud's: "Heidegger's concepts of *Geworfenheit*-man is thrown into the world, unplanned and unintended by himself-and *Entwerfen*-the taking over and actively developing the potentialities of this fact-have grown in the same soil" (quoted in Leavy 1989, p. 234).

Leavy mentions the proliferating concepts Heidegger coined to describe being: not only *Dasein*, thrownness, and project, but also being-in-the-world, being-with, the cyclical nature of experienced time in the interrelatedness of past, present, and future, and care and solicitude for others. These concepts reflect Heidegger's use of multiple perspectives and aspects of being to elaborate the individual's embeddedness in the world. It should be noted, however, that one great difference between the two men highlighted by Loewald and Leavy is the neglect of the conscious/unconscious domain in Heidegger's work.

Leavy sees Heidegger's influence in Loewald's notions of the mother-infant unity, the object-relational origins of instincts, the constitutive nature of processes of internalization recurring throughout development, and of time conceived as an interweaving of the past, present, and future in the directional unfolding of the individual's life. Leavy manages, in a concise and subtle account, to convey the broad thrust and atmosphere of Heidegger's writing manifest in Loewald's extension of it. In summary, Leavy writes that Heidegger and Loewald are discussing a world of human comprehension in which "to be there is to be interested, concerned...with other's being-there; that is, others made manifest, even, to themselves, by being recognized and addressed" (p. 239).

Ten years later, and without knowledge of Leavy's article, Mitchell remarks that Loewald's work could be understood as a "Heideggerian reworking of Freud's basic concepts" (1998, p. 835). He finds this most evident in Loewald's focus on language. Mitchell mentions the centrality of words for Heidegger and, among other aspects of his interest in language, his call to rediscover in "original Greek" or other primary terms the insights these words provided which had become obscured by time (underscored as well by Whitebook 2008). Loewald's exegesis of Freud's terms, his effort to expand rather than narrow the meanings of concepts, and his poetic use of language would all have been influenced by Heidegger. Mitchell also points out that Loewald's perspective bridged dichotomies between the non-verbal and verbal realms of experience in contemporary theories of language. In a second piece on Loewald, Mitchell states that he is most interested in clinical Loewald. Mitchell considers Loewald's most significant revision of Freud's theory to be his model of the mother-infant field from which psychic formation arises. He sees the inspiration for this idea coming from Freud's concept of primary narcissism. He does not mention Heidegger.

The fact that Loewald came to psychoanalysis with a sophisticated understanding of continental philosophy can now be specifically acknowledged and considered. As Downey, a close friend and colleague, observed, "In terms of his intellectual heritage... Hans was captivated by the ideas of Nietzsche, Heidegger and Goethe" (1994, p. 840). Before beginning medical training, Loewald studied philosophy with Martin Heidegger, whom Downey describes as his mentor. At that time, the field was immersed in Husserl's phenomenology of subjective experience and his student Heidegger's search for more radical approaches to man's immersion in the world. These perspectives differed considerably from Freud's positivism, still prevalent in American psychoanalysis in the 1950s (Whitebook 2004). Husserl and Heidegger recognized that an investigator of human experience was using precisely those attributes he was intending to study. Heidegger focused not only on the need to encompass the indivisibility of man and his study of his own being but also on the broader primary interconnectedness of man and his world.

In the Preface to *Papers on Psychoanalysis*, Loewald acknowledges that philosophy was his "first love." "My teacher in this field was Martin Heidegger, and I am deeply grateful for what I learned from him, despite his most hurtful betrayal in the Nazi era, which alienated me from him permanently" (1980, p. ix). The fact that Loewald broke with Heidegger and rarely cited his work has contributed to eclipsing the significance of this intellectual background. Loewald's 'permanent alienation' is more complex than it would appear. Leavy writes that despite Heidegger's "appalling actions," Loewald "has always acknowledged his debt to Heidegger, only after Freud, as his teacher" (p. 232). This may have been true for those who knew Loewald personally, but it was not explicit or evident to those who knew him through his writing only.

I believe Loewald's training in philosophy enhanced his own interests in conceptual rigor, foundational principles, and the construction of theory. It seems evident that Heidegger's major influence was on Loewald's focus on interpersonal, interactional processes, beginning with the mother-infant matrix in which psychological experience emerges on the basis of these processes and extends throughout his work to the ways in which relatedness to others and the world are taken in and transformed into ever more complex integrations and reintegrations. In addition, I believe Heidegger also influenced Loewald's method of scholarly inquiry. Heidegger (1962) used the word "*destruktion*" to describe a necessary approach to the study of being.

> When tradition becomes master, it does so in such a way that what it 'transmits' is made so inaccessible... that it rather becomes concealed... it blocks our access to those primordial 'sources' from which the categories and concepts handed down to us have been in part quite genuinely drawn.
>
> (p. 43)

He advises, "this hardened tradition must be loosened up, and the concealments which it has brought about dissolved" (p. 44). *Destruktion*, then, implies the study of basic terms, attention to their narrowing, restrictive effect over time, and the recovery and expansion of their original illuminating power. This perspective provides a fuller understanding of Loewald's intense focus on Freud's early concepts, his rejection of terms which he believed had become rigid, taken-for-granted or hollow, and his simultaneous appreciation of and regard for the profundity of others, which he strove to enliven. The fact that this method includes strong agreements and disagreements with Freud throws light on the perplexity in psychoanalytic literature about Loewald's degree of allegiance to or departure from Freudian theory. I will return to this below.

The Problem of Defense and the Neurotic Interpretation of Reality

Returning to the trajectory of Loewald's early work, in his second paper, "The Problem of Defense and the Neurotic Interpretation of Reality" (1952), he amplifies his critique of the psyche as defensive, leaving psychoanalysis with a theory too heavily based on conflict and defense as the stimulus for development. Rather than adopting Freud's view of civilization as opposing man's desires, Loewald centers the source of the infant's anxiety and conflict on the discrepancy between the infant's capacity for integration and the environment's far greater complexity. This requires the mother's support and the channeling of developmental processes. Particularly in these earliest stages of what he now labels "the organism-environment field" (p. 447), a lack of adequate support leads to ego deficiencies. Later, on the basis of an ego in which ego/reality distinctions are more firmly established, the ego becomes capable of reacting to internal and external threats; that is to say, defensive functioning becomes possible. The overemphasis on defense and neurotic levels of integration collapses this distinction. Similar oversights occur in considerations of the pleasure and reality principles, which emphasize adjustment to reality, a later integration, at the expense of the role and significance of fantasy, an earlier one. The failure to appreciate integrative forces also occurs in conceptualizations of the transition from primary to secondary process functioning with its novel capacity for language and in the investigation of the various forms of subliminatory activity.

Again, Loewald has raised strong objections to the neglect of early libidinal processes of introjection/projection in the interpersonal field and the resulting misunderstanding of dynamics as primarily defensive. And again, he points to its inhibitory effect on the further understanding of significant areas of psychic functioning.

Hypnoid State, Repression, Abreaction, and Recollection

In Loewald's third paper, "Hypnoid state, Repression, Abreaction, and Recollection" (1955), he focuses more specifically on technique, unusual in his writing. What is at stake are the technical consequences of confusing earlier and later dynamic processes. To demonstrate the significance of such confusions, he examines Freud's reconceptualization of hysteria as a disorder based on repression rather than a hypnoid state. Freud discarded the techniques of abreaction and catharsis associated with the hypnoid state and endorsed interpretations of repression for his revised understanding of hysteria.

He defined repression as a three-stage process: primary repression, in which experience is laid down in unconscious somatic memory traces due to the infantile state of the ego or its inability to absorb and abreact an overstimulating experience; repression proper, in which the ego repels the material associated with the memory traces; and the return of the repressed, in which the repressed material continually reemerges into consciousness in the guise of derivatives and compromises.

Once Freud had rejected the hypnoid state, he and subsequent analysts focused on the last two phases, repression proper and the return of the repressed, in which the technical interventions were interpretations of drive derivatives and defense. This perspective minimized primary repression and the strategies suitable for it. Loewald points out that Freud's technical recommendations for handling unconscious memory traces laid down in undifferentiated sensory experience were the rejected techniques of abreaction and catharsis. The arousal, articulation, and expression of affect from body memories and the detailed recollection of the events connected with them are the methods for lifting material that had never progressed beyond unconscious organization to the level of language and meaning. Loewald and Freud agree that the unconscious resists the "transformation into secondary process" (p. 207) and tends to draw material so transformed back into the unconscious. This "drawing back" is the work of repetition compulsion, not of repression proper. Despite temporary transformation into secondary process, working through consists of repeated efforts to lift unconscious material onto higher levels of organization. As this progression becomes more stable, abreaction and catharsis become intertwined with and enhanced by interpretations of drive and defense. Since they address the earliest registrations of experience, abreaction and catharsis remain fundamental to analytic technique, they are not superseded, that is replaced, by interpretations of drive and defense.

On the Therapeutic Action of Psychoanalysis

To recapitulate, thus far, Loewald has proposed a new model of psychic development originating in an interpersonal mother-infant unity and characterized the processes involved in its early formation, distinguishing them from the later levels of organization which had preoccupied Freud and psychoanalytic theory. Loewald's fourth paper, "On the Therapeutic Action of Psychoanalysis" (1960), offers further details and refinements of the arguments he has been developing. It also contains significant reintegrations of them. Loewald begins by stating that his overarching concern is with the contribution of object relations to psychic structure formation as it applies to the therapeutic processes occurring with the analyst in the treatment situation. He thereby brings forward the interpersonal/interactional perspective underlying his critiques of analytic theory.

In previous papers, the distinctiveness of his model of the mother-infant unity was explicated in the context of the inadequate analytic understanding of earlier and later levels of psychic organization. In the hypnoid state article, the paper just before the therapeutic action one, Loewald proposed different technical strategies for material organized at unconscious and preconscious levels. In an early draft of the therapeutic action paper (Moscovitz 2014), Loewald continues his focus on the confusion of earlier and later levels of organization, objecting to the narrowing of technique to interpretations of transference and resistance. In subsequent drafts, however, he abandons this line of argument and begins to concentrate on the implications of his object-relational model for therapeutic action (Moscovitz 2014). This change in focus is, I believe, the first significant reintegration in the therapeutic action paper.

In the first section of the paper, Loewald begins with an objection to the concepts of the individual as a closed system and the analyst as a reflecting mirror. Instead, analysis, as in development, is the occasion, through interaction, for ego disorganization and reorganization. In the transference with the analyst, disorganization leads to the new discovery of old object relations through the interpretation of transference distortions, a task with which both patient and analyst increasingly identify. The neutrality of the analyst based on the scientific model of an investigator examining the subject of his study is replaced by "objectivity and neutrality the essence of which is love and respect for the individual and for individual development" (p. 20). This stance is analogous to parent–child interaction in which the child's core comes into being as a result of the parent's focus and care.

In the second section, Loewald reviews Freud's concepts of instincts and their relation to libido and the ego. He redefines instincts as urges gaining form and structure through intersubjective interactions organized by and organizing the environment. This stands in opposition to instincts viewed purely as internal stimuli discharging in reflex arcs. Loewald points out that Freud conceptualizes two sources of integration in the psyche: the binding activity of the libido as well as the synthesizing activity of the ego. The usefulness of the concept of organization with its various levels of integration, he believes, has yet to be sufficiently employed in understanding instinctual drives.

In the third section, Loewald reviews the higher level of organization mediated by the mother to the infant in the earliest phases of psychic formation and relates it to the satisfaction in integrative interactions with the analyst based on "the mutual recognition involved in the creation of identity of experience in two individuals of different levels of ego organization" (p. 25). In his discussion of this analogy, satisfaction, understood by Freud as the reduction or abolition of stimuli, has fallen by the wayside. Central to the integrative process is the analyst's mediation of material at the level of instinctual drives into secondary process organization through the use of language.

In the final section, Loewald introduces a less familiar meaning of the term transference: the transfer of the intensity of an unconscious idea to the preconscious, which is the basis for the more usual meaning, the transfer of infantile to contemporary object relations. He uses these transferences to support his famous metaphor of ghosts from the past haunting the individual in his or her current life. It is the ghosts' tasting the blood of the transference that leads to the new discovery of old objects, organized at unconscious levels, which in turn allows for new relationships to the self and the analyst. The transference from the unconscious to the preconscious operates as "the 'dynamism' by which the instinctual life of man" (p. 30) becomes more complex, differentiated, and mature, thereby rescuing it from being seen as simply the pathway for neurotic repetition. Furthermore, the transfer from the unconscious to the preconscious is the internalized form of the intersubjective, interactional processes driving development and resumed in analysis. This multi-layered convergence and reintegration clarifies and elaborates his model of the mother-infant unity and the dynamic organization of the psyche adumbrated in "Ego and Reality" and his two following papers. This expansive reorganization is Loewald's new and innovative understanding of the therapeutic action of psychoanalysis.

Characteristics of Loewald's Writing

With the preceding explication of Loewald's first papers as background, I will discuss three characteristics of Loewald's work that have confused and divided early readers and made it difficult to understand and fully appreciate his work. The first is Loewald's adherence to many of the terms and concepts of classical Freudian thought. Despite this adherence, he has been called a revolutionary (Cooper 1988; Fogel 1991; Mitchell 2000). Whitebook (2004) who calls him a "radical conservative" (p. 97), notes that almost all commentators seek to locate Loewald on the radical/conservative dimension. Friedman (1996) wittily remarks that analysts argue "about what Loewald was really *up* to?" (p. 671). Was he subverting or clinging to tradition, hiding or revealing his true opinions?

To some extent, the effort to read Loewald in one way or another is due to the different traditions and territorial infighting in American psychoanalysis in the later part of the twentieth century, but it is also descriptive of the two opposing currents in Loewald's writing: his adherence to and departure from Freud and the mainstream of psychoanalytic theory. I have tried to emphasize in my discussion of Loewald's early papers that his challenges to and departures from Freud's ideas are not subtle but directly stated and of major import, both in his disagreement with particular concepts and in his recognition of the far-reaching ramifications of his point of view. For Loewald, these agreements and disagreements, a method influenced to a degree by Heidegger, were not a measure of loyalty or repudiation but rather his form of intense scholarly engagement in the task of carrying psychoanalytic theory forward, a task to which he was devoted.

A second and related difficulty in reading Loewald is the vastness of his theoretical universe, filled with Freud's concepts and terms, Loewald's revisions of them, and the many connections and new connections between them. Part of the wish to locate Loewald on the classical/non-classical dimension is due to the effort involved in comprehending what he is saying and determining its implications for theory. In the Loewald archive, Moscovitz (2014) uncovered written responses to Loewald's early papers in which the correspondents summarized his remarks, seeming to ask whether he had really said what they heard. A similar response to the intellectual challenge his work presents occurred in the frequent remarks that Loewald raised more questions than he answered. There were also outright misunderstandings. Rapaport commented that therapists of borderline patients already knew that "the therapist is always, besides being a transference object, a *real* object" (Rapaport quoted in Moscovitz 2014, p. 579), a naïve view of reality, and precisely the misreading Loewald anticipated and attempted to prevent in his paper. It requires a nimble reader to penetrate the density and grasp the scope of Loewald's theoretical discourse.

Loewald's use of poetic language involves a third challenge for the reader of his work. The poetic quality of his language has been criticized as unsystematic, idiosyncratic, and falling short of the precision required by metapsychological discourse (Cooper 1991; Schafer 1991). Cooper cites Loewald's use of metapsychological language in his use of terms such as "the resumption of ego development" and the concepts of transference in dreams or in the relationship to the analyst. He contrasts this language with the phenomenological descriptions of human interaction in passages such as the parent's "bodily handling of and concern with the child, the manner in which the child is fed, touched, cleaned, the way it is looked at, talked to, called by name, recognized and un-recognized" (p. 74). Cooper finds the metapsychological and phenomenological levels unintegrated and therefore unable to provide "scientific guidance in our work" (p. 76). Schafer faults Loewald for his inconsistent and imaginative rather than precise and established use of Freud's terms. Schafer's view is that "The realm of theory-making will never lack for ambiguity and turbulence, but these features have to do with competing and ever-evolving approaches to systematization and consensus and not to literariness" (p. 88). I have chosen Cooper's and Schafer's critiques because both men greatly admired Loewald's clinical descriptions, despite their reservations about the relation of these descriptions to metapsychology. Their admiration, I believe, allowed them to speak for others who may have had much stronger objections to his work.

As with Winnicott's critics, "poetic" was used by some as a term of dismissal (see Jacobs, this volume). It is, however, one of the aspects of Loewald's writing that I and many others find most appealing (Cooper 1991; Mitchell 2000). Heidegger and Loewald were concerned about the dangers of overly abstract and desiccated technical language. The strength of poetic writing is its ability to make experience come alive. Dobyns, a contemporary poet, explains that this is achieved in poetry principally by metaphor, the comparison of a graphic image to an experiential referent. The mind grasps the perceptual image rapidly but then to complete the comparison must review and articulate prior experience at a slower pace. The tension between these separate mental processes stimulates an internal dialogue and the awakening of emotional experience (Brett 2018; Dobyns 2003). Loewald's poetic language communicates the affective and experiential referents of the concepts and theories he creates in his work. A potential liability of this language, however, is that the reader may lose track of the conceptual argument accompanying it, e.g., Rapaport's misunderstanding of the concept of 'the real object.' Ultimately, I believe that abstract theoretical language and poetic language are distinct modes of knowing and communicating about human experience, each having strengths and weaknesses which can be recognized and taken into account. The wish for an authoritative, systematic, psychoanalytic metapsychology is the dream of an earlier era. In our postmodern, pluralistic world, we are much more aware that core concepts have different shades of meaning, of more and less significance, in diverse psychoanalytic traditions, and that hierarchical levels of abstraction are useful but do not provide ultimate answers to understanding the complexities of human experience.[3]

Conclusion

In summary, from his first publications, Hans Loewald presents a model of mother-infant unity, in which psychic development takes place in the tension systems of an interpersonal field. He outlines the almost undetectable and emergent processes in the psyche as psychological functioning begins to form and evolve in its earliest stages, proposing a conception of development based on successive levels of differentiation and integration. All of these proposals, influenced by Heidegger and Loewald's philosophic training, challenged basic concepts of Freud's and of the psychoanalytic theory of the day. Many, especially early readers, were confused by these challenges, particularly given Loewald's strong agreements and disagreements with carefully, explicated positions of Freud's; by the magnitude of the theoretical questions under consideration; and by the attraction to and suspicion of Loewald's poetic writing.

Notes

1 Loewald published four papers before beginning his psychoanalytic writing: three in Italian about psychiatric and neurological topics (1937a, 1937b, 1938), while working at the Neuro/Psychiatric Hospital, La Salutare, in Padua, Italy; and one in English, a book review of Kurt Goldstein's *The Organism* (1942), a holistic approach to studying the mind and body.
2 Ego and Reality has been discussed by many of the authors mentioned and at length by Mitchell (2000), Lear (2000), and Chodorow (2020).
3 For a concise and intelligent review of the history of attempts to systematize psychoanalytic terms, see the "Introduction," especially pp. xxii–xxv, to *Psychoanalytic Terms and Concepts* (Auchincloss and Samberg 2012).

References

Auchincloss, E.L. & Samberg, E. (2012). Introduction. In *Psychoanalytic Terms & Concepts*, eds. E.L. Auchincloss & E. Samberg. New Haven, CT: Yale University Press, pp. xxii–xxv.

Balsam, R. (2008). The essence of Hans Loewald. *Journal of the American Psychoanalytic Association* 56:1117–1128.

Brett, E.A. (2018). The play's the thing. *Psychoanalytic Study of the Child* 71:217–223.

Chodorow, N.J. (2003). The psychoanalytic vision of Hans Loewald. *International Journal of Psychoanalysis* 84:897–913.

Chodorow, N.J. (2004). The American independent tradition: Loewald, Erikson, and the (possible) rise of intersubjective ego psychology. *Psychoanalytic Dialogues* 14:207–232.

Chodorow, N.J. (2020). *The Psychoanalytic Ear and the Sociological Eye: Toward an American Independent Tradition*. New York: Routledge.

Cooper, A.M. (1988). Our changing views of the therapeutic action of psychoanalysis: Comparing Strachey and Loewald. *Psychoanalytic Quarterly* 57:15–27.

Cooper, A.M. (1991). Our changing views of the therapeutic action of psychoanalysis. In *The Work of Hans Loewald: An Introduction and Commentary*, ed. G.I. Fogel. Northvale, NJ: Jason Aronson, pp. 61–76.

Dobyns, S. (2003). *Best Words, Best Order: Essays on Poetry*. New York: Palgrave Macmillan Ltd.

Downey, T.W. (1994). Hans W. Loewald, M.D. (1906–1993). *International Journal of Psychoanalysis* 75:839–842.

Fogel, G.I. (1991a). *The Work of Hans Loewald: An Introduction and Commentary*. Northvale, NJ: Jason Aronson.

Fogel, G.I. (1991b). Transcending the limits of revisionism and classicism. In *The Work of Hans Loewald: An Introduction and Commentary*, ed. G.I. Fogel. Northvale, NJ: Jason Aronson, pp. 153–190.

Fogel, G.I., Tyson, P., Greenberg, J., McLaughlin, J.T. & Peyser, E.R. (1996). A classic revisited: Loewald on the therapeutic action of Psychoanalysis. *Journal of the American Psychoanalytic Association* 44:863–924.

Friedman, L. (1996). The Loewald Phenomenon. *Journal of the American Psychoanalytic Association* 44:671–672.

Friedman, L. (2008). Loewald. *Journal of the American Psychoanalytic Association* 56:1105–1115.

Heidegger, M. (1962). *Being and Time*, trans. J. Macquarrie & E. Robinson. New York: Harper and Row.

Lear, J. (1996). The introduction of eros: Reflections on the work of Hans Loewald. *Journal of the American Psychoanalytic Association* 44:673–698.

Lear, J. (1998). *Open Minded: Working out the Logic of the Soul*. Cambridge, MA: Harvard University Press.

Lear, J. (2000). Introduction. In *The Essential Loewald: Collected Papers and Monographs*, Hagerstown, MD: A Norman Quist Book, University Publishing Group, pp. ix–xl.

Leavy, S.A. (1989). Time and world in the thought of Hans W. Loewald. *Psychoanalytic Study of the Child* 44:23–240.

Loewald, H.W. (1937a). Neurological observations in insulin shock Treatment (In Italian). Milan: Proceedings of the Italian Congress on Modern Treatments in Schizophrenia. In Curriculum Vitae 1953. In Hans W. Loewald Papers (MS1721), Box 1. Manuscripts and Archives. New Haven, CT: Yale University Library.

Loewald, H.W. (1937b). The treatment of chronic arthropathies with intraspinal injections of phenolsulfenphthaleine (In Italian). Rassegna Internationale di Clinica e Torapia 28. In Curriculum Vitae 1953. In Hans W. Loewald Papers (MS1721), Box 1. Manuscripts and Archives. New Haven, CT: Yale University Library.

Loewald, H.W. (1938). Contribution to the measurement of the form and size of the Sella Turcica in intra and parasellar tumors (In Italian). Giornale di Psichiatria e di Neuropatologia. In Curriculum Vitae 1953. In Hans W. Loewald Papers (MS1721), Box 1. Manuscripts and Archives. New Haven, CT: Yale University Library.

Loewald, H.W. (1942). Book Review: Kurt Goldstein, The Organism. Journal of Philosophy and Phenomenological Research. In Curriculum Vitae 1953. In Hans W. Loewald Papers (MS1721), Box 1. Manuscripts and Archives. New Haven, CT: Yale University Library.

Loewald, H.W. (1951). Ego and reality. In *Papers on Psychoanalysis*. New Haven, CT: Yale University Press, 1980, pp. 3–20.

Loewald, H.W. (1952). The problem of defense and the neurotic interpretation of reality. In *Papers on Psychoanalysis*. New Haven, CT: Yale University Press, 1980, pp. 21–32.

Loewald, H.W. (1955). Hypnoid state, repression, abreaction, and recollection. In *Papers on Psychoanalysis*. New Haven, CT: Yale University Press, 1980, pp. 33–42.

Loewald, H.W. (1960). On the therapeutic action of psychoanalysis. In *Papers on Psychoanalysis*. New Haven, CT: Yale University Press, 1980, pp. 221–256.

Loewald, H.W. (1988). *Sublimation: Inquiries into Theoretical Psychoanalysis*. New Haven, CT: Yale University Press.

Mitchell, S.A. (1998). From ghosts to ancestors: The psychoanalytic vision of Hans Loewald. *Psychoanalytic Dialogues* 8:825–855.

Mitchell, S.A. (2000). *Relationality: From Attachment to Intersubjectivity*. Hillsdale, NJ: Analytic Press.

Moscovitz, S. (2014). Hans Loewald's "On the therapeutic action of psychoanalysis": Initial reaction and later influence. *Psychoanalytic Psychology* 31:575–587.

Nields, J.A. (2003). From unity to atonement: Some religious correlates of Hans Loewald's developmental theory. *International Journal of Psychoanalysis* 84:699–716.

Pinsky, E. (2008). Loewald panel: Discussion. *Journal of the American Psychoanalytic Association* 56:1129–1137.

Schafer, R. (1991). Internalizing Loewald. In *The Work of Hans Loewald: An Introduction and Commentary*, ed. G.I. Fogel. Northvale, NJ: Jason Aronson, pp. 77–89.

Strachey, J. (1934). The nature of the therapeutic action of psychoanalysis. *International Journal of Psychoanalysis* 15: 127–159.

Teicholz, J.G. (1999). *Kohut, Loewald, and the Postmoderns: A Comparative Study of Self and Relationship*. Hillsdale, NJ: Analytic Press.

Whitebook, J. (2004). Hans Loewald: A radical conservative. *International Journal of Psychoanalysis* 85:97–115.

Whitebook, J. (2008). Hans Loewald, psychoanalysis, and the project of autonomy. *Journal of the American Psychoanalytic Association* 56:116–1187.

Chapter 6

Loewald, Heidegger, and Freud

A Dialogue

Robert S. White

Introduction

The period between 1923 and 1933 was a pivotal decade in European philosophy. In Germany, several branches of Neo-Kantianism predominated in academic circles. Martin Heidegger began teaching at Marburg and, over the next four years, developed an entire new way of doing philosophy. The publication of *Being and Time* in 1927 set a tone which would dominate European philosophy, for or against, up to the present day. But Heidegger became a Nazi. By his account, he was trying to protect the university, but many others felt a betrayal of his Jewish colleagues and a background of antisemitism. Our story concerns one of those junior colleagues who felt betrayed, Hans Loewald, then studying with Heidegger. Loewald left the field of philosophy, eventually studying medicine and psychiatry and becoming a distinguished psychoanalyst in the United States. He has acknowledged his gratitude to Heidegger (Loewald 1980), yet his published work makes almost no allusions to Heidegger's ideas. I will develop the thesis that Loewald's psychoanalytic ideas, revolutionary in their own right, resulted from a three-way dialogue between himself, Heidegger, and Freud. The dialogue with Freud is conscious and results in a revision of fundamental psychoanalytic concepts, while the dialogue with Heidegger is unstated and unacknowledged, yet perhaps just as fundamental. I will suggest that Loewald used Heideggerian concepts to help psychoanalysis come alive, just as Heidegger wanted to enliven Kantian ideas.

The Participants

Martin Heidegger

Martin Heidegger was born in Messkirch, Baden-Württemberg, in 1889.[1] His interest in philosophy first arose during his high school studies in Freiburg when, at the age of 17, he read Franz Brentano's (1995) book entitled *On the Manifold Meaning of Being according to Aristotle*. By his own account, it was this work that inspired his life-long quest for the meaning of being. Brentano is a central figure in our story, who unites Heidegger, Husserl, and Freud through his intellectual influence. Heidegger entered a Jesuit seminary in 1909 but eventually turned to studies in philosophy, mathematics, and the natural sciences. Having completed a habilitation thesis in 1915, he was appointed a Privatdozent at the University of Freiburg. He taught mostly courses in Aristotelian and scholastic philosophy and regarded himself as standing in the service of

DOI: 10.4324/9781003328230-8

the Catholic worldview. This occurred in the backdrop of WWI, where Heidegger was mostly deferred for medical reasons. He married Elfride Petri in 1917, who, scholars later discovered, was openly antisemitic.

Nevertheless, Heidegger's turn from theology to philosophy was soon to be followed by another turn. In 1916, he became a junior colleague of Edmund Husserl, who pioneered the study of phenomenology. Heidegger's lectures on phenomenology and his creative interpretations of Aristotle earned him wide acclaim. Arendt (1971) puts it thusly:

> Thinking has come to life again; the cultural treasures of the past, believed to be dead, are being made to speak, in the course of which it turns out that they propose things altogether different from the familiar, worn-out trivialities they had been presumed to say.

Laboring over the question of being, Heidegger soon began a radical reinterpretation of Husserl's phenomenology. In 1923, Heidegger was appointed associate professor at Marburg University. He formed close friendships with Karl Jaspers and Rudolf Bultmann, both of whom incorporated Heidegger's ideas into their own philosophies. Hannah Arendt arrived in Marburg in 1923, an 18-year-old Jewish student with a forceful intellect. Heidegger took notice of her in February of 1924, invited her for a talk at his office, and their affair began soon after. Heidegger demanded total secrecy and a type of adulation, yet he had very little interest in her independent academic achievements. Safranski (1998) described her as Heidegger's muse for *Being and Time*. Heidegger suggested in 1925 that she move to Heidelberg, and the affair began to wind down.

Between 1923 and 1928, Heidegger enjoyed the most fruitful years of his teaching career. He attracted the best and brightest of philosophical students, many Jewish, and among these was Hans Loewald. Heidegger's students testified to the originality of his insight and the intensity of his philosophical questioning. He extended the scope of his lectures and taught courses on the history of philosophy, time, logic, phenomenology, Plato, Aristotle, Aquinas, Kant, and Leibniz; however, he had published nothing since 1916, a factor that threatened his future academic career. Finally, in February 1927, his fundamental but also unfinished treatise, *Being and Time* (*Sein und Zeit*), appeared. Within a few years, this book was recognized as a truly epoch-making work of twentieth-century philosophy. It earned Heidegger in the fall of 1927 a full professorship at Marburg University and, one year later, after Husserl's retirement from teaching, the chair of philosophy at Freiburg University. *Being and Time (Heidegger, 1962)* has been hailed as one of the most significant texts in the canon of contemporary European Philosophy. It pushed Heidegger to a position of international intellectual visibility and provided the philosophical impetus for a number of later programs and ideas in the contemporary European tradition: Sartre's existentialism, Gadamer's philosophical hermeneutics, Merleau-Ponty's phenomenological perception, Derrida's notion of 'deconstruction', and Levinas' idea of the ethics of the Other.

Heidegger's life entered a problematic and controversial stage with Hitler's rise to power. When Hitler was appointed chancellor of Germany in 1933, Heidegger, up to then virtually apolitical, became politically involved. He was elected rector of the University of Freiburg by the faculty. He later claimed he wanted to avoid the danger of a party functionary being appointed, but he also seemed to believe that he could steer the Nazi movement in the right direction. He joined the Nazi party, and on May 27, 1933, he delivered his inaugural rectoral address on "The Self-Assertion of the German University" (Heidegger, 1985). The ambiguous text of this speech has often been interpreted as an expression of his support for Hitler's regime (Neske and Kettering 1990). During his tenure as rector, he produced a number of speeches for the Nazi cause and was much more active in supporting the Nazi party than he has publicly admitted to; he never renounced his Nazi affiliation. He participated in the removal of Jewish colleagues from the university, including his mentor, Husserl, and did nothing to help Arendt, who was briefly detained by the Gestapo. There is little doubt that during that time Heidegger placed the great prestige of his scholarly reputation at the service of national socialism and thus, willingly or not, contributed to its legitimization among his fellow Germans (Safranski 1998). What Heidegger's motivation was for joining the Nazi movement remains highly controversial, but in 1934, Heidegger resigned from his office and took no further part in politics. He was then criticized by the Nazi party. Following Germany's defeat in the Second World War, Heidegger was accused of Nazi sympathies, was forbidden to teach in German universities, and in 1946 was dismissed from his chair of philosophy. This ban was lifted in 1949.

More recently, Heidegger's Black Notebooks (2017) from 1931 to 1941 have been published, and they contain scattered antisemitic passages[2]:

> The Jews, with their marked gift for calculating, live, already for the longest time, according to the principle of race, which is why they are resisting its consistent application with utmost violence.
>
> (quoted in Brody, 2014)

Or:

> Jews are "uprooted from Being-in-the World"—that is, incapable of authentically caring and knowing.
>
> (quoted in Brody, 2014)

This makes it clear that Heidegger was a committed antisemite well before the Nazis. Is this the personal opinion of a deeply flawed man, or does it contaminate the whole of his philosophy?

Safranski (1998) suggests that Hannah Arendt's (1958) book, The Human Condition, written after the war without ever mentioning Heidegger's name, criticized his philosophy. I believe it is a criticism that Loewald would have agreed with. She contrasts the *vita contemplativa* with the *vita activa*. Heidegger is the vita contemplativa, the philosopher, whose quest for Being and purity meant that he rejected the ordinary human world, what Heidegger (1962) called the they (*das Man*) (pp. 163–168). *Dasein*, in his view, is opposed to the Others who make up the they; Heidegger speaks of Being that will be taken over by the Others, submerged, subject to averageness, leaving Being to be leveled down. It is tempting for *Dasein* to want to escape into the they, to escape being-onto-death. The self of ordinary life is the they-self, which can be distinguished from the authentic self. Heidegger calls this publicness (*öffentlichkeit*) (p. 165). In one sense, this is right; there is often a need to escape authenticity through submission in a group or culture. But Arendt raises the opposite concern; she argues that Heidegger, in rejecting the ordinary world of the They, is abandoning the ground of the human. She finds openness, not in a clearing toward Being, aloof from the polis, but in the public life of a shared world with other human beings, a place where persons encounter each other and must find a way to live together. She calls this the *vita activa*, the human condition of action. It is inherently political; it creates the conditions for history. Appearance constitutes reality and the existence of a public realm. The term "public" signifies the world itself. We live together in a world that is common, and the things in the world lie among us. It gathers us together and prevents us from falling all over each other. Speech and action are the two modes of how humans appear to each other. By such we insert ourselves into the human world. In taking the initiative to begin to disclose who the others are, the unexpected can happen. This is true human freedom. Arendt's (1971) view of Heidegger is that he, like Plato in *The Republic*, "succumbed to the temptation" of politics but "was young enough to learn from the shock of the collision".

Arendt suggests that Heidegger sees himself as above the they, estranged from ordinary concerns of persons and stuck in the peaks of contemplation. He is left with Nothingness, and no fixed values, which is our modern concern. Heidegger readily becomes unhinged from moral concerns and is prey to the very thing he despises, group mentality, when he takes up Nazi ideology. There was a cult-like aspect to Heidegger. He was charismatic and revered by a large group of students and colleagues, many of them Jewish, yet he was arrogant, never admitted to mistakes, and showed little interest in the work of others. All of this was true for Arendt and, we can imagine, likely true for Loewald as well. Loewald was fatherless and must have embraced this larger-than-life man, only to be bitterly disappointed. I believe that Loewald embodied this contradiction; he applied Heidegger's ideas on ontology to revive psychoanalysis, yet he abhorred Heidegger's Nazism.

I think Arendt's ideas raise more disturbing questions about the basic stance of modernity. We have steadily seen the loss of external moral values through the decline of religious moral codes. If God is dead, then everything is permitted; man is the measure of all things. Heidegger is the heir of Nietzsche. *Dasein* is authentically able to own and project its own projects and futures. But Heidegger's embrace of National Socialism goes squarely against this philosophy. Hitler demanded the allegiance of the masses and projected hate toward outsiders, what Heidegger called the They. Could there be an emptiness and loneliness built into modernity that yearns to be filled? Does man need external support to feel secure? It is not just religious ideas that have been lost; there is a skepticism and loss of confidence in institutions of all sorts. This has led to a rise in authoritarianism and a return to orthodox religions for some, both reactions to this existential loss. Was Heidegger prey to the same forces, looking for a utopian faith in a movement larger than the self? What is the path forward for those of us who do not have faith and want to preserve the freedoms promised us by modern philosophy?

Finally, a number of authors have documented a disturbing trend in German intellectual life. In the eighteenth century, much of continental Europe was divided into numerous city-states (especially Germany and Italy). In the Romantic movement, a kind of romantic nationalism grew up longing to unite the national language with a country (Wilson, 1973). Countries should be built on the traditions and myths of the past rather than existing political boundaries. Instinct and feeling are emphasized over rationality. In Germany, Johann Gottfried Herder (2002) was responsible for the development of these ideas. He argued for the existence of individual cultural types, which he thought were largely determined by the physical environment of the country and language. Each nationality should develop along its own innate lines set out by history and nature. A number of German poets and philosophers were attracted to this ideal. But, in the early twentieth century, there followed a view of German exceptionalism, which included beliefs about the primordiality of the German language, the intellectual superiority of German thought, and the moral purity of the German race (Sluga, 1993). Heidegger added to this belief, as he thought that German culture was the direct heir of classical Greece. This is the dangerous path leading to ideas of racial purity and the holocaust. This suggests that Heidegger was caught up in romantic nationalism and thought that the Nazis would further this aim.

A series of seminars was initiated in 1947 by Dr. Medard Boss, one of the founders of Daseinanalysis, and continued with a yearly visit by Heidegger with a group of Swiss psychiatrists for over 20 years (Heidegger, 2001; Keikhaee and Bell, 2016). Boss had been one of Freud's analysands. Heidegger (2001) thought the main issue in psychology was conflating the ontological with the ontic level of analysis. He considers Daseinanalysis as a description of concrete existential experience on the level of ontic or regional anthropology (p. 125). Heidegger supported Boss's emphasis on "perceptive world openness" and human existence as the clearing or illumination of being. Each person's "world-relations" is an individual way of being human and open to the world. Psychotic patients form a blockage of their world-openness. Heidegger criticized psychoanalysis for settling for the scientific attitude, especially the Cartesian dichotomy of subject and object (p. 207). He thought that Freud failed to see the "clearing" and neglected the ontological characteristics of the being of man (p. 182), basing his theory on forces that reduce the person to urges and wishes:

> Concealment is not the antithesis of consciousness but rather concealment belongs to the clearing. Freud simply did not see this clearing, otherwise, he would have succeeded in understanding the consciousness of children.
>
> (p. 182)

Heidegger is saying that Freud's repression is a hiding, while concealment is a more basic existential structure. He would see psychiatry and psychoanalysis as ontic pursuits, legitimate in themselves, but not to be confused with ontology, the study of fundamental beings. In this view, any psychology is a study of essences and categories, derivatives of a more basic ontological study of Being.

Hans Loewald

Hans Loewald (1906–1993) was a psychoanalyst and theorist born in the Alsace region of Germany (Downey, 1994). His father, who died shortly after his birth, was a Jewish physician with an interest in dermatology and psychiatry; his mother was a gifted musician. After his father died, the family moved to Berlin, where he grew up in the care of his mother, aunt, and maternal grandparents. He was a graduate student in philosophy at Marburg (where Heidegger was teaching) and Freiburg between 1924 and 1926, just before the publication of *Sein und Ziet* in 1927 (Loewald, 1950). From 1924 to 1926, when Loewald was his student, Heidegger gave lecture series on Aristotle, the concept of time, and the work of Wilhelm Dilthey, as well as working out early drafts of *Sein und Ziet* (Kisiel, 1993).

Since Heidegger did not move to Freiburg until 1928, it seems unlikely that Loewald followed Heidegger to Freiburg, as he started medical school in Tuebingen in 1926. It has oft been speculated that Loewald left his study with Heidegger because of his turn toward Nazism, but it is likely more complicated. Heidegger did not become officially a Nazi until 1933 and previously had had little interest in politics. Since we now know that Heidegger held antisemitic views, it is likely that Loewald understood this during his study with Heidegger. Moreover, one cannot go to medical school without preparatory science courses, so Loewald must have been planning this for some time. There is no record of his motivation for medicine, but he told colleagues that even before his break with Heidegger, he had been wary of philosophy's tendencies towards exclusions, other worldliness, and a reason too abstracted from life. He continued medical training in Tuebingen, Freiburg (where he may or may not have had more contact with Heidegger), and Berlin between 1926 and 1932, then fled in 1933 to Bologna and then to Padua, taking a medical degree from Rome University in 1934. While in Italy, he married his first wife and practiced psychiatry in Italy until 1939. In 1939, with fascism growing in Italy, Loewald went to Paris, where he made an attempt to become a French citizen before moving with his family to the United States. He eventually lived and practiced in New Haven, Connecticut, and wrote a series of influential papers on the theory and practice of psychoanalysis.

I knew Loewald when I became a candidate at the Western New England Institute for Psychoanalysis in 1975, and he was assigned as my first supervisor. We worked together for seven years. Of interest was that in supervision, he spoke very little of his own theoretical concepts, focusing only on the basic concepts of transference and countertransference appropriate to my stage of learning. He was a private man, and I knew almost nothing about his private life. He apparently did not speak much about his philosophical experiences, and so we know little about his experience with Heidegger.

You would barely know from Loewald's collected writings that he had studied philosophy or was a student of Heidegger. Stan Leavy (personal communication), a personal friend of Loewald, reports that Loewald carried around a copy of *Sein Und Zeit* like a holy book. Leavy said of Loewald: "His attitude was Heideggerian in the sense of observing someone in their fullness, you must try to live in that fullness, that there is something more there that is going to reappear" (unpublished interview). I took part for a number of years with Stan Leavy and several academic philosophers in a study group on Continental philosophy, where we read *Being and Time* along with other works of Heidegger and his colleagues. At my request, this study group also read papers by Loewald and traced the Heideggerian influences in them. Leavy (1989) was the first to publish about Heidegger's influence on Loewald. This paper attempts to expand on Leavy's views and reflect on discussions in the study group.

I can find only three references to Heidegger in his published work; the first occurs in the introduction to Loewald's collected papers:

> Philosophy has been my first love. I gladly affirm its influence on my way of thinking while being wary of the peculiar excesses a philosophical bent tends to entail.

My teacher in this field was Martin Heidegger, and I am deeply grateful for what I learned from him, despite his most hurtful betrayal in the Nazi era, which alienated me from him permanently.

(Loewald 1980, pp. viii–ix)

The present project aims to elucidate the influence of Heidegger on the themes in Loewald's psychoanalytic thinking by tracing Heideggerian ideas and themes that appear either directly or in parallel in Loewald's thinking. Since none of this is attributed by Loewald directly to Heidegger, we are left to make judgments. But Loewald is quite open to a debate with Freud, having great respect for Freudian concepts yet wanting to offer revisions, re-interpretations, and extensions. Important to Loewald was the idea that psychoanalysis, in his time, had grown stale. The dominant school of psychoanalysis was American ego psychology; the focus was the isolated ego, mechanistic concepts of drive and defense, and an austere, intellectual way of practice. Loewald wanted to re-vitalize psychoanalysis through a re-interpretation of classical Freudian concepts rather than the wholesale revision of language found in the various object-relations schools.

Sigmund Freud

Sigmund Freud was a Viennese medical doctor who, with several close colleagues, was the founder of psychoanalysis. Freud famously said: "Even when I have moved away from speculation, I have carefully avoided any contact with philosophy" (1925, p. 59). This statement turns out to be misleading (Askay and Farquhar, 2006; Tauber, 2010). Freud named Schopenhauer and Nietzsche in particular as forerunners of psychoanalysis. It is clear that he was well versed in philosophy; he had considered a doctorate in philosophy at one point. He took six lecture courses from Brentano and was friendly with him.[3] Brentano taught that there is no mental act without intending an object. The actual object of intentionality is a representation and is situated between the intending and the physical object. Freud adds that the intending is unconscious; drives require an object for discharge; and in narcissism, the ego has a libidinal investment in the narcissistic object. Melanie Klein (1946) takes the intentional object one step further by postulating that unconscious fantasy is always object-seeking. The Freudian ego derives from Descartes, who established that mental states form self-identity. Much of Freud's work is derived from Kant: the synthesizing ego, movement toward rationality, the mind as isolated, and consciousness as a unifying aspect in relation to experience. Nature, organized by cognition, constitutes experienced reality. Freud reportedly equated his idea of the unconscious with Kant's ideas of the thing-in-itself that is unknowable (Tauber 2010, p. 118). The question then becomes: what is the nature of the self? How can the self that knows also be part of the knowable world? Schopenhauer, in opposition to Kant, offers a universal will from which both subject and object differentiate. It is willing, not knowing, that is important; it allows a place for dreams and emotions. The task of philosophy is to inquire into the hidden and unknown. Freud himself commented that the will of Schopenhauer resembles his concept of the instincts. From Nietzsche, Freud borrows the Will to Power as a strife between competing instincts and the ability of the mind to self-deceive.

A Brief Introduction to Being and Time

Arendt (1971) characterizes Heidegger as a passionate thinker: "Heidegger never thinks "about" something; he thinks something". He both penetrates to the depths but is content to stay there, laying down pathmarks[4] constantly rethinking. In this sense, you can see why a psychoanalyst might be attracted to Heidegger, both live in the depths. Heidegger (1962) thinks that the entire tradition of Western metaphysics, since Plato, is dominated by a fascination with theory. This is the idea that you can understand the world by abstracting principles that underlie the multiplicity of visible phenomena, starting with Plato's forms or Aristotelian concepts of substance. The dominant version of metaphysical theory in the modern era starts with Descartes' division of self and object, leading to epistemological questions about what we can know. If all that we can be certain of is our own self, how can we be certain of other objects or other minds? But of course, this creates another problem that remains un-solved if the basic structure of being is subject and object, how do we bridge the gap between mind and body? Heidegger was not against theory, but he thought that theory was an abstraction from something even more fundamental, something that remains hidden in Western traditions.

Heidegger was trained in the neo-Kantian philosophy that dominated the German-speaking world from roughly 1870 until the First World War (Friedman, 2000; Safranski, 1998). Kant (1958) stands in the Cartesian tradition of the isolated cognito. He asks the question, squarely in the epistemological tradition: how can this cognito acquire knowledge of other objects? Is knowledge or true judgment about objects pos-sible? Kant comes to the conclusion that objects of knowledge cannot be outside of our subjective judgments; the object is created or constituted in the mind when unconcep-tualized sensory data is organized by a priori structures of judgment – the categories of time and space. The neo-Kantians then argue about the details of the ideal realm of pure logic, one that is timeless and ahistorical, where value and meaning can be found. Arendt (1970) described the philosophical scene at the time as drowning in an ocean of boredom.

Dissatisfied with Kant's use of pure logic, Heidegger turned to the phenomenology of Edmund Husserl (1970). Phenomenology tries to find certainty in the different ways in which things present to consciousness. Husserl thinks that objects are always found in consciousness, what he calls intentionality. For example, in my consciousness, I see a cat. I see the cat from one angle, but I can imagine that cat from other angles. The cat is my cat; the cat is purring; the cat is hungry; the cat is frightened and hisses. I can recall other cats or see my friend's cats. I remember other cats that I have had in the past. I can think of other types of cats, like a tiger, for example, that I saw in a zoo, and so on. I can also intend my cat with different subjective moods; I love my cat, I hate my cat when it wakes me up, I resent having to clean up the litter box, etc. The intended object is neither subjective nor objective; the traditional boundary between subject and object blurs and tends to disappear. The aim of phenomenology is to find a foundation – a firm ground for cognition – in a pre-perceptual unity. Yet, as Heidegger points out, there is still a transcendental ego set against objects, which he thinks is a false dichotomy.

Heidegger basically thought that philosophy had reached a dead end in the trajectory from Descartes through Kant and Husserl. The subject-object split that Descartes had uncovered could not be healed. In the formalism of Kant and his successors, the person had disappeared. This is the study of ontology, the question of being. He thought that philosophy tended to take being for granted and did not investigate the structure of being. What is a person, what is God, an idea, a substance? Heidegger thought that all these categories were abstractions from something even more fundamental.

Heidegger (1962) states, "We should raise anew the question of the meaning of Being" (p. 19). What does Heidegger mean by Being (*Sein*)? It is not a thing or an entity, such as a chair, a depression, or even Martin. It is the primordial meaning that which makes beings in their concreteness possible. Heidegger calls this a pre-theoretical grasp of prior structures that make possible modes of being, what he calls "fundamental ontology" (p. 34).

> In this everydayness there are certain structures...which, in every kind of Being that factical Dasein may possess, persist as determinative for the character of its Being.
>
> (p. 38)

We might think of Being as the most basic condition to describe existence. Heidegger also speaks of an openness to Being that has been forgotten, "veiled in darkness" (p. 25) in the rush toward scientific theory, and can only be accessed through hermeneutic questioning; "it must be made transparent" (p. 24). *Fundamental ontology* is a search for what it is that unites and makes possible our varied and diverse senses of what it is to be.

Ontology traditionally asks, what is something? What are the facts? What is its category? Heidegger (1962) would have us ask, who is someone (p. 79)? In a new beginning, Heidegger wants to start with human existence, which he calls *Dasein* (p. 32). He starts with *Dasein's* uniqueness, that of being an inquisitive being. What is Being? We can say what Being is not. It is not a specific human being or a conscious subject. It is not the whatness of things. It is not a category, an entity, an essence, or a substance – all traditional descriptions of being. All of these are derivatives of Being, which Heidegger calls ontic. *Dasein*, rather, is the way of being characteristic of human beings. What is it to be *Dasein*? What is fundamental is existence:

> That kind of being toward which *Dasein* can comport itself in one way or another, and always does comport itself somehow, we call existence.
>
> (p. 32)

Dasein is uniquely defined as "being-in-the-world" (p. 78), to be seen as a whole and a priori. The world is not a container but what we are always immersed in, where we "reside" or "dwell in" (p. 80). Rather than the side-by-side characteristic of entities, we are "being alongside" the world, of being absorbed in the world (p. 80). What is the characteristic structure of *Dasein*? *Dasein* is inquisitive; it inquires about itself and asks about its Being. Secondly, human beings are always immersed in an activity that aims for an end. Being is always by its nature temporal (*zeitlich*) (p. 17), seeing itself as projecting into the future. Finally, *Dasein* is characterized by care (*Sorge*) (p. 84). Care is taking one's own being as a question, of finding an authentic way of Being, of absorption in activity, but it also includes attending to, taking care of something

(*Besorgen*), or actively caring for someone else, solicitude (*Fürsorge*). To know the truth is to care about it; the truth is what we allow ourselves to know. Here again, we have a connection to psychoanalysis, which shares this passion.

Let us return to my cat. My cat is attached to me, will follow me around the house, and does not like to be left alone. He wants to be fed, provided with a clean litter box, and wants to be petted (on his terms). But Heidegger would say that my cat does not have *Dasein*.[5] For Heidegger would assume cats cannot self-reflect, do not have concern for others as other *Dasein*, do not plan for the future, and do not contemplate the limitations of time and existence.

Heidegger means to undercut mental activity, such as desiring or thinking, by a more fundamental practical activity or involvement that is pretheoretical. Then concepts, thinking, or categories are a secondary phenomenon, abstracted from activity and involvement.

Heidegger uses hammering as his prime example, but let us examine a psychoanalytic hour. When my patient arrives, we are usually both in a theoretical mode; we each might have a theory of the other, of her or my current motives, what happened in the last session, etc. All of these are ideas that maintain a distance between her and me. They may be useful as a starting point, but something is hidden. Heidegger calls this mode present-at-hand (*vorhandenheit*) (p. 67), a concern with what an object is, universal laws, categories, or theory. As my patient starts to talk, I begin to get drawn into her mental world, to be absorbed by it. Thinking about tends to be replaced by reacting to or being with. Both parties become immersed in the unconscious. A transferential field narrows the gap between subjects, a dialogue and a flow develop. Heidegger calls this readiness-to-hand (*Zuhandenheit*) (p. 98). He notes that we do not encounter mere things, but rather we use the things at hand to get something done, what Heidegger calls equipment (*Zeug*) (p. 97). It is *Dasein's* active engagement and activity with objects that constitute authentic Being. In our patient hour, my task is to elucidate the unconscious motivations of my patient. Equipment might include the setting, the assurance of privacy, or my relative abstinence. Even what shows up in my mind, the countertransference, is a kind of equipment sometimes useful for the task. Equipment is defined not by its properties but by what it is used for, its place in a context of use, or what Heidegger calls manipulation (*handlichkeit*) (p. 98). Being-in-the-world (*In-der-welt-sein*) (pp. 78–86) then is a totality of involvements (p. 116) for acting in the world. We become absorbed in the project, what Heidegger calls circumspection (*umsicht*), a kind of looking around (p. 98). Moreover, being at work on something always entails being toward a purpose, a goal, or a project (p. 99).

Heidegger thinks that, in the experience of being ready-to-hand, we lose ourselves in the task and fail to notice it. It is only when something fails that we become aware of the activity. Let us say there is a miscommunication in the hour, the patient becomes angry or breaks off, and an impasse develops. There are three modes of breakdown: conspicuousness, obtrusiveness, and obstinacy (p. 104). When equipment temporarily malfunctions, we become conspicuous of the activity; the equipment stands out, a kind of unhandiness. Or something protrudes, stands in the way, is missing, or is obtrusive. We likely fall back on deliberation and conscious planning. We are forced to pay attention to the activity. In the hour, we focus on the impasse and find a new way of coping. If there is standing in the way, a total breakdown (obtrusiveness), or a prolonged impasse, we fall back on theoretical reflection and finally just resort to staring at each other. We are back to present-at-hand and the awareness of isolated properties and substances. Arendt (1971) puts it thusly:

> Thinking has come to life again; the cultural treasures of the past, believed to be dead, are being made to speak, in the course of which it turns out that they propose things altogether different from the familiar, worn-out trivialities they had been presumed to say. There exists a teacher; one can perhaps learn to think.

The Dialogue among Heidegger, Freud, and Loewald

Use of Language

In reading Being and Time, we immediately encounter a strange philosophical language, both in the original German and in the English translation. There are hyphenations, unusual prefixes, uncommon suffixes, and redefining of ordinary German words, all to reveal the hidden meanings and resonances of ordinary talk. Vandevelde (2014) suggests that we can read Heidegger in two contradictory ways. We can read Heidegger as a kind of poet-philosopher who is trying, in his use of evocative words and novel phrasing, to recreate for us the experience of Being, or we can develop propositions to make Heidegger's ideas into a conceptual framework. In either case, Heidegger invents a whole new philosophical language.

Being, for example, is a basic concept in Western metaphysics, meaning permanent and unchanging reality, the substance or essence of what is. For Heidegger, Being (*sein*) must be differentiated from beings (*das seiende*). With beings, we can ask, what are they, what are they made of, and what is their constitution? But of man, we ask, who is man, how does he exist, and what are his modes of existence? *Dasein* is Heidegger's invented name for the distinctive mode of Being realized by human beings. *Dasein* is a combination of two German words: *da*, meaning there or here, present or available, and *sein*, meaning modes of being. *Dasein* in ordinary German is used for the being or life of a person. *Dasein* is not to be understood as the biological human being, nor is it to be understood as 'the person'. For Heidegger, *Dasein* "is distinguished by the fact that, in its very Being, that Being is an issue for it" (p. 32). *Dasein* "always understands itself in terms of its existence – in terms of a possibility of itself, to be itself or not itself" (p. 33). The *Da* can be translated as 'open', the possibility of 'taking-as', a preintellectual openness to Being that is necessary for us to encounter beings as beings in a particular way.

Loewald, like Heidegger, wants to subvert the traditional language of psychoanalysis, but he is not interested in a new vocabulary; rather, he wants to redefine traditional Freudian concepts. He (1976) states:

> I use metapsychological concepts, reformulating or reinterpreting some of them, and attempting to integrate them within a broader framework than that in which they first appeared.

(p. 148fn)

In another paper (1978b), Loewald states his opinion that many psychoanalytic concepts "are based on anxious clinging to unimaginative comprehension and to rigid and unduly restrictive definitions of certain Freudian concepts and theoretical formulations" (pp. 191–192). "What psychoanalysis needs might not be a 'new language' but a less inhibited, less pedantic and narrow understanding and interpretation of its current language" (p. 193). In the phrase, 'anxious clinging', we can see an echo of Heidegger's inauthenticity, the clinging to the They. We might contrast Loewald with Melanie Klein, who invents a new psychoanalytic language, much closer in spirit to Heidegger. Concepts such as positions, projective identification, and unconscious fantasy have their roots in Freudian concepts but take on such added meaning as to be totally new.

An example of Loewald's creative use of psychoanalytic terms is found in his description of the Freudian instinct. Freud (1915a) speaks of an instinct as a 'stimulus' (p. 118) arising from within the mind and thus cannot be evaded. But then Freud calls an instinct "a psychical representation" (p. 112), which Loewald re-interprets as a force. The mind's work is not to discharge stimuli but to generate representations. With the formulation of the structural theory (Freud 1923), the mind is seen as an organism, and instincts are active and dynamic forces within that organism. Life and death instincts (Freud 1920) are now broad motivational forces, the tendency toward inertia and toward activity. Loewald (1971b) wants to reinterpret these broad motivational forces in a revolutionary formulation:

> Instincts, understood as psychic, motivational, forces, become organized as such through interactions within a psychic field consisting originally of the mother-child (psychic) unit.
>
> (pp. 127–128)

For Freud (1915a), an instinct is not originally connected to an object but becomes assigned to the instinct in terms of the ability to provide satisfaction. Loewald (1971b) reinterprets instinct and object as a developmental process:

> In the mnemic action pattern, urge and response, environmental engenderment, and the subject's excitation are not differentiated from each other.
>
> (p. 131)

In Loewald's view, the mnemic action pattern is not yet an instinct nor is it represented. Primary narcissism (Freud 1914a) is not a state of non-cathexis of the external world but rather an inability to distinguish the ego from the external world. Pleasure and unpleasure are global events. What we call instinct and object only gradually become differentiated out of the original undeveloped matrix of mother and child.

Another aspect of language is its evocatory aspect. Heidegger (1962) distinguishes between idle talk (*gerede*) and talk (*rede*). Idle talk or chatter is equated with gossiping, passing along, and scribbling (p. 212):

> Idle talk is the possibility of understanding everything without previously making the thing one's own.
>
> (p. 213)

Idle talk is the manifestation of a groundless floating, a kind of protective shelter to remain in the They, a dead language. Talk is a living language, open to experience and to its own history and temporality:

> The ultimate business of philosophy is to preserve the force of the most elemental words in which Dasein expresses itself.
>
> (p. 262)

Similarly, in the last section of his paper on language, Loewald (1978a) speaks of the "magical evocative" (pp. 199–200) quality of language, a sentence that could come straight out of Being and Time. Heidegger (1962) speaks of the call of consciousness (p. 317); it is an appeal to the self, lost in self-absorption, to be brought to itself, back to a more authentic being-in-the-world. This call is not formulated in words but is silent and "calls Dasein forth to its possibilities" (p. 319).

Loewald (1978a) uses a similar language. Words not only name things, but they "summon things and experiences, as bringing them to life" (p. 200). Words have the power of action, rendering them present. Loewald suggests that, in the development of civilization, much of this primordial power of words has been lost, only coming to the fore in great poetry and creative prose, echoing Heidegger's lifelong interest in poetry. It is in this distinction that Loewald discusses secondary and primary process. Primary process are those forms of mentation that promote non-differentiation and oneness, what Loewald calls the primordial density, while secondary process are those forms of mentation that promote differentiation, self and object formation, duality, and multiplicity. In the move to secondary process, there is a danger of losing a connection between the thing-presentation, the "first and true object-cathexes" (pp. 184–185), and the word-presentation, losing its "original unity" (p. 187), similar to Heidegger's contrast between idle talk and authenticity.

Deconstruction

Heidegger (1962) holds that:

> The meaning of Being is one that has not been attended to and one that has been inadequately formulated, but that it has been quite forgotten in spite of all our interest in 'metaphysics'.
>
> (p. 43)

What he means is that Being has been taken as a grounding concept and something self-evident. It is this tradition, in Heidegger's view, that needs to be destroyed (De-strucktion[6]). Metaphysics has become sterile and desolate. He asks, "What is Being?" (p. 49), and he answers that Being must be disclosed from its concealment. Dasein, the human version of Being, in the ordinary world, is hidden:

> The 'they' has always kept Dasein from taking hold of these possibilities of Being.
>
> (p. 312)

The They (*Mann*) means measuring or submerging oneself according to others, the crowd, or the tradition; it is a sign of inauthenticity. The authentic truth remains hidden:

> Truth (uncoveredness) is something that must always first be wrested from entities. Entities get snatched out of their hiddenness. The factual uncoveredness of anything is always, as it were, a kind of robbery.
>
> (p. 265)

Being must be uncovered or disclosed from its everyday absorption. Being ordinarily is "tranquillized" (p. 239) or "addicted" (p. 240). What must be destroyed, then, is the inauthentic tradition, which blocks *Dasein* from accessing the primordial aspects of Being. But deconstruction is not just a negative move; it opens up possibilities. If *Dasein* can grasp its historicity (*Geschichtlichheit*), its temporality, it:

> Becomes the repetition of a possibility of existence…going back into the possibilities of the Dasein that has-been-there.
>
> (p. 437)

Here, repeating (*wiederhalen*) means an attempt to retrieve former possibilities, and it becomes "a moment of vision" (p. 438) and opens up the possibilities of the future.

Loewald, I think, has a different kind of deconstruction in mind. In his dialogue with Freud, his wish is not to destroy but to reform. The impulse is to find new life in concepts that have become stale and overly abstract, much as Heidegger viewed the metaphysical tradition. Let us take the ego as an example. Loewald (1951) here is in dialogue with Freud (1923) and his conception of the ego as a "repressive, defensive agency" (p. 3), a compromise between the demands of the id and the outer world. Outer reality is essentially seen as hostile and threatening – an outside force. Further, Freud tends to personify the father as this outside force. The father is the great castrator, the figure who threatens the boy for his connection to his mother, who reminds the boy that his penis is too small and unsatisfying, and who forms a boundary between masculine and feminine. It is not that Loewald disagrees with this formulation, but he sees a competing reality, drawn from Freud's (1914a) study of narcissism. There is another reality, that of primary narcissism, in which "reality is not outside, but is contained in the pre-ego of primary narcissism" (p. 8).

> It is an undifferentiated phase in which the infant and its world are still one, are only beginning to differentiate from one another, which means also that the differentiation of the psychic apparatus itself into its structural elements still is dormant.
>
> (p. 10)

Loewald calls this "a unitary whole" (p. 11).

Loewald (1952) suggests that psychoanalysis has "understood unquestioningly" (p. 30) a view of reality as "a hostile-defensive ego reality" (p. 30), making it the dominant objective reality. In this "defensive-reactive process" (p. 31), fantasy is split off and leads to an impoverishment of the ego. Is this a parallel to Heidegger, where impoverishment is a product of inauthenticity?

While Loewald's project differs from Heidegger's in its aim and meaning, I believe he has been profoundly influenced by Heidegger's hermeneutics. Traditional psychoanalysis emphasizes a foundational belief, a vertical picture of human knowledge that posits a descending degree of justified beliefs down to core or foundational beliefs. In this sense, Freudian interpretation is the search for a primal meaning, a restoration of meaning, and a reduction of illusion (Ricoeur 1970). Freud (1937b) described the "work of construction, or, if it is preferred, of reconstruction, resembles to a great extent an archaeologist's excavation of some dwelling-place that has been destroyed and buried or of some ancient edifice" (p. 259). The assumption is that analysis can, in principle, uncover a true, justified belief about original trauma.

Loewald (1960) reinterprets the archeological simile as picturing the deeper layers of the id cut off from present reality and influence:

> It is as though the functional relationship between the deeper strata of an excavation and their external environment were denied because these deeper strata are not in a functional relationship with the present-day environment; as though it were maintained that the architectural structures of deeper, earlier strata are due to purely 'internal' processes, in contrast to the functional interrelatedness between present architectural structures (higher, later strata) and the external environment that we see and live in.
>
> (p. 232)

Both Heidegger and Loewald aim to uncover what is hidden – Being or the primal ego, respectively. What is recovered for Loewald (1960) is not primarily a set of unconscious fantasies but the resumption of "ego development" (p. 221). He calls ego development "a process of increasingly higher integration and differentiation of the psychic apparatus" (p. 224). To promote ego growth, the analyst makes himself available as "a new 'object-relationship' between the patient and the analyst" (p. 224). Loewald calls this "a new discovery of objects" (p. 225), to emphasize a new look at old objects. The new object could be understood as seeing the analyst in a new way, but also as the opening up of new possibilities: "the newness consists in the patient's rediscovery of the early paths of the development of object-relations leading to a new way of relating to objects and of being oneself" (p. 229). While Loewald recognizes a mirror aspect of transference, he holds that the analyst has a vision of the "true form" (p. 226) or "the emerging core" (p. 229), "always from the viewpoint of potential growth" (p. 230). This is what the analyst holds and contains for the patient – a vision of what he can become. This is an aspect of identification between patient and analyst, but not of what is or what has been, but of what can become. What does Loewald mean by integration and differentiation? He emphasizes understanding of both conscious and unconscious material, of greater mastery, of putting into words, of overcoming a differential, and of lifting the unconscious into the preconscious. Part of what the analyst does is promote a "true regression" (p. 240) to open up "freer interplay between the unconscious and preconscious systems" (p. 240). To do this, the analyst "must be able to regress within himself to the level of organization on which the patient is stuck" (pp. 241–242).

Being in the World

As Heidegger does, I will start with Aristotle (1984). In his Physics, he divided things into two general categories: artifacts, which require an external principle of change – a house built by a builder – and natural things, which have an internal principle of change – an oak that grows from an acorn. The acorn represents the potentiality of the form, while the mature tree is its actuality. Form can exist at various levels of potentiality and actuality; there are various intermediate forms between the acorn and the mature tree. Creation consists of the imposition of form on matter. Here we have a developmental force which impels the thing toward its realization of its form. The form is a powerful and dynamic force for the realization of structure. *Entelecheia* means continuing in a state of completeness, or being at an end which is of such a nature that it is only possible to be there by means of the continual expenditure of the effort required to stay there. It is the activity that makes a thing what it is; *entelecheia* extends to *energeia* because it is the end or perfection which has been achieved only in, through, and during activity.[7] But Heidegger is adding something to *entelecheia*. The acorn's potential is only to become an oak tree, but *Dasein* has the existential potential to choose its own projects and can project possibilities into the future.

To signify movement in this Aristotelian sense, Heidegger (1962) introduces the German word "*Bewegtheit*" (p. 224), variously translated into English as "movement", "movedness", and "motility". In Heidegger's interpretation of Aristotle, *Bewegtheit* is not something that happens to being; it is constitutive of being, what Heidegger calls "bringing forth" or "coming to presence". He interprets Aristotle's term "*entelechy*" to signify the moment in which movement gathers itself together and comes to rest in the fully realized product. Heidegger's point is that things cannot be understood as a subject of knowledge but rather as interpretations in terms of meaning and use.

Loewald's dialogue is with Freud, yet his model of psychoanalysis is profoundly influenced by being-in-the-world. He examines two models of psychoanalysis that Freud proposes (Loewald, 1971b). The first model is a closed system, describing the mind as a mental apparatus (Freud, 1900). The nervous system is an apparatus which functions to get rid of or reduce stimuli to their lowest levels. "The mind is an instrument – however complex – that processes incoming stimuli to discharge them again in some modified form" (p. 120). The mind works on instinctual forces by forming mental representations of biological stimuli, what Loewald (1971b) thinks of" as the most primitive element or unit of motivation" (p. 119). Loewald counters Freud in thinking that:

> the basic postulate concerning the general function of the psychic apparatus is no longer that of getting rid of the (organismic) stimuli that reach it, but that of generating mental representations of these stimuli.
>
> (p. 119)

The introduction of the structural model (Freud 1923) is an advance on the psychic apparatus. The ego can now be understood as a set of personal motivation structures, "an interplay of psychic forces and structural layers" (p. 121). The mind "is embedded in its environment in such a way that it is in living contact and interchange with it; it modulates and influences the environment by its own activities, and its activity is modulated and influenced by the environment" (pp. 119–120).

Loewald proposes a third model, an interactive model, where instincts are now conceived as broad polar forces or urges of living matter. Fogel (1989) suggests that internalization is the central concept for Loewald (1973):

> Internalization…is conceived as the basic way of functioning of the psyche, not as one of its functions.
>
> (p. 71)

By internalization, a movement from outside to inside, Loewald does not mean the taking in of objects under threat of loss, as it does for Freud, as in an internal schema or map. He thinks of internalization as a growth process, an acceptance of the external world, and an enrichment of the ego.

> In internalization, in contrast, the ego opens itself up, as it were, loosens its current organization to allow for its own further growth.
>
> (p. 75)

The external world is assimilated; objects are destroyed and reincorporated into the ego structure. For Loewald, ego growth through internalization is opposed to repressive forces, which aim to inhibit growth and maintain infantile forms of functioning.

> In internalization it is a matter of transforming these relationships into an internalized, intrapsychic, depersonalized relationship, thus increasing and enriching psychic structure: the identity with the object is renounced.
>
> (p. 83)

But internalization is not a one-way process. Human life is inseparably embedded in a matrix of object-relations. As the ego grows through internalization processes, so are objects constituted and grow in complexity.

What about inside and outside? How might the coherent ego influence external relations? This is not well developed in Loewald's thinking, but we might turn to his use of projection (Loewald, 1988a), not merely defensive but a recognition of the call of unconscious forces located in the external world, "acknowledging live, driving forces beyond and encompassing those operating in individual existence" (p. 53). For Loewald, projections are called or summoned by the unconscious of others, much as Heidegger thinks of *Dasein* as being summoned into existence. Loewald is suggesting movement toward individuation/internalization and the connectedness found in the "transindividual matrix" (p. 51) of mother–child unity.

Perhaps another indication of inside to outside is found in Loewald's (1986) discussion of transference/countertransference where he explicitly states that the patient and analyst have equal and symmetrical transferences to each other. Then, he states, "countertransference, in this general sense, is a technical term for the analyst's responsiveness to the patient's love-hate for the analyst" (p. 286). This responsiveness, this need for love and dependency with our objects, is what draws out the patient's projections.

Instincts originally are the same as the life of the body, only becoming separate as the organism becomes more differentiated. The ego is always "a constellation or field of motivational activity composed of two centers of such activity" (Loewald, 1971b, p. 105). Loewald reinterprets Freud's (1914a) concept of primary narcissism as a manifestation of the interactions within the mother-child psychic field. Instincts and objects become gradually constituted within that field through differentiation and integration. Instinct and object both contribute to the organization of the other. "Satisfaction is a creative process in which appropriate environmental activity…engenders and organizes excitation processes" (p. 130). Instincts, in this sense, only come into being in psychic growth. In this sense, psychic structure formation is dependent on object-relations, established by way of internalizations and externalizations in which both mother and child participate (Loewald, 1973).

In another formulation, Loewald (1988b) describes sublimation as "passion transformed" (p. 9). By this, he means that in the process of differentiation out of an original unity, a symbolic linkage remains of the original instinctual charge:

> The elements we call instinctual and deinstinctualized each acquire a measure of autonomy without losing the other.
>
> (p. 13)

He goes on to suggest a vast reciprocal play between the development of objects and ego out of primary narcissism, what Freud called object libido, and the internalization of external objects back into the unity of the ego, what Freud called narcissistic libido. This internal binding Freud (1923) called "desexualized Eros" (p. 44). Loewald (1988b) states:

> Sublimation, in this view, involves an internal re-creative turn toward that matrix, a reconciliation of the polarized elements produced by individuation and, one may suspect, by sexual differentiation…it brings external and material reality within the compass of psychic reality, and psychic reality within the sweep of external reality.
>
> (pp. 21–22)

This is a version of being-in-the-world; the self is connected to the world by internal loving connections; the self reaches out to the world through object connections, while at the same time, taking the world into itself through internalizations. Loewald believes in non-climactic satisfactions that could be described as sublimatory in various intimate relationships, in play, and in creativity, which he calls "reconciliation" (p. 33).

Death

The concept of death is central to Heidegger's (1962) philosophy. By death, he does not mean "coming-to-an-end" (p. 286), an individual death. Rather, he means a way to be (*Zorn*):

> Death is something that stands before us – something impending.
>
> (p. 294)

The realization of the death of the subject brings *Dasein* to face its own "uncanniness" (*unheimlichkeit*) (p. 233) and opens up the possibility of an authentic existence (*eigentlich*). In "the basic state of mind of anxiety" (*angst*) (pp. 228–235), something vague and shadowing, *Dasein* is forced to confront Being. It takes away any standing outside or the familiar. The other mood for Heidegger is boredom (*Langeweile*), which he takes up at length in *The Fundamental Concepts of Metaphysics* (Heidegger 1995). Boredom, in its first form, is "Being bored with" (p. 113), where time drags. But profound boredom, with its emptiness, discloses a fundamental temporality of *Dasein*. For Heidegger, moods, in both cases, are not subjective states in an objectively given world but rather are aspects of what it means to be in a world. Death is a possibility of Being that we constantly flee from. Death is not something chosen by us, we are thrown into it.

> Anxiety in the face of death must not be confused with fear in the face of one's own demise…it amounts to the disclosure of the fact that Dasein exists as thrown Being toward its end.
>
> (p. 295)

Heidegger thinks of the awareness of death as a release from illusions, as "an impassioned freedom toward death" (p. 311).

Loewald (1972b) has a dialogue with Freud about the death instinct. He notes that Freud's original conception of the death instinct (1923, 1924, 1937a) emphasized aggression turned inward and a punishing sense of guilt, what Loewald calls "a deep-seated unconscious resistance" (p. 316). But for Loewald, this represents an upward interpretation of a phenomenon far less structured. He is pointing to aggression that arises before instincts become organized in the matrix of very early mother-infant interactions:

> But in severe cases such an imbalance [between eros and Thanatos] is rooted in problems of early psychic development, in the precursors of morality, conscience, and guilt that antedate the Oedipus complex and the formation of the superego – where destructive forces got out of hand, as it were, and affected the very fiber of the person before it could be bound.
>
> (p. 320)

The death drive, in this formulation, is not yet instinctual but results from "tensions within the mother-child matrix" (p. 321) and reflects an in-balance between destructive and creative tendencies. Loewald is speaking of death as something primal to be faced in all of us; we do have a parallel conceptualization with Heidegger's view of death as the possibility of Being.

Authenticity

Heidegger's existentialism comes from Friedrich Nietzsche (1956) and Soren Kierkegaard (1941). To be meaningful is to reject conventional morality or to take a leap of faith to truly become what I already am. Heidegger was also influenced by Wilhelm Dilthey (1996) who conceived of the subject as a living person with a history in need of interpretation. I believe that, like Nietzsche and Kierkegaard, Heidegger wanted to rescue philosophy from its formalism and find its passion and humanity, what he called authenticity, yet at the same time not reject metaphysical structure.

For Heidegger, authenticity (*eigentlich*) and inauthenticity (*uneigentlich*) are two modes of Being (p. 68). Inauthenticity is not a lessor mode; rather, it is one way of existing – what Heidegger calls falling-in-the-world – a groundless and nullity. It is *Dasein* in its everydayness, characterized by hustle and tranquillization; it drifts along toward an alienation (*Entfremdung*) (p. 222). It is lost in the 'They'. Heidegger thinks of this as looking away from a realization of finitude:

> Dasein is proximally and for the most part lost in that which it concerns itself. In this lostness, however, Dasein's fleeing in the face of authentic existence which has been characterized an 'anticipatory resoluteness', has made itself known; and this is a fleeing which covers up. In this concernful fleeing lies a fleeing in the face of death – that is, a looking away from the end of Being-in-the-world.
>
> (p. 477)

Moods (*stimmung*), for Heidegger, are fundamental states of attunement (pp. 172–179). Most moods are found in everyday *Dasein*, happiness, irritation, and sadness – and do not provide any existential awareness. They accompany an inauthentic existence. It is anxiety (*angst*), the attunement to nothingness which is at the heart of *Dasein*. Heidegger differentiates fear from anxiety. Fear is inauthentic (p. 391), a "bewildered making-present" (p. 392). But the mood of anxiety discloses, confronts, and reveals this nothingness. Anxiety is not a fear but rather a dread of the awareness of death and finitude. In anxiety, there is a breakdown, resulting in a state of confusion and a loss of the everyday comfort of inauthentic existence. It is an uncanny awareness of not being at home. But this allows *Dasein* to make a claim of authentic existence, of being face to face with its personal being-in-the-world.

> *Dasein* finds itself face to face with the 'nothing' of the possible impossibility of its existence.
>
> (p. 310)

Anxiety "merely brings one into the mood for a possible resolution" (p. 394). *Dasein* must choose itself authentically or not, actively taking on the responsibility of its death and the nothingness of its current existence. This is the meaning of resoluteness (*entschlossenheit*), which accepts this anxiety and can act without fear of it:

> Anxiety can mount authentically only in a Dasein which is resolute. He who is resolute knows no fear; but he understands the possibility of anxiety as the possibility of the very mood which neither inhibits nor bewilders him. Anxiety liberates him from possibilities which "count for nothing", and lets him become free for those which are authentic.
>
> (p. 395)

The essence of *Dasein* is a basic having-to-be-open to our primordial connectedness, an understanding and fascination with the world, providing, looking after, foreseeing, and awareness of the time horizon. The experience of anxiety leaves *Dasein* homeless and unguarded, exposed to authentic Being as standing out against the background of nothingness. The experience of nothingness is a shock, but this may allow a focus on something creative. Anxiety reveals that everyday life is fleeing from Being. Nothing changes, only our attitude towards it. Care (*sorge*) is a basic characteristic of the human condition (pp. 227, 235–246), an orientation toward its world in a totality of practical involvement and projects. Care means providing, looking after, foreseeing, and being aware of the time horizon. It is a basic having-to-be-open to our primordial connectedness, an understanding and fascination with the world. In care, the world is disclosed to us as "Being-uncovered" (p. 261). The existential structures of care are disposedness, thrownness, projection, fallenness, and understanding (p. 264). Disposedness (*Befindlichkeit*) can be translated as a state of mind, a receptivity. Richardson (2003) renders Befindlichkeit as 'already-having-found-oneself-there-ness'. Thrownness (*Geworfenheit*) is an acceptance of the world we have not chosen and end up in. Falling is the state of being lost in the world. Projection is not conscious planning, nor is it the wish to get rid of undesirable parts of the self; projection "has nothing to do with comporting oneself towards a plan that has been thought out" (p. 185). Rather, projection is being aware of possibilities and having an understanding of the freedom to choose.

Loewald (1978b), in a lecture given at Yale University, spoke of Man as Moral Agent. The process of mental growth means an assumption of taking responsibility for oneself. This means taking responsibility for one's own history, by which he means both "the history that has been lived and the history in the making" (p. 11). This responsibility is to transform raw experience into meaningful contexts at higher levels of organization, which Loewald conceptualizes as an ego function. Yet the opposite is also true. The ego can become rigid and frozen, "an unyielding rationality" (p. 16), and needs to rediscover its links to the unconscious. Loewald draws this from Freud's (1933) statement: "where id was, there ego shall be" (p. 80) Loewald's translates *werden* as to come into being. He is emphasizing the potentiality of id processes to evolve into ego organization. Unconscious levels of functioning can be appropriated as potentially me, as ego. Loewald calls this an existential task. It is here that Loewald (1978b) cites Heidegger[8]:

> Heidegger's concept of Geworfenheit – man is thrown into the world, unplanned and unintended by himself – and Entwerfen – the taking over and actively developing the potentialities of this fact – have grown in the same soil.
>
> (p. 19)

Loewald goes on to make clear (in a footnote) that the factuality of human existence in Heidegger's sense has a different dimension than the psychological meaning for Loewald, but what is in common is the dictum: "become what you are" (p. 19). Loewald calls the superego "the representative of futurity" (p. 23). "It represents the care and concern we have for ourselves, in past and present, as continuing on into a future that is to be shaped" (p. 23).

Likewise, Loewald's (1960) idea of a true regression contains a version of the search for authenticity. He has a vision of ego development, a dynamic organization consisting of internalizations of increasing higher integration and differentiation between the infant and important objects in his environment. He calls this "synthetic ego activities" (p. 228). Ego growth is promoted by one or more parents who both understand the child's current development and hold a vision of the child's future and mediate this vision to the child, "always from the viewpoint of the future" (p. 230). Needs are beyond the ability of the infant:

> The understanding recognition of the infant's need on the part of the mother represents a gathering together of as yet undifferentiated urges of the infant, urges that in the acts of recognition and fulfillment by the mother undergo a first organization into some directed drive.
>
> (p. 237)

These interactions are a mutual responsiveness in which both drive the direction and organization of the environment happen simultaneously. The analyst, like the mother, "operates as a representative of a higher stage of organization" (p. 239). Loewald uses the metaphor of "*per via de levare*"[9] (p. 226), as in sculpture, "chiselling away the transference distortions" (p. 225) to bring out the "true form" (p. 226).[10] There is a circularity of interpretation in the reciprocity of chiseling away and revealing, aiming at a "new object-relationship" (p. 226). Interpretation "makes available" (p. 240) previous unconscious material, through steps toward a "true level of regression" (p. 242), promoted by the analyst's interpretation of defense and the analyst's ability to regress to the same organizational level of the patient, "whereby the preconscious regains its originality and intensity" (p. 240). The analyst:

> reveals himself to the patient as a more mature person, as a person who can feel with the patient what the patient experiences and how he experiences it, and who understands it as something more than it has been for the patient.
>
> (p. 243)

Then, in a further move, Loewald thinks that psychic growth is not just an interaction between psychic apparatus and the object-world but an interplay between unconscious and preconscious intensities. It is these unconscious intensities that give current experiences their full meaning and emotional depth. This is the meaning of Loewald's well-known evocation of Odysseus's journey to the underworld, where ancestor-ghosts need to taste blood in order to reawaken to life and be released from their ghost life.

Loewald (1951) has a biphasic view of anxiety. In one of his few references to Heidegger, Loewald (1953) notes that Heidegger sees anxiety as an "expression of nothingness, of man's possibility of finding himself unrelated, confronted with 'the abyss of naught'" (p. 3),[11] which Loewald sees as parallel to Freud's use of anxiety as the threat of loss of love, another kind of nothingness. Loewald goes on, in Heideggerian fashion, to equate the experience of anxiety with the call for freedom. Once the ego and the instincts become structuralized by integrated processes, conflict, signal anxiety, and defense become aspects of the mind:

> Defense, in the sense in which we speak of it in neurosis, and therefore to a certain degree in normal development, is based on that stage in the development of individual-environment configuration, of ego-reality integration, in which an organized ego and organized reality have been differentiated from each other.

What I mean here by organized reality may be indicated by saying that it implies (among other things) the establishment of distinct, libidinally invested (parental) figures mutually related to each other and the ego, such as they come into being in the development of the Oedipus situation. Only then is a stage in the constitution of ego and of reality reached in which a defense struggle between an ego and an 'external' object-world and the resulting defense against id impulses can occur.

(p. 25)

Repression, for Loewald (1952), is opposed to internalization, a kind of anti-growth, a lack of authenticity. Projective identification and introjective processes of "a narcissistic and magical" (p. 26) character predominate in pre-Oedipal development. Quoting Karen Horney (1932), Loewald (1951) proposes a male "dread of the vulva" (p. 13), a "fear of...being drowned, sucked in, overpowered" (p. 13). Loewald calls it "an unstructured nothingness of identity" (p. 16), a regression to a loss of boundaries between ego and objects. It is here that we see a hint of Heidegger in characterizing early development as a state of nothingness and equating repression with a loss of authenticity.

For Loewald (1962b), emptiness and loneliness are examined in the context of object loss through separation or death. If the loss cannot be mourned and internalized, then either the loss or its significance can be denied, a substitute must be found, or depression results. Mourning is a process of acknowledging the loss, examining in detail its pain, and relinquishing external objects. But at the same time, we internalize aspects of the lost object and incorporate these aspects into ourselves. Internalization is meant to abolish the pain of separation and loss. But in considering early development, where there is "no difference exists between the 'I' and the 'not-I'" (p. 265), such loss and frustration are "boundary-creating processes" (p. 266) establishing externality and internality. There is then always a tension between wanting to return to the security of mother-child unity and the mastery and freedom of separation, which for Loewald is exemplified in the ego ideal:

> The ego ideal, in contrast to the child's frequent experiences of an impotent, helpless ego, is then a return, in fantasy to the original state; it is an ego replenished, restored to the wholeness of the undifferentiated state of primary narcissism.
>
> (p. 268)

It is the establishment of a secure inner world of objects that provides security to withstand adult external losses. Further, in adult life, the intensity of unconscious processes and access to primary process experiences need to have an interplay with more conscious and rational experiences (Loewald, 1960). If this linkage is severed due to repression or splitting, then a defensive isolation results; "human life becomes sterile and an empty shell" (p. 250), leading to an excessive reliance on external objects for security. Might this be Loewald's reply to Heidegger's deflection to the Nazis, a wish to return symbolically to the unity of primary narcissism?

Time

Heidegger (1962) differentiates between the ordinary conception of time and primordial time. Ordinary time is duration – my hour is 50 minutes; a measurement – this pill is 20 mg; it is earlier or later – I will see you later in the afternoon. Clock time is what is counted (pp. 472–480). In this view, time is an endless sequence of nows – it comes into being and passes away – as an uninterrupted sequence; it has no beginning and no end.

What Heidegger calls primordial time is what underlies and makes possible ordinary time:

> Temporality is the primordial 'outside' of itself (p. 377).

Dasein is always situated in a place and a time. Temporality is one of the determining properties *of Dasein*; it is always situated in its personal history, finding its meaning in time. Heidegger does not mean a personal history of one person, but that history defines being and its possibilities. What we need to grasp in its primordial temporality is finitude – that *Dasein's* life is limited. We are thrown into a world not of our choosing, and we die. This being-toward-death is usually evaded by fleeing into idle talk and ordinariness. We can only uncover primordial time by authentically facing death and its finitude. *Dasein* projects "ahead-of-itself" (p. 386) to the possibilities of its existence and lays hold of the way its past lives on as "having-been" (p. 373) within the present. *Dasein's* nature is to project, not in the psychoanalytic way of putting one thing into another, but that its very character is one of having possibilities and projects. Thus, time is "stretched" (p. 425) within this threefold model. Being-toward-death then discloses possibility (pp. 304–311). Heidegger means the potential of opening up – what he calls the openness of the clearing, a moment of vision (p. 463). Then, in a second move, we return to the things encountered to make them meaningful in the present. What is disclosed is anticipatory resoluteness (pp. 370–380), a kind of opening up to" being oneself, an impassioned freedom toward death – a freedom that has been released" (p. 311). It is "the working out of possibilities projected in understanding" (p. 189). This allows "for a freedom of choosing itself and taking hold of itself" (p. 232).

What is Heidegger saying here? If we can authentically accept our finitude as human beings, if we truly understand that our time is limited, that can free us up to our inner potential. The determinism of the past can be balanced by an orientation toward projects and possibilities. Inauthentic existence means to be "lost in the They" (p. 313). Authenticity can be claimed by a call of conscience (p. 314), a "summoning to its innermost Being-guilty" (p. 314). Guilt is being lost in the They. For Heidegger, being guilty means "being responsible for" (p. 327). Then conscience is a summoning of *Dasein* toward this potentiality-for-being, which alone is the issue; it "is a call for care" (p. 322).

Heidegger sums up the following:

> Once one has grasped the finitude of one's existence, it snatches one back from the endless multiplicity of possibilities which offer themselves as closest to one—those of comfortableness, shirking and taking things lightly—and brings Dasein to the simplicity of its fate. This is how we designate Dasein's primordial historizing, which lies in authentic resoluteness and in which Dasein hands itself down to itself, free for death, in a possibility which it has inherited and yet has chosen.
>
> (p. 435)

Loewald states (1972a) that in the early years of psychoanalytic thought, the past was seen as an absolute determinism where unconscious forces from the past controlled and determined our present behavior. Unacceptable impulses are repressed

(Freud 1915b) and forgotten, then return as substitute formations or are repeated in action (Freud 1914b). Finally, Freud (1920) found a compulsion to repeat that accompanied trauma and overrode any pleasure. In a dialogue with Freud, Loewald notes that there is a dialogue between past and present modes of time. The psychic past is activated in the psychic present by transference. But the psychic present also impacts the psychic past. Reminiscences, Freud's (1893) term for immature memory traces, pull the psychic present back to reenactment (hypnoid states) (Loewald 1955). In Freud's concept of nachträglichkeit, the past is constantly reworked by more mature understandings in the present. Leavy (1989) suggests that for Loewald:

> our "thrownness" is better conceived as one into a world that is prior to defense. Not only the infant lives in this unitary world; the parents also, especially the mother, have the wherewithal, the persisting capacity, to "regress" to the infantile level sufficiently to be one with the child. Interaction with the environment at this stage is not defensive.
>
> (p. 236)

Loewald (1955, 1960, 1962a, 1971a, 1972a) adds to Freud's vision of psychoanalysis in the interrelatedness of the three modes of time – past, present, and future. Almost alone among classical analysts, Loewald highlights the future mode of time. "The superego functions from the viewpoint of a future ego" (Loewald 1962a, p. 45), to what we might be, or should be, "potentialities that we envisage for ourselves or of which we despair" (p. 46). Loewald postulates three successive stages in superego development. First is the stage of ideal ego, a magical return to the original state of perfection, a state of unity with the environment. Gradually, an ego ideal forms where the future state is "attained by merging with the magical object" (p. 47), leaving it dependent on external structures to have any claim. In the superego proper, the "ego envisages an inner future of itself" (p. 47) "in terms of psychic time, the relationship between ego and superego can be seen as a mutual relation between psychic present and psychic future" (p. 52).

Conscience for Loewald (1960) is a call from the future:

> Only insofar as we are ahead of ourselves, insofar as we recognize potentialities in ourselves, which represent more than we are at present and from which we look back at ourselves as we are at present, can we be said to have a conscience.
>
> (p. 273)

In his paper on memory, Loewald (1976) speaks of the human being as an "historical being" (p. 171):

> In such memorial activity, which weaves past, present, and future into a context of heightened meaning, each of us is on the pathway to becoming a self.
>
> (p. 172)

In his paper on internalization, Loewald (1973) speaks of:

> Inner ideals, expectations, hopes, demands, and, equally, inner doubts, fears, guilt, despair concerning oneself – all this is reaching toward or feeling defeated by a future.
>
> (p. 273)

The voice of conscience tells us what we should do or should have done, speaking from a future that we ask ourselves to reach or tell ourselves we are failing to reach – perhaps a future which should bring back a lost past, but certainly a future whose image in the course of development becomes imbued with all that is still alive from the hopes, expectations, demands, promises, ideals, aspirations, self-doubt, guilt, and despair of past ages, ancestors, parents, teachers, prophets, priests, gods, and heroes.

> The superego, insomuch as it is the internal representative of parental and cultural standards, expectations, fears, and hopes, is the intrapsychic representation of the future... The voice of conscience speaks to us as the mouthpiece of the superego, from the point of view of the inner future which we envision.
>
> (p. 273)

This echoes Heidegger's (1962a) call for the unity of past, present, and future as the potential for Dasein.

The Body

It is a common criticism that Heidegger neglected to say much about the body (Aho 2013; Dreyfus 1991; Li 2015). He makes the distinction between ontological, by which he means the basic structures of *Dasein*, and ontic, which is the regional manifestation of *Dasein* in practical activities. The care structure, authenticity, categories of time, aspects of thrownness, and death are all ontological categories to describe the structure of *Dasein* being in the world. The body, for Heidegger (1962), is an ontic category, something present at hand and not a primary constituent of existence. He thinks it is a mistake to reduce *Dasein* to a merely physical being rather than a being with a particular relationship to being:

> ...the perverse assumption that the entity in question has at bottom the kind of Being which belongs to something present-at-hand, even if one is far from attributing to it the solidarity of a occurrent corporeal Thing.
>
> (p. 153)

Perhaps Heidegger fears that reducing *Dasein* to a merely biological being would be to situate *Dasein* in the present as a biological system determined by its physical characteristics, being present-at-hand, rather than its orientation toward future prospects. The rebuttal to this absence is found in Merleau-Ponty (2014), who asks, how can we discuss ready-to-hand without involving the body? Is not the body to be equally disclosed in *Dasein's* involvements? *Dasein* always has a body, and it is not a separate structure in its world. We can make a similar analysis of involvement with our bodies and its disruption in illness and pain.

Heidegger (2001) participated for many years in a yearly seminar with Swiss psychiatrists organized by Menard Boss and L Binswanger, published as the *Zollikon Seminars*, three decades or more after the publication of *Being and Time*. It is evident in the book that the group pushed Heidegger about his stance on the body, and, to my reading, he is quite evasive and doesn't really answer. He does try to answer such criticism by making the distinction between the lived body (*Lieb)* and the corporal body (*Körper*). In my lived body, I am already "bodying-forth" (*Leiben*) (p. 86) in my pretheoretical state:

> How does the body participate in this assertion? The body participates by hearing and seeing. But does the body see? No. I see. But certainly my eyes belong to such a seeing, and thus to my body...I see through my eyes.
>
> (p. 88)

Loewald would not likely have had access to the *Zollikon* lectures and thus would be left with Heidegger's exclusion of bodily functions.

Conclusion

Martin Heidegger was Hans Loewald's teacher in Germany from 1924 to 1926. Loewald does acknowledge his profound gratitude to Heidegger but cannot forgive him for his antisemitic betrayal. I have tried to convey that Loewald's psychoanalytic conceptions result from two profound influences: Loewald has a conscious dialogue with Freud in an effort to evolve Freudian concepts into modern usage, while he has a hidden and unconscious dialogue with Heidegger in translating concepts of Being into psychoanalytic terms. While Heidegger wants to battle traditional metaphysics by destruction and replacement, laying the groundwork for modern attempts at deconstruction, Loewald is more of a "quiet revolutionary" (Fogel et al. 1996), profoundly altering Freudian language but not inventing new vocabulary. Both Heidegger and Loewald feel their respective fields are deadened by a sterile use of language. Loewald feels that words could lose their "magical evocative" power if the link between conscious and unconscious mentation is lost. Loewald is, by personality, not a Klein or Lacan who wants to overturn the Freudian enterprise. I would hold that Heideggerian concepts, such as being-in-the-world, authenticity, death, and time, permeate Loewaldian thinking. Being-in-the-world is a subversion of the traditional distinction between subject and object, actually coming from a variety of sources, not just Heidegger. For example, the relational sense of being embedded in the world can be traced back to Ferenzci (Wolstein 1997). Heidegger characterizes Being as inseparable from its place in the world. Loewald similarly characterizes self and object as differentiating from the original unity of a mother-child matrix. For Loewald, instincts and defenses, indeed all mental structures, are originally global events which only evolve out of this unity. In Heidegger's view, the authenticity of *Dasein,* the human form of Being, is predicated upon its acceptance of thrownness, finitude, and death. This frees *Dasein* to authentically care about itself and its projects, an orientation toward the future. Loewald, almost alone in the field, calls on psychoanalysts to think about the future as a meaningful category. Loewald thinks that the clinical psychoanalyst carries a future vision of what his or her patient can become while at the same time reaches into the past to identify true regressions and restart psychic growth. For Heidegger, anxiety can disclose a fleeing from authenticity, but this awareness of fleeing can free *Dasein* to attend to its future projects, for Loewald, he posits a relationship between the time modes of the past, present, and future. Loewald characterizes the call of conscience as serving a similar role to Heidegger's expression of basic anxiety. I will finish with this quote from Loewald (1971b), which is profoundly Heideggerian:

I have implied that the object of psychoanalysis is the individual human person. Only in this entity do we encounter what psychoanalysis calls psychic life and psychic reality.

(p. 104)

Notes

1 From Safranski (1998), a biography.
2 See Rothman (2014) and Brody (2014) for a general description of the issues involved, and Tawny (2015) for a detailed exposition.
3 Both Husserl and Freud took courses from Franz Brentano, who originated the idea of intentionality.
    Brentano stated: "Every mental phenomenon includes something as object within itself, although they do not all do so in the same way. In presentation something is presented, in judgement something is affirmed or denied, in love loved, in hate hated, in desire desired and so on. This intentional in-existence is characteristic exclusively of mental phenomena" (1995, p. 89).
4 The title of a collection of Heidegger's (1998) essays (*Wegmarken*) meant to convey the activity of a woodsman working in the depths of the woods.
5 This is an area of controversy, as Heidegger draws a sharp distinction between humans and animals and others would attribute partial consciousness to animals.
6 Alternately translated as destroyed or deconstructed.
7 See Lear (1988) for the complete argument.
8 The second reference is to Heidegger.
9 From Freud (1905), p. 260.
10 The metaphor of sculpture picks up the Aristotelian discussion of potentiality and actuality found in the section on Being-in-the-world, which Heidegger interprets as bringing forth.
11 The third reference is to Heidegger.

References

Aho, K. (2013). "The Body." In *The Bloomsbury Companion to Heidegger*, eds. F. Raffoul & E. Nelson. New York: Bloomsbury Publishing, pp. 269–274.

Arendt, H. (1958). *The Human Condition*. Chicago, IL: The University of Chicago Press.

Arendt, H. (1971). Heidegger at Eighty. New York Review of Books, October 21, 2021. https://www.nybooks.com/articles/1971/10/21/martin-heidegger-at-eighty/

Aristotle (1984). *The Complete Works of Aristotle*. Vol. 1, ed. J. Barnes. Princeton, NJ: Princeton University Press.

Askay, R. & Farquhar, J. (2006). *Apprehending the Inaccessible: Freudian Psychoanalysis and Existential Phenomenology*. Evanston, IL: Northwestern University Press.

Brentano, F. (1995). *Psychology from an Empirical Standpoint*, ed. L. McAlister. London: Routledge.

Brody, R. (2014). Why Does It Matter if Heidegger Was Antisemitic? *The New Yorker*, March 27.

Dilthey, W. (1996). *Selected Works, Hermeneutics and the Study of History*, Vol. 4, eds. R.A. Makkreel & F. Rodi. Princeton, NJ: Princeton University Press.

Downey, T. W. (1994). Hans W. Loewald, M.D. (1906–1993). *International Journal of Psychoanalysis* 75:839–842.

Dreyfus, H. (1991). *Being-in-the-world: A Commentary on Heidegger's Being and Time, Division I*. Cambridge: The MIT Press.

Fogel, G. I. (1989). The Authentic Function of Psychoanalytic Theory: An Overview of the Contributions of Hans Loewald. *Psychoanalytic Quarterly* 58:419–451.

Fogel, G. I., Tyson, P., Greenberg, J., McLaughlin, J. T. & Peyser, E. R. (1996). A Classic Revisited: Loewald on the Therapeutic Action of Psychoanalysis. *Journal of the American Psychoanalytic Association* 44:863–924.

Freud, S. (1893). *On the Psychical Mechanisms of Hysterical Phenomenon*. Standard Edition, London: Hogarth Press Limited, vol. 2, 3–17.

Freud, S. (1900). *The Interpretation of Dreams*. Standard Edition, London: Hogarth Press Limited, vol. 4–5.

Freud, S. (1905). *On Psychotherapy*. Standard Edition, London: Hogarth Press Limited, vol. 7, 255–268.

Freud, S. (1914a). *On Narcissism: An Introduction*. Standard Edition, London: Hogarth Press Limited, vol. 14, 67–102.

Freud, S. (1914b). *Remembering, Repeating and Working-through (Further Recommendations on the Technique of Psychoanalysis II)*. Standard Edition, London: Hogarth Press Limited, vol. 12, 145–156.

Freud, S. (1915a). *Instincts and their Vicissitudes*. Standard Edition, London: Hogarth Press Limited, vol. 14, 109–140.

Freud, S. (1915b). *Repression*. Standard Edition, London: Hogarth Press Limited, vol. 14, 141–158.

Freud, S. (1920). *Beyond the Pleasure Principle*. Standard Edition, London: Hogarth Press Limited, vol. 18, 3–64.

Freud, S. (1923). *The Ego and the Id*. Standard Edition, London: Hogarth Press Limited, vol. 19, 3–66.

Freud, S. (1924). *The Economic Problem of Masochism*. Standard Edition, London: Hogarth Press Limited, vol. 19, 157–70.

Freud, S. (1925). *An Autobiographical Study*. Standard Edition, London: Hogarth Press Limited, vol. 20, 1–74.

Freud, S. (1933). *New Introductory Lectures on Psycho-Analysis*. Standard Edition, London: Hogarth Press Limited, vol. 22, 1–182.

Freud, S. (1937a). *Analysis Terminable and Interminable*. Standard Edition, London: Hogarth Press Limited, vol. 23, 211–253.

Freud, S. (1937b). *Constructions in Analysis*. Standard Edition, London: Hogarth Press Limited, vol. 23, 255–270.

Friedman, M. (2000). *A Parting of the Ways: Carnap, Cassirer, and Heidegger*. Chicago, IL: Open Court.

Heidegger, M. (1962). *Being and Time*, transl. J. Macquarrie and E. Robinson. New York: Harper and Brothers.

Heidegger, M. (1985). The Self-Assertion of the German University and The Rectorate 1933/34 Facts and Thoughts. *Review of Metaphysics* 38:3.

Heidegger, M. (1995). *The Fundamental Concepts of Metaphysics*, transl. W. McNeill & N. Walker. Bloomington: Indiana University Press.

Heidegger, M. (1998). *Pathmarks*, ed. W. McNeill. Cambridge: Cambridge University Press.

Heidegger, M. (2001). *Zollikon Seminars*, transl. F. Mayr & R. Askay. Evanston, IL: Northwestern University Press.

Heidegger, M. (2017). *Ponderings II–VI, Black Note Books 1931–1938*, transl. R. Rojcewitz. Bloomington: Indiana University Press.

Herder, J. (2002). *Philosophical Writings*, eds. D. Clarke & M. Foster. Cambridge: Cambridge University Press.

Horney, K. (1932). Observations on a Specific Difference in the Dread Felt by Men and by women Respectively for the Opposite Sex. *International Journal of Psychoanalysis* 13:348–360.

Husserl, E. (1970). *Logical Investigations*, transl. N. Findlay. London: Routledge and Kegan Paul.

Kant, E. (1958). *Critique of Pure Reason*, transl. N. Smith. New York: The Modern Library.

Keikhaee, A. and Bell, S. (2016). On the Concept of Anxiety in Heidegger's Thought. *International Journal of Humanities* 23:1–26.

Kierkegaard, S. (1941). *Fear and Trembling*. Princeton, NJ: Princeton University Press.

Kisiel, T. (1993). *The Genesis of Heidegger's Being and Time*. Berkeley: University of California Press.

Klein, M. (1946). Notes on Some Schizoid Mechanisms. *International Journal of Psychoanalysis* 27:99–110.

Lear, J. (1988). *Aristotle: The Desire to Understand*. Cambridge: Cambridge University Press.

Leavy, S. A. (1989). Time and World in the Thought of Hans W. Loewald. *Psychoanalytic Study of the Child* 44:231–240.

Li, M. (2015). "The Lived Body in Heidegger, Merleau-Ponty and Derrida." Louisiana State University Master's Theses. 11. https://digitalcommons.lsu.edu/gradschool_theses/11

Loewald, H. W. (1950). Curriculum Vitae. Hans W. Loewald Papers (MS1721). Box 1. Manuscripts and Archives. New Haven, CT: Yale University Library.

Loewald, H. W. (1951). Ego and Reality. In *Papers on Psychoanalysis*. New Haven, CT: Yale University Press, 1980, pp. 3–20.

Loewald, H. W. (1952). The Problem of Defense and the Neurotic Interpretation of Reality. In *Papers on Psychoanalysis*. New Haven, CT: Yale University Press, 1980, pp. 21–32.

Loewald, H. W. (1953). Psychoanalysis and Modern Views on Human Existence and Religious Experience. *Journal of Pastoral Care* 7:1–15.

Loewald, H. W. (1955). Hypnoid State, Repression, Abreaction and Recollection. In *Papers on Psychoanalysis*. New Haven, CT: Yale University Press, 1980, pp. 33–42.

Loewald, H. W. (1960). On the Therapeutic Action of Psychoanalysis. In *Papers on Psychoanalysis*. New Haven, CT: Yale University Press, 1980, pp. 257–276.

Loewald, H. W. (1962a). Superego and Time. In *Papers on Psychoanalysis*. New Haven, CT: Yale University Press, 1980, pp. 43–52.

Loewald, H. W. (1962b). Internalization, Separation, Mourning, and the Superego. In *Papers on Psychoanalysis*. New Haven, CT: Yale University Press, 1980, pp. 43–52.

Loewald, H. W. (1971a). Some Considerations on Repetition and Repetition Compulsion. In *Papers on Psychoanalysis*. New Haven, CT: Yale University Press, 1980, pp. 87–101.

Loewald, H. W. (1971b). On Motivation and Instinct Theory. In *Papers on Psychoanalysis*. New Haven, CT: Yale University Press, 1980, pp. 102–137.

Loewald, H. W. (1972a). The Experience of Time. In *Papers on Psychoanalysis*. New Haven, CT: Yale University Press, 1980, pp. 138–147.

Loewald, H. W. (1972b). Freud's Conception of the Negative Therapeutic Reaction with Comments on Instinct Theory. In *Papers on Psychoanalysis*. New Haven, CT: Yale University Press, 1980, pp. 315–325.

Loewald, H. W. (1973). On Internalization. In *Papers on Psychoanalysis*. New Haven, CT: Yale University Press, 1980, pp. 69–86.

Loewald, H. W. (1976). Perspective on Memory. In *Papers on Psychoanalysis*. New Haven, CT: Yale University Press, 1980, pp. 148–173.

Loewald, H. W. (1978a). Primary Process, Secondary Process, and Language. In *Papers on Psychoanalysis*. New Haven, CT: Yale University Press, 1980, pp. 178–206.

Loewald, H. W. (1978b). *Psychoanalysis and the History of the Individual*. New Haven, CT: Yale University Press.

Loewald, H. W. (1980). Preface. In *Papers on Psychoanalysis*. New Haven, CT: Yale University Press, 1980, pp. vii–ix.

Loewald, H. W. (1986). Transference-Countertransference. *Journal of the American Psychoanalytic Association* 34:275–287.

Loewald, H. W. (1988a). Psychoanalysis in Search of Nature: Thoughts on Metapsychology, "Metaphysics," Projection. *Annual of Psychoanalysis* 16:49–54.

Loewald, H. W. (1988b). *Sublimation: Inquiries into Theoretical Psychoanalysis*. New Haven, CT: Yale University Press.

Merleau-Ponty, M. (2014). *Phenomenology of Perception*, transl. D. Landes. London: Routledge.

Neske, G. & Kettering, K. (ed.) (1990). *Martin Heidegger and National Socialism*. New York: Paragon House.

Nietzsche, F. (1956). *The Genealogy of Morals*, transl. F. Golffing. New York: Doubleday and Company.

Ricoeur, P. (1970). *Freud and Philosophy: An Essay on Interpretation*. New Haven, CT: Yale University Press.

Richardson, W. (2003). *Heidegger through Phenomenology to Thought*. New York: Fordham University Press.

Rothman, J. (2014). Is Heidegger Contaminated by Nazism? *The New Yorker*, April 28.

Safranski, R. (1998). *Martin Heidegger between Good and Evil*, transl. E. Osers. Cambridge, MA: Harvard University Press.

Sluga, H. (1993). *Philosophy and Politics in Nazi Germany*. Cambridge: Harvard University Press.

Tauber, A. (2010). *Freud, The Reluctant Philosopher*. Princeton, NJ: Princeton University Press.

Tawny, P. (2015). *Heidegger and the Myth of a Jewish World Conspiracy*, transl. A. Mitchell. Chicago, IL: University of Chicago Press.

Vandevelde, P. (2014). Language as the House of Being? How to Bring Intelligibility to Heidegger While Keeping the Excitement. Philosophy Faculty Research and Publications, 417. https://epublications.marquette.edu/phil_fac/417

Wilson, W. (1973). Herder, Folklore and Romantic Nationalism. *Journal of Popular Culture* 6:819–835.

Wolstein, B. (1997). The First Direct Analysis of Transference and Countertransference. *Psychoanalytic Inquiry* 17:505–521.

Chapter 7

Future Tense and the Unthought New

The Not Yet—Something More—and
the Horizons of Time

Alfred Margulies

It is in the nature of our being that we develop, unfold, and achieve growth within an arc and boundary of time. We move toward an unfolding we do not fully understand. Loewald (1962, p. 243) called this arc of becoming the "something more", believing that the clinician holds this potentiality, a potentiality-for-being, even as—especially as—the patient is unclear and moving toward what it might be. Building on phenomenological-existential scholarship so integral to Loewald's psychoanalytic insights about time and the human situation—building on their potential—this paper will explore how, from the perspective of our contemporary understandings, we might situate ourselves within and towards time, highlighting the often background presence of the future. In this chapter, we take up the entangled modes of time—past-present-future; the potential of transference-countertransference enactment as an opportunity to operationalize—to bring forward—this nexus of time; and the place of the "inner future", the not-yet, the something more, of Being and becoming. This will take us to the uncharted possibilities of existence, how, as clinicians, they are entrusted to us, and how we might hold these potentials even when we too are in the dark, holding possibilities of the unthought new.[1]

Something More

> Only insofar as we are ahead of ourselves, insofar as we recognize potentialities in ourselves, which represent *more* than we are at present and from which we look back at ourselves as we are at present, can we be said to have a conscience...the inner future toward which to move.
>
> (italics in the original, p. 273) Hans Loewald (1962)

Many find Loewald mind-expanding, fascinating, and yet somehow elusive, hard to capture within a psychoanalytic tradition. He seems to stand alone, unique. Indeed, he does. Though Loewald is inspiring and much cited, it's not widely appreciated that he straddled the worlds of phenomenological-existential studies and classical psychoanalysis. As a student of philosophy, Loewald absorbed Heidegger's (1962) deep conceptions of time and anxiety, bringing these insights to psychoanalysis in a highly creative and distinctive fashion. But here's the rub: in the preface to his collected essays, Loewald (1980) comments:

DOI: 10.4324/9781003328230-9

Philosophy has been my first love... My teacher in this field was Martin Heidegger, and I am deeply grateful for what I learned from him, despite his most hurtful betrayal in the Nazi era, which alienated me from him permanently.... Freud is close enough to my generation to have been a commanding living force as I grew up and became a psychiatrist, although I never met him in person. He has remained for me, through his writings, that living presence.

(pp. xlii–xliii)

And here for me came a surprising realization: Loewald implicitly bridges from Heidegger to Freud, but, because of his betrayal by his mentor, Loewald left his Heideggerian connections largely unstated throughout the rest of his work. I have come to appreciate how elegant Loewald's implicit syntheses are, jewel-like, a gift to those of us who have dwelled at the overlap of phenomenological-existential studies and psychoanalysis.

In this chapter, I reimagine the potential of Loewald's theories about potential, taking them into a conceptual framework he had not seen but one that we now inhabit, in particular our modern conceptions of (1) the power of memory (that is, *Après-coup*, deferred action, *Nachträglichkeit*) and (2) the power of transference-countertransference enactment. These complex concepts expand and amplify Loewald's theories of time, taking his work into new possibilities. If only he might now participate in this exploration! My empathic imagination will have to do.

Potentialities—or the Possibility of Possibilities

Why does this quote from Loewald (1962) seem deep and right?

The parent *ideally* is in an empathic relationship of understanding the child's particular stage in development, *yet ahead in his vision of the child's future and mediating this vision to the child...*

(italics added, p. 229)

What a powerful vision a parent holds for a child's unfolding—a vision of the future! Loewald wisely remarks that the parent is "*ideally* in an empathic relationship", that is, ideally the parent feels into this child's uniqueness, attempting to be ahead in a vision of who this child might become. Implicitly, Loewald is foregrounding the parallel relationship of the analyst and analysand; that is, to paraphrase, the analyst, too, is ahead in a vision of this singular person's future and mediating this vision as unfolding possibilities. I would call this visioning an "empathic imagination" of the future for the person before us, within their unique, unfolding potential (Margulies, 1989).

But this glimmer of potential is often nebulous, not yet clear. It remains a possibility. And, to be sure, the reason that holding this potential is a profound and fraught responsibility for parents and clinicians is precisely because there are deep and unknown consequences. Which is to say, this empathic holding of imagined possibilities might go terribly awry—and I'll return later to show how this might happen.

To reframe: parents hold open possibilities for a child that the child is not yet aware of. By analogy, the clinician holds open possibilities for the patient that the patient is not yet aware of. Moreover, because the analytic therapist may not yet be aware of the contours of these potentials, *the clinician holds open the possibility of still unknown possibilities—and all of this in the face of the possibility of no possibilities at all.* That is, time is limited, possibilities evaporate, and opportunities are missed as we unfold over an arc of Being that is always there, on the horizon, a horizon that is fragile, uncertain, and yet, precisely because we are humans, terribly certain. This is what it means to be a person, to be mortal, and what we mean (what Heidegger [1962] meant) by "Being-towards-death".

Here's an all-too-common, urgent example: A depressed patient sees no way out, feeling trapped by life and an overwhelming sense of being weighed down by a present that extends endlessly, without change. With severe depression, the markers of time seem to collapse into an endless void of no-where and no-when. This collapse of the horizons of time is precisely what we mean by hopelessness. Bringing such spatial-temporal experiences forward, the pioneering psychological existential phenomenologists, for example, Minkowski (1970) and Binswanger (1975), boldly re-conceptualized psychopathology through a taxonomy, a diagnostic system, of the pathologies of time itself. In this sense, the future could be sick or broken (Margulies, 2016, 2018).[2] As clinicians, we are alert to utter hopelessness, because here temporal collapse can turn lethal. The clinician's task is both to protect the patient—if need be, even physically—and to protect a yet unimagined future, holding on to the possibility of a path to emerge. We play for time while we free the capacity to envision a new, unthought of, future. This wording surprises me: a "new future", such a strange thing to say—versus the old, stale, lethal futures—an emerging future that frees up possibilities. In a sense, we are lending our temporal empathic imagination to the Other before us.

The Entangled Modes of Time, Past-Present-Future

From Loewald's "The Experience of Time" (1972):

> We encounter time in psychic life primarily as a linking activity in which what we call *past, present, and future are woven into a nexus.* The terms themselves, past, present, and future, gain meaning only within the context of such a nexus. The nexus in itself is not so much one of succession but of interaction... as modes of time which determine and shape each other, which differentiate out of and articulate a pure now.... There is no irreversibility on a linear continuum, as in the common concept of time as succession, but a reciprocal relationship *whereby one time mode [past, present, future] cannot be experienced or thought without the other and whereby they continually modify each other.* As terms they are correlative, like the terms father and son; *as experiential phenomena they interpenetrate.*
>
> (italics added, 1972, pp. 143–144)

Let me pause to condense: The modes of time, past-present-future, are always already interconnected, they are figure ground to one another, they define and bring one another into being. They are correlative, like the terms father and son, they imply one another, even if unstated. Loewald continues:

> The microdynamics of memory is the microcosmic side of historicity, i.e., of the fact that the individual not only *has* a history that an observer may unravel and describe,

but that he *is* history and makes his history by virtue of his memorial activity in which past-present-future are created as mutually interacting modes of time.

(italics in original, 1972, p. 146)

My reframe: in our very own being, then, it is our nature, our way of being, to have a history that we create and recreate in the very remembering. Compare the "individual not only has a history... but that he is history" with Heidegger's conclusion in *Being and Time* (1962): not only does Being have time, but human Being is always becoming, past-ing, and presence-ing; Being is an action, a verb; all of which is to say (and Heidegger does): Being is Time. Note, too, that in translation (as in Loewald, 1972, p. 146) the hyphens that interconnect past-present-future parallel a similar conception with Heidegger's (1962) Being-in-the-world to indicate the correlative, interpenetrating nature of time and space. *That is, past-present-future and Being-in-the-world are also entangled: space-time-Being.*

The Entangled Transference and the Unthought New

For me, Loewald brings forward further implications of these entwined existential and psychoanalytic insights: *the centrality of transference to psychoanalytic technique is a brilliant operationalizing of time because past-present-future are always already entangled in the experience of transference.* Indeed, by interrogating this basic point of the centrality of transference phenomena within psychoanalysis, Loewald (1972) further opens to us the existential *phenomenology,*[3] that is, the lived experience as it presents itself, of transference:

> The phenomenology of transference may serve as example: not only is the present relationship to the analyst partially determined by the patient's past (which is, as we say, still active in the present) and by a wished-for or feared future (itself codetermined by the past). It is also true that the present relationship, and the expectations it engenders, activate the past and influence how it is now experienced and remembered. *This reintegration of the past, in its turn, modifies the present relationship with the analyst* (and of course with other people as well) and *has a bearing on the envisaged future. The modification of the past by the present does not change 'what objectively happened in the past,' but it changes that past which the patient carries within him as his living history.*

(italics added, p. 144)

Here is Loewald's profound, crystallized insight: *"Transference" serves as an operationalized prism for time, refracting the white light of time into its components, into a spectrum of time, that is, through the analytic relationship itself.* A clinician working within the transference implicitly—and, with interpretative activity, explicitly—carries forward this entanglement of time to achieve insight, or awareness, and *change.*[4] This brings the present analytic relationship into conjunction with past relationships, with the implication that the grip of past relationships might now be relaxed to free up new possibilities. The pregnant implication: the recasting of the present in terms of the influence of the past potentially changes the future. This is, precisely, the rationale of psychoanalytic awareness.

As an example of holding the future, patients sometimes want me to hold the possibility of other possibilities, even, especially, as they are caught in the grip of compulsive repetitions which they do not want to let go of—not yet.[5] Indeed, they rely on me to hold a bookmark for the future, something to return to, a still unfinished story, whatever that might be. If I suggest that perhaps the repetitive choices are what they might actually be looking for—though they haven't yet fully acknowledged or owned it—because this is the way of life that they are persistently choosing to live, I will often get a strong, even panicky, push-back from the patient, as if: "No! This isn't what I want, it makes me miserable, but I'm just not ready, not yet—and I need you to hold on to a different possibility for me". That is, I am asked to hold a still vaguely imagined, hoped-for new path, flooded with anxiety and uncertainty precisely because of the risk of letting go of the familiar for—and here let me coin a phrase—the "unthought new". Yes, there are no guarantees—embracing the future is always risky.

And now I more fully apprehend the subtle enactment that we are caught in, the complex role that I now inhabit in their struggle to free themselves. Someone else, the patient feels, perhaps a parent, would not, could not, help with this uncertainty. There is a vague inner vision that is working itself out—an aspiration to be something more. In this sense, the belief I am entrusted with is not quite in the future per se, but, more precisely, within the person before me, that is, the person-in-time-in-the-world-with-me, filled with an unknown future and the arc of who they might become.

"The inner future": The "not-yet"—the "something-more"— of Being

Here's Loewald from "On the Therapeutic Action of Psychoanalysis" (1960):

> The patient... attempts to reach the analyst as a representative of higher stages of ego reality organization... It is this *something more*, not necessarily more in content but more in organization and significance... here represented and mediated by the analyst... for which the individual is striving... The patient, being recognized by the analyst as something more than he is at present, can *attempt to reach this something more...*
>
> (italics added, p. 243)

How stunning this is! "The patient, being recognized by the analyst as something more than he is at present, can attempt to reach this something more..."

Now, note how Loewald (1962) unpacks this "something more":

> The superego, inasmuch as it is the internal representative of parental and cultural standards, expectations, fears, and hopes, is the intrapsychic representation of the future. Only insofar as we are ahead of ourselves, insofar as we recognize potentialities in ourselves, which represent *more* than we are at present and from which we look back at ourselves as we are at present, can we be said to have a conscience. The voice of conscience speaks to us as the mouthpiece of the superego, from the point of view of the inner future which we envision... the inner future toward which to move.[6]
>
> (italics in original, p. 273)

Note, too, how Loewald is linking the superego, the ego ideal, not only with guilt but with the deep existential sense of who we might become, that is, the inner future, the not-yet, the-being-toward, the something-more:

> We have a sense of guilt concerning past or present thoughts, feelings, and deeds, but only inasmuch as they represent a nonfulfillment of the inner image of our-selves, of the internal ideal we have not reached, of the future in us that we have failed.
>
> (p. 274)

Such powerful language, the "voice of conscience speaks to us" of our "nonfulfill-ment", of an "ideal we have not reached", of "something more" that still awaits us. Loewald is implicitly echoing Heidegger, who referred to this voice explicitly as "the call", as in (Heidegger, 1962, p. 317, subhead 56): "The Character of Conscience as a Call".

A Contemporary Re-visioning

Working within a classical theoretical framework, Loewald understood deeply that the phenomenon of transference could operationalize the existential nexus of time. And now years later we have new (or different) conceptual tools to take us further in revising his work, *après coup*, through our spiraling, evolving understanding of uncon-scious processes and psychoanalysis.

My claim: *Enactment takes transference entanglement with time right into the inter-subjective field.* That is, if transference entangles time, then this nexus is further com-pounded by the irreducible entanglement of the countertransference within enactment. And—this is crucial, though seldom explicit—our contemporary privileging of enact-ment, the right here/right now between patient and clinician, implicates the entangled nexus of past-present-future. Moreover, precisely because elements of enactment are unconscious to both patient and analyst, being caught up in enactment is only more fully understood after the event. And it is here in this continual, spiraling loop of un-derstanding that new perspectives emerge (Compare Laplanche's spiraling images of *Après-coup* [2017]).

Après-coup: Kierkegaard famously observed that we only understand backwards, but we must live forwards.[7] To this wonderful insight, let us now add a contemporary psychoanalytic perspective, afterwards. In understanding backwards, that is, in re-understanding/re-inscribing the significance of the past, a new understanding emerges of the past that, in its very newness, carries forward to change our understanding of the present, which then carries forward to our future. And this new future orientation now spirals backwards to change how we understand the past. We are, in our very becoming, this spiral of entangled time. Recall Loewald (1972):

> The reintegration of the past…modifies the present relationship with the analyst… and has a bearing on the envisaged future. The modification of the past by the present does not change 'what objectively happened in the past,' but it changes the past which the patient carries within him as his living history.
>
> (p. 144)

Loewald did not specifically take up *Après-coup*,[8] but he captures its essence. My reframe: old experience acquires new significance, and, with this new significance, the old experience now has renewed power to change present and future; that is, the old becomes new again (I am basing this conception on Laplanche and Pontalis [1973]). Loewald (1962) summons the essence of *Après-coup* with powerful images from Freud evoking the underworld of Homer's *Odyssey* in "The Interpretation of Dreams" (Freud, 1900, p. 553n.):

> The transference neurosis, in the technical sense of the establishment and resolution of it in the analytic process, is due to the blood of recognition, which the patient's unconscious is given to taste so that the old ghosts may reawaken to life.
>
> (Loewald, 1962, pp. 248–249)

Seemingly abstract yet underpinning the psychoanalytic process, the spiral of *Après-coup* is precisely why therapeutic awareness can be transforming. That is, perspective, insight, and the psychodynamic process all come together, change our understandings of our past, present, and future, offering a new path, a new potentiality.

Case Example: On Being Lost[9]

Some years ago, a young lawyer came to me feeling lost, angry, and disillusioned. Work seems a sham; his supervisors are hypocritical, immoral, and disgusting. He's filled with contempt for these supposed adults; they are idiots. And he can't keep his mouth shut; he knows he's making trouble for himself. So, what is he to do? Is there a place for him? He's smart, motivated, and frustrated precisely because he's idealistic. But he's never trusted those in power. Like many, he felt fate had thrown him into the wrong family—and so his deep disappointment. But, to his great surprise, he also came to realize that his parents felt the same way—he was the wrong son—and so his bitter grievance. How did it all come to this? Deep cynicism seemed like a deep truth. And now, his future seems bleak.

No surprise (well, it's always a surprise); he's sharply supercilious and patronizing to me, too. He's cynical about therapy and my motivations. And he decides this is a real problem, because if I'm not the one he's looking for, it's probably because all therapists are hopeless. But he's not sure.

And I'm not either. A year into it, we seem to be getting nowhere. He's tiresome, annoying, and provokes me to spar with him. And I do, by aggressively taking him up on his undermining therapy with his constant arsenal of withering attacks. I try to check my patronizing him, but it's frustrating—the same old, same old that never gets traction. Actually, I often wish he would leave.

Almost. Not quite. Not yet… I'm searching for something more, too. After all, he's smart, capable, can be blisteringly funny, and would seem to have much promise—there should be potential here. I worry that if we both end up too cynical, he may not get into another therapy—because our therapy will have simply repeated his expectations. And, if *we* enact his expectation—that is, if I act it out, too—it will become just another confirming instance in his life's story, his being on his own, stuck in these near irresistible, self-defeating patterns, past-present-future entangled, repetitive, predictive, and life-draining.

Speaking of mismatch, I needed to remind myself of what he bravely chose to tell me early on, fearing that I might misuse it. Born into the wrong family, he felt cheated. And, surely, it's a possibility that, from any perspective, it was a terrible, even tragic, mismatch. The existentialists would call this his thrownness, his facticity,[10] the so-called facts of his history that he gives particular significance and fantasy elaboration, and indeed, finds repeated everywhere. And so, his bitter grievance—it's not fair. And here we are continuing that history, both wondering whether to quit and move on. It's here between us now, as our old-new burning question.

Still, I know that the *potential* of our mismatch is precisely that we feel in the grip of an airtight, future-collapsing mutual enactment. In a sense, this potential is what the therapy brought us to, if only we had the imagination to engage it, to escape this possibility. This intense, bitter grievance and how it might get played out between us became my touchstone of our engagement of his future.

Here's the fuller story he told, reflecting his style of presenting his history as a kind of legal brief. He argued that none of the adults in his life gave useful direction matched to his needs. His father was a jerk, mostly, especially when he deferred to his vapid and grasping mother. When things became most unbearable as an adolescent, he'd gone to his father feeling misunderstood, pissed off, and at wit's end. Mother was willfully intolerable, father was unsupportive, and he was just not going to take it anymore. My patient took a stand and set an ultimatum: If the family wouldn't change, he'd pack up and leave. This threat really covered over a plea to his father, and, given his upper middle-class, striving background, it seemed inconceivable that father wouldn't hear him out and capitulate.

But father shocked him, agreeing that it would be best for him to go. My patient felt the ground cut from beneath him. He didn't have a Plan B. And so, he would leave emotionally, willful, proud, and icy in his interactions, biding his time until he had the resources, stamina, and moment. This simmering, inner rage energized him. Given his intelligence and privilege, he did well enough in college but, no surprise, remained sour about relationships and lost in his directions. Despite his intelligence, given his mistrust, he was not someone who attracted mentors. His aloneness became self-fulfilling.

Our rocky relationship—so clear to me now—enacted this crucial history. Like those toy bamboo finger locks, the more you struggle, the more you are caught. Other than to bail out, these critical enactments have no way out except through—and together— into awareness. And so, it all rests on a hope that both must hold, a possibility that all the therapy turmoil will be worth it. Fuller understanding must wait; now was our moment. And this possibility is what I held out to him, to us both: "You and me: can't we do better than this? Do we have to replay this yet again? I don't know how, but can't we find another way than what you experienced with your father?"

This stopped us both in our tracks, both of us relieved. What I said was, in essence, aspirational, something to work toward: together, maybe we could rewrite the future. This was now our shared question: "Can't we find another way?" Our relationship first changed gradually and then decisively. We both relaxed, and we were now able to experience each other freshly. Though before he seemed complex and difficult, setting logical traps as if playing chess, he now seemed simpler. Almost boyish and guileless. His legalistic, paranoid style would flare up at work and sometimes with me, but our relationship was remarkably devoid of the hatred we'd experienced before.

To be sure, he seemed a bit naïve about how the world actually works and how it can crush you. And here I felt protective—a different, more workable countertransference enactment. He was thoughtful and appreciative. And likeable. Surely, I was more likeable, too. He wanted to open up. And he did. And I did… Indeed, we enjoyed one another. All of which is to say, by becoming aware of how history kept writing us into its script, we stopped and wrote the possibility of a new possibility to replace the old, deadening one. We re-wrote our future, and so we re-wrote the possibility of his having a new future, even though that possibility remained on the further horizons of time.

(A footnote—or bookmark to the future: Years after our therapy had ended, I ran into him. He thanked me and vaguely, sheepishly, recalled: "I kind of remember I was a real pain in the ass—I apologize for that". I replied, "Yeah, but that was a good thing, we really got into it—that's what we needed to do. And why it worked". He filled me in about his life, and like those ending movie credits where you are told what happened to the characters, I got to fast-forward to a future that was unclear to us back then. Over time, he'd become the successful leader of a prominent NGO that fought on behalf of the marginalized. A charismatic leader with a mission, he carried himself with a mature, dignified, passionate, witty, and even fierce presence, a residue of the old anger creatively sublimated, harnessed, into a fight for social justice. Who could have predicted? I hadn't seen this particular possibility, but here it was, as if waiting all along for him to take hold of it. Ironically, his fulfilling *this* potential now seems almost inevitable. But little could we have predicted this future-realized-present back then.[11]

Afterwords: The Call of Something More

Loewald situates "something more" with the evolution of the superego, one's growing sense of values and conscience. Implicit is that this something more is part of our existential background, a reminder, a call to us, of our transience, our finitude: we must not waste time, which is, after all, our very being, as in Heidegger's Being is time. Re-call: Loewald is here summoning up Heidegger's (1962) "the call" of the inner voice of existential conscience: we aim for a life more fully lived, feeling as Loewald puts it: "a sense of guilt concerning …. the future in us that we have failed" (Loewald, 1962, p. 274).

Loewald envisions a growth model of therapeutic action, an approach familiar to anyone who spends time with children, students, or gardens—a growth model imagines an unfolding, a growing-towards. Further, a model rooted in evolving potentials implicitly counters clinical-theoretical reductionism through the vision of emerging and unknown horizons. The philosopher Emmanuel Levinas (1987a,b), like Loewald, a profoundly disillusioned student of Heidegger, diverged sharply from his teacher by reimagining the primordial essences of Being. Levinas recognized that Being itself must be grounded in an *a priori* ethics conjoined to the presence of the Other, who is apprehended as never fully knowable. The first experience of infinity, Levinas asserted, is precisely the otherness of the Other before us: "The infinite is the radically, absolutely, other" (p. 107). This disquieting unknowability of the Other can impel us towards explanation, thereby covering over the disconcerting essence—the humanity—of the Other. Levinas asserted that the infinity of possibilities of the Other, that essential something more and beyond us, thereby obligates us to care for their being and, indeed, grounds our own Being in ethics. By "totalizing" (Levinas, 1987a,b) the Other through our explanations, we risk effacing their unknowable humanity and possibilities—opening the door, as history has repeatedly shown us, to awful consequences.

How then to balance the demands of knowing and not knowing? As analytic clinicians, we, of course, reflexively search for explanations—dynamics, repetitions, patterns, diagnoses. Hard-won knowledge meshed with clinical experience creates theoretical mappings, compelling guides through dense forests. But we need to remain vigilant that such explanations in and of themselves must never be enough, by luring us into reductionistic, "totalizing", complacency. Moreover, totalizing is always constellated within the dynamics of power.

As analysts, we are aware of myriad unconscious reductions of the Other, out-of-awareness patterns, and biases that may pull us toward the seductive feel of familiar clarity. Indeed, this is our stock-in-trade as analysts: the power of unconscious patterns that shape us and dominate our ways of being. We must continually return to the dialectic tension of knowing and not-knowing at the same time.[12]

Loewald doesn't foreground how the holding of the potential of the other might go awry. The analyst, though, feels the weight of responsibility of holding the future of another precisely because of the possibility of enacting the limitations of the past, thereby introducing new hazards. And let us be clear, because the future is also imagined, it saturates fantasy with force and direction; this imagined, internalized future becomes realized in its consequences. Many who come to us are still trying to escape their proscribed, internalized, and externalized futures, the limitations of possibilities imposed by others: family, culture, patriarchy and the symbolic order, privilege and discrimination, racism, sexism, and the foreclosure of what might be. It is grievous that our society neglects or destroys the future of so many of our young. And so, we must ask: as clinicians, where do we fit into this arc of foreclosed possibilities and the struggle for new futures?

How often a child is both held and lost within another's nexus of time. Structuring and orienting, the imagined future becomes woven into a familiar way of Being. Sometimes this holding of time is traumatic: the child's future is held ambivalently, destructively, sadistically, abusively, hatefully—the child's future is a kind of throwaway. But perhaps more often the damage is subtle, even hidden, because a child, especially an exceptional child with clear but untold potential, becomes an extension of the parents (who might have been an extension of their own parents), who want the child to redeem and enhance their thwarted lives, their limitations, trauma, and lack of possibilities. They might experience their urgent concern as in the child's best interests, particularly given the confines of their childhood, their experience of the harshness of the world, and the shortness of life. But still, this love of the child's potential—shot through with fantasy—can be rooted in limitations and conflicts of imagination. Throughout, the question remains: Just whose future is it? How did this omnipresent, sometimes multigenerational traumatized and traumatizing, internalized future come to be this way? And where is it now headed? The struggle for who owns the future is, then, always ripe for enactment and totalizing reduction. As clinicians, we must continually check ourselves against our values, assumptions, desires, and needs. It is our ethical obligation to the Other before us.

And here is a note of concern for the clinician: Therapists can feel scorched when things go badly, feeling that they are unable to hold open a future for their patients, who seem hell bent to pursue failure or self-destruction. So, let us revise: The analytic therapist tries hard, sometimes intrepidly against the odds, to hold open the possibility of possibilities in the face of the possibility of no possibilities at all. Many clinicians suffer terribly here at their perceived failures. The lost future can be tragic, irreversible. Did this becoming have to end this way? As clinicians, as healers, it is our way of Being to hold on to the potential of possibilities, even knowing that this can break our hearts. And so it is that we perpetually return to the threshold of becoming, to the something more, the not yet known, and the unthought new.

Notes

1 This chapter began as notes and a brief talk for an ongoing Discussion Group titled "The Critics of Psychoanalysis" in collaboration with Jonathan Lear for the February 15, 2018, annual meetings of the American Psychoanalytic Association. My deep thanks to Jonathan Lear and the group for your invaluable conversations. Also, a recently published paper (Margulies, 2023) on Loewald, Lacan, and Apres-coup complements this chapter (which was actually written first).

2 Soon after their 1879 revolution, the French victors, wanting a new beginning, broke apart and restructured time and space to wrest cultural ways away from religion to Enlightenment ideals, for example, by changing the names of months and holidays, resetting the calendar, converting the measure of space (metric), and re-structuring the length of the week (ten days).

   Jonathan Lear's *Radical Hope* (2006) interrogates the breaking of time through the devastation of the culture of the Crow Nation. As familiar ways of being in the world—symbols, customs, words—lose their richly constellated, entwined significance, time becomes incoherent, and the links between the past-present-future impoverished. As the great chief recounted to a white historian, "After this nothing happened" (p. 2).

3 Roughly here approximated by my use of the term "lived-experience", phenomenology within continental philosophy is especially associated with Edmund Husserl, Heidegger, Sartre, Merleau-Ponty, Binswanger, and Minkowski and indicates a rigorous philosophical approach to explore how experiential phenomena present themselves.

4 I use the wording "carries forward" as a way of capturing the nuances of *"nachträglich"*.

5 Here Freud enters the conversation: this resonates with his basic conception of libidinal fixation or regression in the creation of neurotic symptoms—one fixates or retreats from the anxiety of the next stage.

6 Compare Heidegger's (1962) conception of "Being-towards".

7 See C. Carlisle (2020) for how central and iterative this conception was throughout Kierkegaard's life.

8 See Laplanche and Pontalis (1973); Laplanche (2017).

9 Disclaimer: For reasons of confidentiality, my clinical examples must be disguised and amalgams, losing some texture—but I have taken pains to remain true to the process and experience.

10 "By "facticity", I am drawing on Heidegger's language (1962)—which echoes Loewald's "historicity" (as above, 1972, p. 146): "The microdynamics of memory is the microcosmic side of historicity, i.e., of the fact that the *individual not only has a history... he is history and makes his history...* created as mutually interacting modes of time" (italics added, p. 146).

11 And a footnote to a footnote: The example here is to illustrate a more delimited focus on the future in psychotherapy. For an example of a fuller psychoanalytic exploration over time, see Margulies (2014).

12 So aptly captured by John Keats' conception of "Negative Capability" (see Margulies, 1989).

References

Binswanger, L. (1975). *Being in the World: Selected Papers of Ludwig Binswanger* (J. Needleman, Trans.). London: Souvenir Press.

Carlisle, C. (2020). *Philosopher of the Heart: The Restless Life of Soren Kierkegaard*. New York: Farrar, Straus and Giroux.

Freud, S. (1900). *The Interpretation of Dreams*. Standard Edition, vol. 5. New York: Norton, 1953.

Heidegger, M. (1962). *Being and Time* (J. Macquarrie & E. Robinson, Trans.). New York: Harper Collins.

Laplanche, J. (2017). *Après-coup* (J. House, Trans.). New York: The Unconscious in Translation.

Laplanche, J. & Pontalis, J.-B. (1973). *The Language of Psycho–Analysis* (D. Nicholson-Smith, Trans.). New York: W. W. Norton & Co.

Lear, J. (2006). *Radical Hope: Ethics in the Face of Cultural Devastation*. Cambridge, MA: Harvard University Press.

Levinas, E. (1987a). *Collected Philosophical Papers* (A. Lingis, Trans.). Phaenomenologica, vol. 100. Dordrecht-Boston: Nijhoff.

Levinas, E. (1987b). "Philosophy and the Idea of the Infinite" (A. Lingis, Trans.) (1993). In A. Peperzak, ed., *To the Other*. West Lafayette, IN: Purdue University Press, pp. 88–119.

Loewald, H. (1960/2000). "On the Therapeutic Action of Psychoanalysis" (1960). In *The Essential Loewald: Collected Papers and Monographs*. Hagerstown, MD: University Publishing Group, 2000, pp. 221–256.

Loewald, H. (1960/2000). "On the Therapeutic Action of Psychoanalysis" (1960). In *The Essential Loewald: Collected Papers and Monographs*. Hagerstown, MD: University Publishing Group, 2000, pp. 257–276.

Loewald, H. (1962/2000). "Internalization, Separation, Mourning, and the Superego" (1962). In *The Essential Loewald: Collected Papers and Monographs*. Hagerstown, MD: University Publishing Group, 2000, pp. 257–276.

Loewald, H. (1972/2000). "The Experience of Time" (1972). In *The Essential Loewald: Collected Papers and Monographs*. Hagerstown, MD: University Publishing Group, 2000, pp. 138–147.

Loewald, H. (1980/2000). "Preface" (1980). In *The Essential Loewald: Collected Papers and Monographs*. Hagerstown, MD: University Publishing Group, 2000, pp. xli–xliii.

Margulies, A. (1989). *The Empathic Imagination*. New York: Norton.

Margulies, A. (2014). After the Storm: Living and Dying in Psychoanalysis. *Journal of the American Psychoanalytic Association*, 62: 863–905.

Margulies, A. (2016). Hidden in Plain Sight on Locked Wards: On Finding and Being Found. *American Journal of Psychotherapy*, 70 (1): 101–16.

Margulies, A. (2018). Illusionment and Disillusionment: Foundational Illusions and the Loss of a World. *Journal of the American Psychoanalytic Association*, 66 (2): 289–303.

Margulies, A (2023). It's about Time: Loewald, Lacan, and Après-coup in America. *Journal of the American Psychoanalytic Association*, 71 (5): 823–841.

Minkowski, E. (1970). *Lived Time: Phenomenological and Psychopathological Studies* (N. Metzel, Trans.). Chicago, IL: Northwestern University Press.

Chapter 8

On Being Grown-Up
Loewald's Concept of Maturity[1]

Joel Whitebook

I.

In "What is Enlightenment?" Immanuel Kant identified maturity (*Mündigkeit*) as a fundamental value of that wave of historical and cultural innovation known as the German *Aufklärung* (1784: 11). Like Mozart's *The Marriage of Figaro*, which was written at roughly the same time, that canonical text expresses the growing confidence of the ascendant European bourgeoisie in pre-revolutionary Europe, albeit in a more restrained fashion.[2] In our day, however, much of the air has gone out of the idea of maturity—along with that of the Enlightenment itself. Theoretically, Kant's moral philosophy, in which the idea of maturity is embedded, has been criticized from a number of directions. The critical theorist T. W. Adorno, for example, who was steeped in Freud, argues that, insofar as Kant's moral theory demands the subordination of our bodily based inclinations to the understanding—which, in psychoanalytic terms, means the domination of unconscious-instinctual life by the rational ego—it is essentially repressive. At the same time as the critical theorist commends Kant for refusing to soft pedal the intrinsic conflict between society's demand for stability and order and the embodied individual's demand for happiness, he criticizes him for coming down in favor of the former, in other words, on the side of repression (see Adorno 2001: 15. See also Whitebook 1985, 2004a).[3] From a cultural perspective, in today's post-patriarchal and less stringent environment, which places a high premium on individual fulfillment, the notion of maturity often has a puritanical, Victorian, if not downright stuffy, ring to it. And more recently, post-colonial theorists have rejected the Enlightenment's moral framework in its entirety, arguing that it consists of Eurocentric prejudices, which are often used to rationalize Western imperialism.

There are those who argue that, in light of these considerations and others, the ideas of the Enlightenment and Maturity are unredeemable and should be completely abandoned. I would maintain, however, that besides the uncritical acceptance of these ideas, on the one hand, and their outright rejection, on the other, a third option can be identified: that we take these criticisms seriously and reconceptualize central Enlightenment ideas in light of them—or, even more strongly, that we follow Adorno's admonition to do justice to the anti-Enlightenment objections and place them "in the service of" deepening, expanding, and enriching "the progressive Enlightenment"

DOI: 10.4324/9781003328230-10

(Adorno 2020: 192).[4] What I am suggesting, in other words, is a strategy of "immanent critique." In it, rather than being rejected, the central tenets of the Enlightenment are to be subjected to the anti-Enlightenment's critique and then reappropriated in light of those criticisms. In this paper, I will try to show that this is the strategy that Loewald adopts in his interpretation of Freud in general and of Freud's concept of maturity in particular.

Freud was another representative of the Enlightenment, and as such, he also adopted maturity as a fundamental norm for his theoretical and practical project.[5] However, because he joined that movement roughly a century after Kant, his relation to it—and to the concept of maturity—differs in fundamental ways from the philosopher's. In contrast to the eighteenth-century Enlightenment, Freud belonged to a more disillusioned, conflicted, tragic, and, I would argue, for that reason, more mature stage of that tradition which the philosopher Yirmiyahu Yovel refers to as the "Dark Enlightenment":

> [T]his process of dark enlightenment proved a sharp awakening from religious and metaphysical illusions, incurring pain and conflict in its wake. For it challenged accepted self-images and enshrined cultural identities, and thereby endangered a whole range of vested psychological interests. But for those very reasons, it was also a movement of emancipation, serving to inspire a richer and more lucid self-knowledge in man, even at the price of unflattering consequences which often shock and dismay. This was the true "Oedipal drive" — not of Freud's Oedipus but of the original protagonist of Sophocles' tragedy, of whom Freud himself is an avid follower.
>
> (Yovel 1992: 76)

This is not to deny that what Loewald calls Freud's "official position," with its dualistic antagonisms—for example, between the Reality Principle and the Pleasure Principle or between the ego and the id—and one-sided rationalist tendencies, can in fact be Kantian in the bad sense and suffer from the predictable difficulties as a result.[6] It is true that Freud was capable of affirming a "dictatorship of reason," but my claim is that, at his best, he not only took seriously the demands of anti-Enlightenment, which is to say, the demands of "the irrational," but that he also pursued the strategy advocated by Adorno (Freud 1933: 213).

Several factors contributed to Freud's becoming a dark enlightener. For one, it is clear that Nietzsche's thinking had a profound impact on him, his disingenuous claims to the contrary notwithstanding. And that being the case, it would have been impossible for him to accept the Enlightenment notions of reason, morality, science, and the subject without seriously rethinking them. Furthermore, after the optimism of the nineteenth-century bourgeoisie was traumatically shattered in the trenches of the First World War, it became next to impossible for one to hang on to a Whiggish idea of progress.

The arena in which Freud's most profound and most personal *Auseinandersetzung* with the anti-Enlightenment took place was his seven-year relationship with Jung, who embraced "the world of the Knights of the Grail and their quest" as his own personal world and who called for the re-enchantment of the world (Jung 1989: 165. See also Whitebook 2002, 2017: Chapters 8 and 9). In his struggle to defeat his "crown prince,"

Freud was not only forced to confront the challenge of the anti-Enlightenment but also to grudgingly enter the realm of archaic, undifferentiated, and preverbal experience, where Jung was more comfortable and adept owing to his character as well as his extensive treatment of psychotic patients. Freud's *agon* with the Swiss analyst culminated in "On Narcissism: An Introduction," in which he attempts to definitively exorcise the "Odium Jungianum" and, with it, the specter of the anti-Enlightenment. That effort, however, was far from conclusive. He acknowledged this as much in a letter to Karl Abraham, where he wrote that the paper was the result "of a difficult birth and bears all the marks of it" (Falzeder 2002: 222). One of the most serious difficulties with the argument of "On Narcissism" is this: insofar as it threatens to sexualize the ego, it skates dangerously close to a theory of sexual monism, precisely the thing Jung accused him of. And if the argument threatens to sexualize the ego—which would mean to naturalize the ego—it also threatens to collapse the distinction between nature and a knowing subject that can stand outside nature and comprehend it, that is, the assumption upon which an enlightened scientific worldview is predicated.[7] Yet, at the same time, despite its difficulties—or, better yet, because of its difficulties—"On Narcissism" proved to be an enormously fertile work. Though Freud does not explicitly flag that this was what he was up to, many of his later, substantial theoretical revisions that expanded and deepened his position—including the introduction of his second instinct theory and the structural model of the psychic apparatus—constituted attempts to work out the unresolved difficulties churned up in his encounter with the anti-Enlightenment, personified by Jung, in that crucial text.

Like Freud, Loewald's "first love" was, as he tells us, philosophy.[8] Indeed, before becoming a psychoanalyst, he studied with Martin Heidegger, who, at the time, was not only the most prominent philosopher in the German-speaking world but also a major exponent of the anti-Enlightenment—and as such, Adorno's arch-nemesis.[9] While Loewald, who was the son of a Jewish physician, acknowledges deep gratitude "for what he learned from" Heidegger "despite his most hurtful betrayal during the Nazi era," he also makes it clear that he "permanently" broke with his mentor after Heidegger assumed the Rectorship at the University of Freiburg and joined the Nazi Party (Loewald 2000: xlii–xliii).[10]

Loewald does not, however, tell us what he appropriated from his mentor's teachings, but there are at least two items that can be identified. The first, as Stephen Mitchell recognizes, pertains to his hermeneutical mode of theorizing. Heidegger characteristically developed his position by reinterpreting basic concepts from Greek philosophy and German Idealism, often in a radical and even violent fashion. Similarly, as Mitchell observes, Loewald also likes "old words," and, to a large degree, his mode of theorizing consists in reinterpreting traditional and fundamental Freudian concepts—a fact "that has made [his] innovations so easy to miss for many readers" (Mitchell 2002: 12–13). This theoretical decision, Mitchell suggests, was based on Loewald's belief that …

… Freud's language, the language of drive theory, is the archaic language (like ancient Greek for Heidegger) of psychoanalysis. It contains within itself, and evokes, powerful affective resonances with both early infantile, bodily experiences and the revolutionary breakthrough of Freud's genius.

(Mitchell 2002: 13–14)

And these remarks apply to Loewald's reinterpretation of the basic Freudian concept that we are concerned with: maturity. As we will see, for him, ideal maturation does not consist in a process of unidirectional progressive development but in a reworking and integration of the archaic material of infantile experience.

A second item that Loewald appropriated from Heidegger was the critique of modern scientific rationality, which, by "enframing" the external world as *res extensa*, as a mathematical manifold, not only reifies nature as a resource for technological domination but also excludes less superficial forms of truth (see Heidegger 1993: 329–333).[11] And following Heidegger, Loewald argues that it is "necessary and timely to question the assumption, handed down from the nineteenth century, that the scientific approach to the world and the self" constitutes the highest and most mature "evolutionary stage of man" (Loewald 1960: 228). As we can see from his remarks in In *Totem and Taboo*, this was an assumption that the "official" Freud subscribed to: "The scientific view of the universe," which has its "exact counterpart in the state at which an individual has reached maturity... no longer affords any room for human omnipotence; men have acknowledged their smallness and have submitted resignedly to death and the other necessities of nature" (Freud 1913: 88 & 90). What is more, in a highly speculative paper that has received little attention in the literature, Loewald suggests that a new science of nature is in fact emerging and that the recent developments in psychoanalysis, which are the subject of his investigations, can contribute to it (Loewald 1988).

But this is only half the story, for, unlike his mentor, Loewald never became a reactionary anti-enlightener. And although there is no mention of Adorno in his work, I would maintain that, as mentioned above, Loewald pursues a strategy that closely resembles the one advocated by the critical theorist. That is, he takes up the challenges of the anti-Enlightenment as they appear in psychoanalytic theory and attempts to formulate a chastened but not defeated—and at the same time richer—conception of the Enlightenment. In his description of Freud's moderated commitment to disenchantment (and maturity), I believe Loewald is also describing his own outlook. "Freud," he writes, "was engaged in what Max Weber has called the disenchantment of the world," which he "saw ... as a necessary step, for the individual and for humanity as a whole, in the development toward greater maturity and sanity." He continues, however, that Freud "did not proclaim it the end of all wisdom (1977: 406)."[12] That is to say, he did not overvalue and idealize the Enlightenment but subscribed to it in a modulated and de-centered way that is appropriate to the finite mind of the human animal.

We can observe Loewald's attempt to do justice to the demands of both the anti-Enlightenment and the Enlightenment, while ultimately siding with the latter, in his exemplarily even-handed review of the *Freud/Jung Letters*. As "a man of a younger generation"—a generation, I would add, for which Nietzsche and Wagner were cultural heroes—Jung, according to Loewald, "was less confined by the positivist philosophy that constricted the idea of science and its very scope during the period of Freud's scientific training." Consequently, Jung better recognized that "psychoanalysis as a new science implicitly eroded the boundaries of positivist science," and he therefore had less difficulty treating the realm of archaic experience as a legitimate domain for scientific research. And in conjunction with this, Loewald continues, Jung "did not share Freud's rationalistic prejudice against religion," nor did he seek to analyze it as a symptom of immaturity that should be overcome (1977: 416).[13] Furthermore, his freedom from this prejudice allowed Jung to acknowledge that psychoanalysis was not only a product of the western scientific tradition, but that it also grew out of another one, namely, "the tradition of the trance," which includes medicine men, mystics, Mesmerists, Spiritualists, and so on (see Whitebook 2002). This is an assessment that Loewald agrees with, writing that "despite Freud's strong disclaimer... even the dividing line between priest or shaman and physician and investigator is less than neatly fixed in the case of psychoanalysis" (1977: 411).

Jung attempted to turn the tables on Freud and accused him of deifying sexuality and treating it as "a sort of *numinosum*" (Jung 1989: 150). Loewald does not entirely reject this accusation, but his interpretation of it differs substantially from Jung's. What Jung gets right, as Loewald sees it, is Freud's failure to appreciate the significance of religious phenomena and the legitimacy of the demand for spirituality, which not only resulted from what Habermas calls his "scientistic self-misunderstanding," but, at a deeper level, also from his inability to fully explore the realm of preverbal and pre-individuated experience (Habermas 1973: 214).[14] But, on the other hand, Loewald argues, Freud's concerns about the defensive and escapist functions that religion and spirituality often serve regarding what he liked to call "the exigencies of life" are wellfounded. Freud's "insistence on the centrality of sexuality vis-à-vis Jung," according to Loewald, "was in good part a fight against the religiosity and theologically tinged" separation "between instinctual life and spiritual life," which often leads to "what he saw as religious or philosophical escapism in the fact of the human condition" (Loewald, 2000: 413–414).

There is no denying that the "official Freud"—who, in "*The Future of an Illusion*," proudly situates himself in the eighteenth-century tradition of anti-clerical enlighteners like Hume and Voltaire—deploys a genealogical critique in an effort to debunk religion. But Loewald identifies another "unofficial Freud" who adopts a different strategy, in which the legitimate demands of religion and spirituality are *aufgehoben* (sublated), to use a Hegelian term, rather than eliminated through a reductionist analysis. In this case, "what Jung labeled Freud's concretistic terminology" is justified because it reflects the fact that "authentic transcendental experiences and insights ('spirituality') are anchored in the individual's personal life history and its instinctual roots." On this view, endorsed by Loewald, Freud sought "to develop, as it were, spirituality out of the biological-archaic roots of man's existence" (Loewald 1977: 415). For it is only "in the concreteness of one's personal life, including the ugliness, trivialities and sham that go with it," he insists, that one can do justice to the demands of religion and spirituality "without escapist embellishments, other worldly consolations, and going off into the clouds." In short, "genuine transcendence" is not to be found in "the collective unconscious, myth, archetypes, religiosity, and 'spirituality,'" but in "sublimation and ego expansion," which are the goals of psychoanalysis as Loewald understands them (Loewald 1977: 416).

The text where Loewald most clearly sets out to elucidate the relation between the demands of the Enlightenment and the anti-Enlightenment is "The Waning of the Oedipus Complex," which has surely become a psychoanalytic classic (see Ogden 2006). However, rather than pursuing his analysis strictly at the level of theory, the philosophically schooled psychoanalyst also pursues it clinically by examining the pre-Oedipal turn that occurred in psychoanalysis after Freud's death. What he seeks to determine are the consequences that working with "non-classical" patients, who increasingly presented themselves for psychoanalytic treatment after the Second World War, have had for

Freud's "official," Oedipal, and Enlightenment positions. Loewald observes that "there is something archaic about their mentality," which is not only "archaic in the sense of antiquated, but also in the sense of belonging to the origins of human life and therefore of its essence or core" (Loewald 1979: 400). Perhaps the most essential thing that clinical work with non-classical patients has revealed, he argues, is "the validity" of the demand "for unity, symbiosis, fusion, merging or identification—whatever name one wants to give to this sense of and longing for nonseparateness and undifferentiation" (Loewald 1979: 402). And by so doing, it has called into question the presumed foundation of scientific rationalism prior to the twentieth-century revolutions in psychoanalysis and post-Newtonian physics, namely, "the objectivity of the object, and the subjectivity of the subject" (Loewald 1979: 399). *These observations represent Loewald's articulation of the "truth content" of the anti-Enlightenment's demands in psychoanalytic terms.*

But this raises a serious problem, for acknowledging that "the quest for irrational nondifferentiation of subject and object contains a truth of its own... fits badly with our rational worldview and quest for objectivity." This, however, is, in fact, nothing new, for psychoanalysis has always been in an "awkward position" with regard to its commitments to rationality and objectivity. What the findings of the pre-Oedipal turn constitute is simply another episode in psychoanalysis' ongoing process of disillusioning and yet enlightening self-reflection, which continually subverts formerly held conceptions of rationality and objectivity—and, we might add, of normality as well. "While [psychoanalysis] has been intent to penetrate unconscious mentality with the light of rational understanding, it also has been and is intent," Loewald observes, "to uncover the irrational unconscious sources and forces motivating and organizing conscious and rational mental processes." Consequently, at the same time, "unconscious processes became accessible to rational understanding... rational thought itself and our experience of the world as an 'object world' became problematic" (Loewald 1979: 402). This enterprise is based on a wager, namely, that the open-ended process of psychoanalytic research and reflection will produce a less reassuring but nevertheless more adequate, indeed, truer, understanding of rationality and objectivity. If it does not, psychoanalytic critique will result in its own version of Nietzschean nihilism, as postmodernist interpreters often claim it does.

The individual is a related concept where psychoanalysis also finds itself in an "awkward position." For not only "is psychoanalysis," as Loewald notes, "a form of "individual treatment" which takes place "between two individuals," but the clinical undertaking "seems to stand and fall with the proposition that the emergence of a relatively autonomous individual is the culmination of human development." Yet, what research into pre-Oedipal development has taught us about narcissistic strivings for fusion and non-differentiation makes the received conception of the individuated and autonomous subject problematic. And this fact returns us to our earlier question. Should the concept of the autonomous individual, like the concept of maturity, therefore be rejected as such? Or should we reject the "Cartesian" way it has traditionally been conceived—namely, as a transparent and centered subject that dominates its "internal foreign territory"— while seeking to develop a more adequate concept of it? And Loewald makes another apt observation in this context: given what we now know, a concept of the individual that excluded "the whole realm of identification" would not only be viewed as theoretically inadequate, it would also bear "little resemblance to actual life" (Loewald 1979: 403). With these considerations in mind, let us turn to the concept of Maturity.

II.

The strategy that Loewald follows in his immanent critique of the concept of Maturity, then, is one iteration of the general strategy that he pursues in his critical appropriation of Freud. The extent to which it was already present *in nuce* in his first two publications, "Ego and Reality" and "The Problem of Defense and the Neurotic Interpretation of Reality," is striking (Loewald 1951, 1952). It was in those papers that he introduced the distinction, mentioned above, between Freud's "official" and "unofficial" positions, which he continued to deploy throughout his career. And his strategy consists in reconstructing the latter through a close reading of Freudian texts and then seeking to determine the proper relation between the two positions.

Before proceeding further, however, a comment is in order. Because the Ego Psychologists who dominated American Psychoanalysis during the period when Loewald wrote many of his important papers tended to subscribe to Freud's "official position," his critique is more or less explicitly directed at them.[15] The situation changed, however, in the last decades of the twentieth century when the Ego Psychologists were challenged by the Relational School and others, and their hegemony gave way to the new pluralism. Today, partly as a result of Loewald's contribution, most of the tenets of Freud's "unofficial" theory have been integrated into the mainstream of the Freudian (and ego psychological) tradition, and one would be hard-pressed to find an analyst defending an unmodified version of the "official" doctrine.[16] When "the official Freud" is invoked today, it is generally as a straw man that anti-Freudians want to polemicize against.

What Loewald calls "the paternal concept of reality" is at the center of Freud's official position.[17] "If we understand the Oedipus conflict and the castration threat as the prototype of the demands of reality," he writes, "it should be clear how strongly for Freud the concept of reality is bound up with the father" (1951: 7). The movement toward "reality acceptance," to use Winnicott's term, begins with the separation-individual process and culminates with the Oedipus Complex, in which the boy (sic) submits under the pressure of the father's threat, relinquishes his desire for the gratifying mother, renounces the pleasure principle, and adapts his "thoughts and actions to the demands of reality" (Loewald 1951: 3). Because reality is personified by the "alien, hostile, [and] jealous" father, it is not only viewed as an external and dangerous "force" which must be defended against, but the "official" ego and the tension-reduction model of the psychic apparatus that corresponds to it—Loewald does not always systematically distinguish between the two—are understood as essentially *defensive* structures that are charged with fulfilling that task (Loewald 1951: 7). Their job is not to bind and organize stimuli into more comprehensive organizations, but to discharge or "gets rid" of them as quickly as possible in order to maintain the homeostasis of the psychic apparatus and protect the supposed coherence and stability of the ego (see Loewald 1971: 119).

In Loewald's opinion, however, the "acceptance of reality" is an inadequate notion for describing the task confronting the ego. Instead, he proposes "ego-reality integration," which is a task that can fail in two directions, as a more adequate concept. It can fail through the loss of the object, on the one hand, or the loss of the ego, on the other. And he argues that at the same time as the Oedipus complex promotes "the acceptance of reality" in one sense, it also poses a threat to "ego-reality integration," since insofar as the paternal relation to reality threatens to create too much distance between ego and object, it threatens to lose the object.

Although we are not surprised to learn that the "maternal concept of reality" corresponds to Freud's "unofficial" position, Loewald makes another point which, though not immediately apparent, is fundamental to his argument. It is that the synthetic function, whose origins he traces to the early unified state of the infant-mother relationship, occupies a central place in the "unofficial" doctrine. Whereas the "paternal concept of reality" only comes into play after a certain degree of ego-object differentiation has been established, "the maternal concept" is in place *ab initio*, with the original state of non-differentiation and oneness—that is, the state of "dual unity," described by Mahler, which contains both the pre-ego and the pre-object (see Mahler et al. 1975: 55). Therefore, with "the maternal concept," reality, far from being experienced as alien and hostile, is experienced as intimate and gratifying. Loewald draws on Freud's discussion of the oceanic feeling in the first Chapter of *Civilization and its Discontents*—a text that plays an important role in his thinking—and argues that development does not begin with the situation described by Freud in "Two Principles," where a self-enclosed psychism faces an external and alien reality with which it must somehow "hook up." Instead, it begins at the point where "the (primitive) ego detaches an external world from itself" (1951: 10). Then, after the initial separation, the early ego is pulled by the "magnetic attraction" that the memory-traces of the original experience of unity exert on it and attempts to reconnect with the early object (Castoriadis 1987: 302).[18]

Loewald's more original thesis is that "the synthetic, integrative function of the ego can be understood" in terms of this pull for reunification (1951: 11)[19] While it was commonly assumed that it was the death instinct that lay "beyond the pleasure principle," Loewald was one of the first analysts to correct this misconception and demonstrate that the introduction of Eros—which is to say, of a synthetic force in the psyche that binds things together into larger unities—comprises the new element in Freud's thinking (see Whitebook 2004b: 104–105 and Lear 1996).[20] Loewald points to another aspect of Freud's larger failure to appreciate the full significance of Eros: although he came to recognize the synthetic function of the ego, he tended to "see the synthetic function itself as a defense." This means that he tended to assimilate his discovery of the synthetic function to his "official" position, thereby blunting the novelty and magnitude of what he had discovered. Indeed, according to Loewald, "the defensive function of the ego has never ceased to play a predominant role in [Freud's] concept of the ego and again and again has overshadowed other aspects of the ego in psychoanalytic thinking" (Loewald 1951: 3–4).

The identification of the synthetic function does not simply add a new item to the list of the ego's functions. It is not on the same par as perception, impulse control, affect regulation, judgement, reality testing, and so on. *It can in fact be argued that synthesis occupies a superordinate position in mental life, indeed, that synthesizing, integrating, and organizing, or however one chooses to call it, constitutes the mind's fundamental function.*[21] Because psychoanalysis grew out of the Western tradition of rationality and science, it inherited a topic that was as central as it was perplexing to the Greek philosophers, namely, the problem of "the one and the many." In the *Philebus*, for example, Socrates tells Protarchus that the propositions "that the many are one and the one many" are "amazing statements" which create "difficulties for everyone" (14c–14d.

Plato 1997: 402). As we are about to see, the psychoanalyst faces the same vexing question as the philosopher but in a specific form: namely, how does one properly elucidate the simultaneous coexistence—the synthesis—of the one and the many?

Since the Greeks, Western philosophers have had to steer between two extremes in their attempt to answer that question. On the one hand, they have faced the Parmenidean pole, which does justice to Oneness and intelligibility at the expense of multiplicity and becoming. And on the other hand, they have confronted the Heraclitan pole, which captures difference and becoming at the expense of stability and intelligibility. The particular way in which psychoanalysis confronts the problem of "the one in the many" is in fact articulated to Protarchus in his response to Socrates. "Do you mean this," he asks, "in the sense that someone says that I, Protarchus, am one by nature but then also says that there are many 'me's' and even contrary ones?" (Plato 1997: 402). In other words, the question of "the one and the many" presents itself in psychoanalysis as the question of *the unity, that is, the integration or synthesis of the self.* Psychoanalytic theory must steer a course between the "obsessional" pole, which achieves the integration of the ego while sacrificing the fluidity and spontaneity of unconscious-instinctual life, and the "hysterical" pole, which allows for the expressiveness of internal nature and archaic experience while sacrificing the unity of the ego.

Our first impulse is understandably to affirm Eros as "the builder of larger unities" as opposed to the death drive—to "attacks on linking"—which breaks things down and into more simplified states. Before we can valorize Eros, however, a qualification must be introduced, for unification *per se* is not necessarily a positive thing. As the reference to the obsessional indicates, there are more and less desirable modes of unification, integration, or synthesis—indeed, there are simplifying processes of integration that can be located on the side of the death instinct. Loewald therefore distinguishes between two modes of integration or synthesis in psychic life (see also Lear 1992). Integration in the desirable sense unifies the ego through the canalization of the contents of unconscious-instinctual life and the synthesis of it into a larger and more differentiated structure, that is, into a "higher and richer organization" of the psychic apparatus (Loewald 1952: 30; 1973: 74). On the other hand, the mode of integration to be rejected, which derives from reflex arch and is based on the tension-reduction model of the psychic apparatus, accomplishes ego-unification by "getting rid of"—discharging, repressing, projecting, and splitting-off—instinctual stimuli, thereby resulting in a more constricted and less differentiated psychic configuration.[22]

In addition to constituting the superordinate function in mental life, it can be argued that synthesis also occupies a superordinate position in Loewald's thinking. His project can, as I mentioned, be understood as an attempt to integrate the findings of the pre-Oedipal turn in psychoanalysis with Freud's "official" Oedipal theory, and a central aspect of that project consists in attempting to integrate the paternal and maternal concepts of reality through an assessment of their relative advantages and disadvantages. With the pre-Oedipal turn in psychoanalysis—which, as Elisabeth Young-Bruehl observers, partly dovetailed with the rise of second wave feminism—one could often observe a tendency to idealize the early mother (see Young-Bruehl 1994). And insofar as the maternal concept of reality is characterized by relatedness and gratification as opposed to distance and hostility, there are obvious reasons for finding it more appealing than its paternal counterpart. Yet, the maternal relation contains its own threat to "ego-reality integration," which, not unexpectedly, is the mirror opposite of the one based on the paternal relation. While the paternal concept's threat to ego-object integration consists in the danger of object-loss, with the maternal concept, it consists in ego-loss resulting from maternal engulfment and dedifferentiation. And seeing this brings the positive function of the paternal relation view: "Against the threatening possibility of remaining in or sinking back into the structureless unity from which the ego has emerged, stands the powerful paternal force" that can serve as a barrier between the child and the pre-Oedipal mother (Loewald 1951: 10; see also Winnicott 1989: 242–243). Loewald, in short, is not an anti-Oedipal thinker.

As a virtuoso of integrative thinking, it stands to reason that Loewald would oppose the theoretical splitting where one is obliged to choose between ego psychology and object relations theory. In fact, he rejects this spurious opposition, which is often motivated more by the political competition between psychoanalytic groups than by theoretical and scientific considerations. He describes the ongoing feedback process that occurs in ego development and object formation: just as the "shadow of the object falls on the ego," thus creating a new stage in ego formation, so "the shadow of the altered ego falls" on the object, thereby constituting a new stage in object relations (Loewald 1987: 460). In the vocabulary we are considering, this means that one is not obliged to choose between the maternal and paternal concepts of reality. The task is, rather, to integrate them. As Loewald asks, "Do we then advocate swinging from the paternal concept of reality to a maternal one?" (Loewald 1951: 12).[23] Beyond simply answering in the negative, he goes on to suggest that recognizing the "features of primary identification and symbiosis," which are contained "in its very core ... may give new luster to the Oedipus Complex in the present psychoanalytic climate" (Loewald 1970: 399).

III.

Like the proverbial man on the street, it has all-too-often been the case that the "official" psychoanalytic understanding of maturity has equated "the acceptance of reality" with the "realism of the disillusioned adult" (Loewald 1975: 368). And there is little doubt that the prevailing psychoanalytic culture of Loewald's day tended to conflate "adaptation" with "conformity," so that "health" meant "fitting-in." This was the target of both Adorno's and Lacan's critique of American Ego Psychology (see especially Adorno 1967, 1968).[24]

The analysts of the Hartmann Era—which roughly overlapped with the 30-year ascendance of the American liberal-capitalist order—also tended to follow the "official" Freud in understanding the concept of Maturity in terms of the Enlightenment's progressivist understanding of science. Undoubtedly, because of his studies with Heidegger, Loewald was sensitive to the difficulties associated with the Enlightenment's Whiggishness and Scientism. According to him, not only did the "official" Freudians insist "that the analytic activity was a strictly scientific one," they also took over the assumption that "the scientific stage of the development of man's conception of the universe has its counterpart in the individual's state of maturity." They therefore posited maturity, as the scientific enlightenment conceived it, as the goal of individual development as well as of psychoanalytic treatment. On this account, the disenchantment of the psyche through the psychoanalytic process parallels the disenchantment of the external world through the steady march of scientific progress: "the patient is led towards the maturity of scientific man who understands himself and external reality not in animistic and religious terms"—not in terms of fantasy or transference—"but in terms of objective science" (Loewald 1960: 228). In an analysis, the elimination of the transference, the exorcism of all vestiges of magic, comprises the point where maturation *qua* disenchantment has been completed and thus constitutes the criterion for termination (see Whitebook 2002).

Loewald quotes from a 1948 paper, which he believes is typical of "many analysts" at the time, where William Silverberg equates transference with immaturity and presents an especially stark, indeed chilling statement of the Enlightenment program of disenchantment articulated in analytic terms:

> The wide prevalence of the dynamism of transference among human beings is a mark of man's immaturity, and it may be expected in ages to come that, as man progressively matures ... transference will gradually vanish from his psychic repertory.
>
> (cited in Loewald 1960: 250)

But, contrary to Silverberg's claim that transference represents "the enduring monument of man's profound rebellion against reality and the stubborn persistence in the ways of immaturity," Loewald argues that the preservation of transference—of fantasy, the creativity of the psyche, or what Jan Abram calls "a magic which is not psychosis"—*in the right way* is an essential ingredient of what makes life "worth living," to use a Winnicottian phrase (quoted in Abrams 2018: 211; Loewald 1960: 250; Winnicott 1971: 65). This is not to deny, of course, that transference can assume pathological and destructive forms that impoverish life. It is only to say that when "unconscious needs" do not find creative means of expressing themselves in contemporary objects—when, in Winnicott's terms, "primary creativity" is not sublimated into "living creatively"— "life becomes sterile and an empty shell" (Loewald 1960: 250; Winnicott 1990).[25]

For Loewald, the scientist worldview, propounded by Silverberg, invites comparison with the obsessional's worldview, as well as with the paternal and defensive concept of the ego-reality relation. Insofar as the "psychoanalytic theory" of the psychic functioning "in its dominant current" seeks to "get rid of" the energy of the libido and the contents of the unconscious, exorcise magic, or, to use a familiar metaphor, drain the id-sludge from the Zuider Zee, it has "unwittingly taken over much of the obsessive neurotic's experience and conception of reality and taken it for granted as 'the objective reality'" (Loewald 1952: 30).[26] Loewald is sometimes criticized for pulling his punches, but in this case, he makes his opinion abundantly clear both about the psychoanalysis and the general culture:

> It is this neurotically impoverished reality, a form of reality that is exercising its great destructive power on all of us, in whose image the psychoanalytic concept of reality has been formed.
>
> (Loewald 1952: 32)

When psychoanalysts adopt this version of reality, they mistake a limited, if not pathological, mode of ego formation for the optimal one and fail to recognize the very "weakness of 'the strong ego.'" The "official" ego is in fact only "strong in its defenses," that is, in its capacity to exclude the energy of the libido and the material of unconscious-instinctual life from its borders through repression, isolation, or projection, instead of canalizing them and taking them up into more integrated and more differentiated organizations (Loewald 1960: 241). Because the "official" ego exercises its "strength" to tighten and reinforce its boundaries and to prevent alien but potentially enriching material from entering its territory, it is in fact narrow, impoverished, and brittle.

The first chapter of *Civilization and its Discontents* is a crucial text for Loewald because it provides him with rich material for reconstructing Freud's "unofficial" position and elucidating the ego's synthetic function. There, in his attempt to account for the origins of "the oceanic feeling," Freud addresses a "subject [that] has hardly been studied yet," namely, the "general problem of preservation in the sphere of the mind," which is to say, how things are integrated in mental life (Freud 1930: 69). He takes the history of his beloved "eternal city" as a model for the development and structuralization of the psychic apparatus and attempts to explain, as Loewald puts it, "the psychological survival of original stages beside the later stages of development" (Loewald 1951: 10). It is here that we arrive at the "unofficial" concept of maturity. According to the "official" view, development is pictured as a unidirectional progressive process in which the earlier, "immature" stages of development are abandoned and replaced by later and more "mature" ones. In the "unofficial" view—as in Rome's historically stratified urban structure, which Freud calls to our attention as he takes us on a virtual stroll through the city—the archaic strata of the psychic life coexist alongside the more advanced layers. Therefore, on this model, we should not think of the "fully developed, mature ego [as] one that has become fixated at the presumably highest or latest stage of development, having left the others behind." Instead, we should think of it "as an ego that integrates its reality in such a way that the earlier and deeper levels of ego-reality integration remain alive as dynamic sources of higher organization," thus comprising a "higher and richer" organization of the psychic apparatus (Loewald 1951: 20; 1973: 74).

Nor should we think of maturity as something that is accomplished once and for all. On the contrary, Loewald claims not only that psychopathology is defined by the cessation of development but also that the clinical task for psychoanalysis is to unfreeze frozen development and set it back into motion by facilitating a regressive transference process. This claim, in turn, leads to a somewhat unexpected conclusion. The analyst's professional maturity, that is, her specialized skill, which is constitutive of the asymmetry of the analytic situation, does not consist in her capacity to assume the role of a neutral scientific observer. On the contrary, it consists of her familiarity with and capacity for regression. For it is this that allows her to facilitate, contain, and interpret the therapeutic regression which is the necessary condition for a productive analysis. Without sufficient regression, an analytic process worth its name never gets off the ground, but with too much regression, an analysis miscarries.

Rather than constituting a fixed state, maturity prescribes a task, understood as an ongoing process, involving, as Castoriadis puts it, "*another attitude* of the subject with respect to himself or herself, in a profound modification of the activity-passivity mix," in which the subject continually takes up and integrates the material of unconscious-instinctual life into more inclusive, differentiated, and vital psychic configurations (Castoriadis 1987: 104). Loewald stresses the dynamic nature of this process.

"It is not," he observes, "merely a question of survival of former stages of ego-reality integration," but of the changeable relations between them, for "people shift considerably, from day to day, in different periods of their lives, in different moods and situations, from one such level to other levels." And in a statement that someone looking for a reassuring concept of maturity might find disconcerting, he adds: "In fact, it would seem that the more alive people are (though not necessarily more stable), the broader their range of ego-reality levels is" (Loewald 1951: 20). Maturity, surmounting infantilism, not only means surmounting the infantile wish that life could be and should be devoid of conflict and difficulty but also appreciating that they are essential to a vital and meaningful existence.

Notes

1 I would like to thank Richard Armstrong, Seyla Benhabib, Werner Bohleber, Peter Dews, Pierre-Henri Castel, and Robert Paul for their helpful comments and criticisms.
2 "The Count Thun Dream" provides evidence that Freud, who must have known that Emperor Joseph II had banned the performance of *Figaro* in Vienna, associated Mozart's opera with the emancipatory impulses of the Enlightenment. We will recall that, In the dream, he found himself humming the opera's *Se vuol ballare* aria in defiance of the reactionary count's arrogant behavior (Freud 1900: 208).
3 Though Freud also articulated the conflict between the collective and the individual, he was much more circumspect than Kant in taking sides.
4 Their divergent attitudes toward the anti-Enlightenment are a topic that separates Adorno's position from Habermas' in general and their positions on psychoanalysis in particular. Adorno, as I have just noted, seeks to do justice to the demands of the anti-Enlightenment and appropriate them to strengthen the Enlightenment. In contrast, Habermas, in most instances, simply seeks to refute the anti-Enlightenment's objections. This difference is clear in their respective attitudes toward Nietzsche. Whereas Habermas generally views him as an irrationalist whose threat to the Enlightenment must be blocked, Adorno sees him as a central Enlightenment figure and expresses an entirely different attitude towards him (see Habermas 1990: Chapters III & IV). "Of all the great philosophers," he states somewhat remarkably, "I owe [Nietzsche] by far the greatest debt—even more than to Hegel" (Adorno 2001: 172).
5 For Freud, the normative status of maturity follows from a fundamental fact of our anthropological condition, namely, the prematurity of the human infant. According to a well-known anthropological theory, nature's solution, as it were, to a critical problem that was threatening hominoid evolution was to shorten the human infant's gestation period, which meant that it was born "prematurely." "The intrauterine existence" of "the young of the human species," Freud observes, "seems to be short in comparison to most animals, and it is sent into the world in a less finished state," which means in a state of "helplessness" (Freud 1926: 154). Though it may seem somewhat schematic, my claim is that positing maturity as the goal of development follows from the prematurity and helplessness of our original situation. My claim gains some content, however, when we examine what Freud means by maturity. On first blush, one might take Freud's declaration that "surely infantilism is destined to be surmounted" to mean that maturity consists in vanquishing helplessness (Freud 1927: 49). But his position is more complicated than that. The idea that helplessness can be overcome *sans phrase* is in fact an omnipotent, which is to say, an infantile fantasy. For Freud, rather, maturity, surmounting infantilism, consists in mitigating our omnipotence, "coming to terms" with our anthropological helplessness, and reconciling ourselves to our situation in an infinite and indifferent universe. As I have argued elsewhere, this cluster of ideas defines maturity as the basic norm of Freud's psychoanalytic-scientific *ethos* (see Whitebook 2017: 386–401).

6   One might say that Freud was a Hegelian in that some of Freud's most fruitful ideas, such as sublimation and frontier concepts, represent examples of what André Green calls "tertiary processes" (Green 1980).

7   Though I do not know what to make of it, I have often been struck by the fact that Freud completed this crucial article (March 1914), where the structure that underpinned his scientific worldview is in danger of collapsing, at the very moment when the nineteenth century's belief in progress was about to collapse in the trenches of the Great War.

8   The "official" Freud claimed that philosophy had never held any attraction for him and promulgated the myth, later taken up and disseminated by Ernest Jones, that he was an anti-philosopher (see Herzog 2015). But this is simply false. In 1896, he informed Fliess that "as a young man [he] knew longing other than for philosophical knowledge" (Masson 1985: 180). And there is no doubt that Freud retained a deep interest in philosophical questions through his second year at the University of Vienna. Although we cannot determine what it was, something occurred during the summer break preceding his third academic year when he was visiting his older half-brothers in Manchester, England, which caused him to perform an about-face and violently turn against philosophy. Upon returning to Vienna, he abandoned his plans to pursue a double major in physiology and philosophy, adopted the mantle of a sober-minded man of science, and proceeded to inveigh against the errors of philosophy for the rest of his career (see Whitebook 2017: 86–110).

9   The 1929 Davos Debate between Heidegger and Ernst Cassirer is often seen as an epochal confrontation between the anti-Enlightenment, represented by Heidegger, and the Enlightenment, represented by his opponent. (For a vivid account of the debate, see Gordon 2012; and for Adorno's criticisms of Heidegger, see Adorno 2003: Part One & Adorno 2013.) One can also say that, whereas Jung was the spokesperson for the anti-Enlightenment in psychoanalysis, Heidegger played that role in philosophy.

10   The Heidegger dossier poses a profoundly disturbing question for contemporary philosophers. It must be asked how one of the two most important philosophers of the twentieth century, Ludwig Wittgenstein being the other, could have been seduced by the lure of Nazism and joined the party. Although Loewald does not address this question directly, he says something suggestive which might have a bearing on it, namely, that he was "wary of the particular excesses that a philosophical bent tends to entail" (Loewald 2000: xlii). One wonders not only about the nature of that wariness but also whether it led him from Heidegger to Freud and from philosophy to psychoanalysis. At the same time as Freud's knowledge of philosophy was clearly limited and his criticisms of the field are rather elementary, they nevertheless contain a valid intuition: that a tendency toward the "omnipotence of thoughts" is an intrinsic danger in philosophical speculation and that the discipline of science— whatever one means by that—is necessary to contain and discipline it. (I discuss the nature of Freud's conception of science beyond his "official" positivist rhetoric elsewhere [see Whitebook: 398–406]). If this is so, it is not simpleminded l psychologizing to suggest that an unmastered wish for omnipotence lay behind Plato's quest for the philosopher king and Heidegger's attraction to the *Führer*.

11   Despite their crucial differences, Heidegger's critique of technique and Adorno's critique of instrumental reason share much in common. This is a result of the fact that they both belong to a philosophical tradition which grew out of Nietzsche's critique of European nihilism and Max Weber's theory of rationalization, which was shared by many thinkers on the Left as well as on the Right.

12   Loewald carves out a similar position with respect to science (see Loewald 1987: 181).

13   Loewald's own attitude towards religion helps to account for his sympathetic reading of Jung. Indeed, until recently, Loewald, together with Winnicott, was one of the few analysts who did not "share Freud's rationalist prejudice against religion" and who sought to understand the positive psychological and cultural significance of religious and spiritual experience (see Loewald 1978: Chapter 3). It should be pointed out, however, that although Loewald advocates a more positive attitude towards religious experience, at no point does he affirm the existence of a transcendent and providential deity.

14 The same criticism of Freud was later raised by Romain Rolland with regard to Freud's inability to appreciate "the oceanic feeling" (see Whitebook 2017: 409–411).

15 Roy Schafer reported that the members of Loewald's seminar in New Haven urged him to be more direct in his criticisms of the psychoanalytic establishment. (Personal communication).

16 Similarly, John Gedo writes that by the 1960s, "psychoanalysis had caught up" with Ferenczi and that many of the Hungarian analyst's ideas that had formerly been condemned as heretical were now part of the mainstream (Gedo 1986: 36).

17 Heidegger's influence can be observed in Loewald's account of "the paternal relation to reality." For his conceptualization of it bears a strong resemblance to Heidegger's description of the reified way that modern science constitutes the world.

18 Compare Freud's analysis of how the infant's experience of "narcissistic perfection" is projected ahead, thereby becoming the "ego ideal" (Freud 1914: 94).

19 Relational analysts often seek to deny the existence of a symbiotic or undifferentiated stage of development because they believe it threatens a view of the self as fundamentally related. Interestingly, for Loewald, the situation is just the opposite. In fact, for him, our striving for relatedness and connection throughout life is animated by the enduring pull that the original experience of unity exerts over us.

20 The death instinct, as a drive towards stasis, is in fact a logical consequence of the constancy hypothesis, the pleasure principle, and the tension-reduction model of the psychic, ideas which Freud introduced in *The Project* of 1895 (Freud 1895/1900).

21 Winnicott equates "thinking" with "gathering" (Winnicott 1974).

22 The philosopher Peter Dews notes a fundamental difference between Adorno and the French Poststructuralists, which is relevant to our investigation (Dews 1995). What they have in common, he argues, is a critique of bad synthesis, as it were, or of what Adorno calls "Identity Thinking." It consists of a form of thinking that imposes unifying qua reifying conceptual grids on inner and outer nature. But that is where the similarity ends. For Adorno takes a further step and seeks to envisage desirable forms of integration and synthesis. The Poststructuralists, however, view all forms of unification as intrinsically violent and repressive. As a result, they reject "Oneness" as such while simultaneously idealizing non-identity and difference, as, for example, in Lyotard's celebration of the flux and the young Foucault's championing of the dissolution of the self into madness. Though Lacan belonged to an earlier generation, these same criticisms apply to his critique of the ego. For him, the ego is false in virtue of the discrepancy between the actual unintegrated state of the infant, who is "still trapped in his motor impotence and nursling dependency," and the integrated "imago" that he perceives in the mirror. Lacan argues that when the falsely integrated "imago" is internalized and set up in the psyche as the ego, it launches the child on a "fictional" and "alienating" developmental trajectory (Lacan 2006: 76). What must be seen here is that the judgment that the ego is "fictional" and "alienating" is based on the assumption that the infant's original, unintegrated state is the true one. In short, it hypostatizes unintegration as the true condition that should be preserved. Though the two analysts are often compared because they both discuss the mirror stage, Lacan's position is in fact the exact opposite of Winnicott's (and Loewald's). For the British analyst, when the good-enough mother's integrated imago of her infant is returned to him and internalized, it becomes the basis for a desirable developmental process which seeks to achieve further and more felicitous modes of psychic integration. In contrast, Lacan's thinking not only excludes a desirable mode of integration, but, owing to its foundation in Structuralism, it is also anti-developmental.

23 André Green makes the same point, albeit somewhat more vividly: "I do not believe that it is useful to replace the Father of the horde with the Great Mother Goddess." Green then raises a question that is behind many of my reflections in this investigation: "I only wonder why analysts persist in this quarrel of precedence" (Green 1980: 253).

24 A critical point must be made here. Not only was Hartmann's introduction of the concept of adaptation an important and necessary theoretical innovation, he clearly distinguished adaptation from conformity. Regarding the first point, at the same time as Freud's theory needed to explain "reality acceptance," it lacked the theoretical resources to do so.

Introducing the concept of adaptation therefore corrected that critical lacuna in Freudian theory. It is odd that, while critics of Hartmann often embrace attachment theory, they do not recognize that he introduced the concept of adaptation for the same reason that Bowlby introduced the concept of attachment, namely, to make up for that lacuna. Regarding the second point, Hartmann explicitly states that adaptation is not equivalent to conformity. He introduces the distinction between "autoplastic" and "alloplastic" adaptation and argues that, rather than autoplastically conforming to society, an individual can alloplastically set out to transform it (see Hartmann 1959: Chapter 2). However, while this is theoretically correct, in the actually existing psychoanalytic practice of the fifties, adaptation was regularly equated with conformity. In Joyce McDougall's vocabulary, this meant that the "normopath" was regularly elevated into the normative (McDougall 2013). This was the socio-cultural phenomenon that was the target of Adorno's and Lacan's critiques.

25 Employing a different vocabulary, the Greco-French philosopher-analyst Cornelius Castoriadis expresses the same idea with considerably more umph: "How can we conceive of a subject that would have entirely 'absorbed' the imaginative function, how could we dry up the spring in the depths of ourselves from which both alienating phantasies and free creations truer than truth, unreal deliria and surreal poems, this eternally new beginning and ground of all things, without which nothing would have a ground, how can we eliminate what is at the base of, or in any case, what is inextricably bound up with what makes us human?" (Castoriadis 1987: 104).

26 Robert Paul has suggested a less rationalist interpretation of draining the Zuider Zee, namely, that the sludge be used to fertilize and enrich ego development (Personal communication).

References

Abram, J. (2018) *The Language of Winnicott: A Dictionary of Winnicott's Use of Words*, New York: Routledge.

Adorno, T. W. (1967) Sociology and Psychology (Part 1), *New Left Review*, 46(1), 67–80.

Adorno, T. W. (1968) Sociology and Psychology II, *New Left Review*, 47(1), 79–97.

Adorno, T. W. (2001) *Problems of Moral Philosophy* (ed., T. Schröder, trans., R. Livingston), Stanford, CA: Stanford University Press.

Adorno, T. W. (2003) *Negative Dialectics* (trans., E. B. Ashton), New York: Routledge.

Adorno, T. W. (2013) *The Jargon of Authenticity* (trans., K. Tarnowski & F. Will), New York: Routledge.

Adorno, T. W. (2020) *Minima Moralia: Reflections from Damaged Life* (trans., E. F. N. Jephcott), New York: Verso.

Castoriadis, C. (1987) *The Imaginary Institution of Society* (trans., K. Blarney), Cambridge, MA: MIT Press.

Dews, P. (1995) *Adorno, Poststructuralism and the Critique of Identity, in The Logics of Disintegration*, New York: Verso.

Falzeder, E. (ed.) (2002) *The Complete Correspondence of Sigmund Freud and Karl Abraham 1907–1925*, Completed Edition (trans., C. Schwarzacher), New York: Karnac.

Freud, S. (1895/1900) *Project for a Scientific Psychology*, Standard Edition, London: The Hogarth Press, vol. 1, 281–392.

Freud, S. (1900) *The Interpretation of Dreams*, Standard Edition, London: The Hogarth Press, vol. 4 & 5, xi–630.

Freud, S. (1913) *Totem and Taboo*, Standard Edition, London: The Hogarth Press, vol. 13, xi–164.

Freud, S. (1914) *On Narcissism: An Introduction*, Standard Edition, London: The Hogarth Press, vol. 14, 67–104.

Freud, S. (1926) *Inhibitions, Symptoms and Anxiety*, Standard Edition, London: The Hogarth Press, vol. 20, 77–178.

Freud, S. (1927) *The Future of an Illusion*, SE Vol. 21, 1–56.

Freud, S. (1930) *Civilization and Its Discontents*, Standard Edition, London: The Hogarth Press, vol. 21, 3–148.

Freud, S. (1933) *Why War?* Standard Edition, London: The Hogarth Press, vol. 22, 197–215.

Gedo, J. E. (1986) *Conceptual Issues in Psychoanalysis: Essays in History and Method*, Hillsdale, NJ: The Analytic Press.

Gordon, P. E. (2012) *Continental Divide*, Cambridge, MA: Harvard University Press.

Green, A. (1980) Passions and their Vicissitudes: On the Relation between Madness and Psychosis. In: *On Private Madness*, Madison, CT: International Universities Press, 214–253.

Habermas, J. (1973) *Knowledge and Human Interests* (trans., J. J. Shapiro), Boston, MA: Beacon Press.

Habermas, J. (1990) *The Philosophical Discourse of Modernity: Twelve Lectures*, Cambridge, MA: The MIT Press.

Hartmann, H. (1959) *Ego Psychology and the Problem of Adaptation, Journal of the American Psychoanalytic Association Monograph Series Number One* (trans., D. Rappaport), New York: International Universities Press.

Heidegger, M. (1993) The Question Concerning Technology. In: *Martin Heidegger: Basic Writings* (ed., D. F. Krell), San Francisco, CA: Harper San Francisco, 307–342.

Herzog, P. (2015) The Myth of Freud as Anti-Philosopher. In: *Freud: Appraisals and Reappraisals: Contributions to Freud Studies* (ed., P. E. Stepansky), Hillsdale, NJ: The Analytic Press, vol. 2, 163–189.

Jung, C. J. (1989) *Memories, Dreams, Reflections,* trans. Clara Winston, New York: Vintage.

Kant, I. (1784) An Answer to the Question: What Is Enlightenment? In: *Immanuel Kant: Practical Philosophy* (trans. & ed., M. Gregor), New York: Cambridge University Press, 11–22.

Lacan, J. (2006) The Mirror Stage as Formative of the I Function as Revealed in Psychoanalytic Experience. In: *Écrits: The First Complete Edition in English* (trans., B. Fink), New York: W.W. Norton & Co, 75–81.

Lear, J. (1992) Inside and Outside the Republic, *Phronesis*, 37(2), 184–215.

Lear, J. (1996) The Introduction of Eros: Reflections on the Work of Hans Loewald. *Journal of the American Psychoanalytic Association*, 44(3), 673–698.

Loewald, H. (1951) Ego and Reality. In: *The Essential Loewald: Collected Papers and Manuscripts*, Hagerstown, MD: University Publishing Group, 3–20.

Loewald, H. (1952) The Problem of Defense and the Neurotic Interpretation of Reality. In: *The Essential Loewald: Collected Papers and Manuscripts*, Hagerstown, MD: University Publishing Group, 21–32.

Loewald, H. (1960) On the Therapeutic Action of Psychoanalysis. In: *The Essential Loewald: Collected Papers and Manuscripts*, Hagerstown, MD: University Publishing Group, 221–256.

Loewald, H. (1970) Psychoanalysis as Art and the Fantasy Character of the Psychoanalytic Situation. In: *The Essential Loewald: Collected Papers and Manuscripts*, Hagerstown, MD: University Publishing Group, 277–301.

Loewald, H. (1971) On Motivation and Instinct Theory. In: *The Essential Loewald: Collected Papers and Manuscripts*, Hagerstown, MD: University Publishing Group, 102–138.

Loewald, H. (1973) On Internalization. In: *The Essential Loewald: Collected Papers and Manuscripts*, Hagerstown, MD: University Publishing Group, 174–177.

Loewald, H. (1977) Book Review: Essay on The Freud/Jung Letters. In: *The Essential Loewald: Collected Papers and Manuscripts*, Hagerstown, MD: University Publishing Group, 405–439.

Loewald, H. (1978) Psychoanalysis and the History of the Individual. In: *The Essential Loewald: Collected Papers and Manuscripts*, Hagerstown, MD: University Publishing Group, 531–579.

Loewald, H. (1979) The Waning of the Oedipus Complex. In: *The Essential Loewald: Collected Papers and Manuscripts*, Hagerstown, MD: University Publishing Group, 384–404.

Loewald, H. (1987) Sublimation: Inquiries into Theoretical Psychoanalysis. In: *The Essential Loewald: Collected Papers and Manuscripts*, Hagerstown, MD: University Publishing Group.

Loewald, H. (2000) *The Essential Loewald: Collected Papers and Manuscripts*, Hagerstown, MD: University Publishing Group.

Loewald, H. W. (1988) Psychoanalysis in Search of Nature. Thoughts on Metapsychology, "Metaphysics," Projection, *Annual of Psychoanalysis*, 16, 49–54.

Mahler, M., Pine, F., Bergman, A. (1975) *The Psychological Birth of the Human Infant: Symbiosis and Individuation*, New York: Basic Books.

Masson, J. M. (ed.) (1985) *The Complete Letters of Sigmund Freud to Wilhelm Fliess: 1887–1904*, Cambridge, MA: Harvard University Press.

McDougall, J. (2013) *Plea for a Measure of Abnormality*, New York: Routledge.

Mitchell, S. A. (2002) *Relationality: From Attachment to Intersubjectivity*, Hillsdale, NJ: The Analytic Press.

Ogden, T. H. (2006) Reading Loewald: Oedipus Reconceived, *The International Journal of Psychoanalysis*, 87(3), 651–666.

Plato (1997) Philebus. In: *Plato: Complete Works* (ed., J. N. Cooper, trans., D. Frede), Indianapolis, IN: Hackett Publishing Co, 398–456.

Whitebook, J. (1985) Reason and Happiness: Some Psychoanalytic Themes in Critical Theory. In: *Habermas and Modernity* (ed., R. Bernstein), Cambridge, MA: The MIT Press.

Whitebook, J. (2002) Slow Magic: Psychoanalysis and "The Disenchantment of the World", *Journal of the American Psychoanalytic Association*, 50, 1197–1217.

Whitebook, J. (2004a) Weighty Objects: on Adorno's Kant-Freud Critique. In: *The Cambridge Companion* (ed., T. Huhn), New York: Cambridge University Press, 51–76.

Whitebook, J. (2004b) Hans Loewald: A Radical Conservative. *The International Journal of Psychoanalysis*, 85: 97–115.

Whitebook, J. (2017) *Freud: An Intellectual Biography*, New York: Cambridge University Press.

Winnicott, D. W. (1971) Creativity and Its Origins. In: *Playing and Reality*, New York: Tavistock Publications, 65–85.

Winnicott, D. W. (1974) Fear of Breakdown. *International Review of Psycho-Analysis*, 1, 103–107.

Winnicott, D. W. (1989) The Use of an Object in the Context of Moses and Monotheism. In: *Psychoanalytic Explorations* (ed. C. Winnicott et al.), Cambridge, MA: Harvard University Press, 217–246.

Winnicott, D. W. (1990) Living Creatively. In: *Home is Where We Start From* (ed., C. Winnicott et al.), New York: W.W. Norton & Co, 35–54.

Young-Bruehl, E. (1994) What Theories Women Want. *American Imago*, 51(4), 373–396.

Yovel, Y. (1992) *Spinoza and Other Heretics*, vol. II, Princeton, NJ: Princeton University Press.

Part III

Clinical Loewald

Chapter 9

Gender Formation

Building from Hans Loewald

Rosemary H. Balsam

Introduction

Hans Loewald says little directly about gender development. However, I would like to contemplate this topic as it relates to his work. Gender portraiture and expression are central features in the formation of the individual mind. In this, I follow Freud and thus grant centrality to the role of the human body as a vehicle for the forming and working mind. It is in the spirit of Loewald's thinking to investigate all trajectories that feature in the sentient mind's gradual maturation.

Curiously, despite no direct discussion of gender, it was Hans Loewald's supervisory and teaching influence on my own development as an analyst that helped my thinking and appreciation of where I was both excited by and differed strongly from Freud. I saw immediately how seriously awry was Freud's view of female body development, and, given how central to sex and gender development were his "psychosexual stages," how distorted must be all affected elements of his general theory of mind. If the "ego is first and foremost a bodily ego," I believe that the fundaments of "the ego" need to include *two* intact and very differently sexed bodies, which otherwise have all operational aspects in common, from procreation to brain, motor, circulation or digestion functions (Balsam, 2012). In turn, Freud's declarations about women seemed to have led astray many of his followers (e.g., see an account of the history in Balsam, 2015b). In contrast, the unrestricted "atmospherics" of Loewald's teaching attitudes and supervision sanctioned my own inclination to listen for an analysand's corporeal internalizations of early embodied and sensual mothering and caretaking influences. Gradually, in tune with Freud, given my old and abiding love of medical studies, the physicality of female or male bodies with their sexual and procreative powers and potentials, as I saw them, became key foci for the building blocks of the ego and embedded gender development. Loewald's emphases on maturation toward autonomy and personal ethical responsibility deftly challenges "biological essentialism," that erroneous and restrictive notion of gender that is a bugaboo for feminist scholars (Chodorow, 2011, see also Balsam, 2018 for such an argument with Kleinian theory). Nothing that is written about the body's mental representations needs to imply any mandate whatsoever for an individual's intended

DOI: 10.4324/9781003328230-12

usage of his, hers or their body's capabilities. A natal female may be strong and energetic, but in no way does she need to be an athlete. Likewise, their reproductive organs may function perfectly, but this does not mean that they need to have children. A natal female who gives birth may choose to call themselves "they." That is the sole responsibility of the owner of that body. The individual's psychic reaction, then, to sexed and procreative human bodies – their own and those in their impacting surroundings – and their ownership and inhabiting of these precious housings become an illumination for understanding more about gender development. Loewald's combined interests in instinctual drives blended with object relations and psychic structure movements throughout the life cycle, plus his interest in autonomy and responsibility for oneself, lead to both the very beginnings of life and the end of life. Women's bodies are, in fact, the alpha and omega of that existence. Listening carefully to a woman's physical and mental experience of her own actual or anticipated pregnancies, then, regardless of her chronological age, flows from this approach. In other words, a natal female may be assumed to have had experiences of inhabiting her sexed body, whatever the nature of those experiences were. And this object/drive sensibility invites similar materials regarding male bodies too. Psychoanalysis has been much more familiar with the latter, however, due to our field's over-comfort with male social bias.

Loewald's (or Winnicott's too, for Loewald was very fond of his work) vital "mother-and-baby" imagoes morphed especially for me into the primal significance of a mother's bodily expression that is in tune or discord with the physicality of her baby, and the language in which this dialogue is represented psychically and encoded over time. Later in my career, I discovered, to my joy, the richness of Julia Kristeva's work in this regard. Her feast of resonant language transforming physical experience as semiotics, blended with psychic operations that call to empathic experiences in the reader, is captivating to me (and others). I have felt deprived by Hans's passing, that I cannot know what he thought of Kristeva. He never mentioned her. I feel frustrated too that so little is available about how he read Laplanche,[1] whom he acknowledges, and who, too, is a later discovery for me. The French who evolved away from Lacan (but not Lacan himself), whom I knew Loewald actually said once was a "charlatan" (personal communication shortly after Lacan's visit to Yale University in 1975), seem so compatible with Loewald's view of the role of the mothering person as being a key co-constructor of the mind's sexual and genderized responses. (See Doris Silverman's chapter on Laplanche in this volume for more information.)

I therefore glean the rich crumbs from Loewald's writing about gender, and I fill in the spaces for myself, using thinking tools from his approach to and presentation of theory. I have also developed doubts about Hans's ideas about "parricide" in the Oedipal situation as such a generalizable psychic phenomenon. He and Freud seem ultimately biased toward male development in this regard and lack interest in the female as a separate but equal "other" in that developmental world. Lastly, as I grow older both chronologically and as an analyst, like him and other old analysts, we seem to end our days in sheer awe of physical creation, procreation, the human mind and the universe. I hope to touch on all these themes as they affect gender, but especially the growth of natal females.

Places of Gender Interest in Loewald's Writings

There are four places in Loewald's work that stand out as being relevant to the formation of an individual's gender portrait.

1) The first allusion is in his famous portrait of mother and child, which is at the heart of how he conveys the melding of instinct theory and object relations. The earliest psychic formations seem to encode archaic gendered and embryonic sexual expressions that are communicated between a mother and her infant, of whose tiny, sexed body she is exquisitely aware, as she holds it close to her own sexed and highly gendered body and ministers to its basic needs for survival. These sensory communications are especially acute in the aftermath of birthing this child. Loewald says,

> In one and the same act—I am tempted to say, in the same breath and the same sucking of milk—drive direction and organization of environment into shapes or configurations begin, and they are continued into ego organization and object organization, by methods such as identification, introjection, projection. The higher organizational stage of the environment is indispensable for the development of the psychic apparatus and, in early stages, has to be brought to it actively. Without such a differential between organism and environment no development takes place.
>
> (1960, p. 238)

This quotation is from his "On the Therapeutic Action of Psychoanalysis." And what is "brought to it actively" (p. 238) communicates all the encoded gendered and sexed messages that the mother or caretaker is imparting to this infantile sensibility, especially through the medium of the infant's bodily perceptions, via his or her own bodily perceptions, actions and attentions. From this underpinning and the fact that a daughter has been birthed by a mother, any analyst then can hear more clearly how, for women's development, her own female-gendered and embodied mother is closely channeled into a female subject's responses.

2) The second keynote to the topic of gender formation is in Loewald's view of the Oedipus situation (1979). He is frank and clear that "Oedipus" applies *only* to males (which Freud also definitively asserted but his followers have ignored, perhaps in their casually unconscious misogyny). Loewald says in "The Waning of the Oedipus Complex" (1979), while both extending and stressing Freud's lesser emphasized notion of the actual *destruction* of the incestuous object, "...the child's ego turns away from the Oedipal complex *(this account refers to the boy)*." (italics, but not parenthesis, mine, p. 385). As it is with all analytic writers who acknowledge that Freud's "oedipal" configurations are specifically male, Loewald thus acknowledges that the scenarios being described in the paper imply that like males, females develop *some* fashion of object relation *triangulation,* because this is important to the mind's continuing growth beyond the dyadic patterning of earlier development. He does not specify a path for females. Loewald later in the paper, like Freud,

acknowledges "...*the less-well explored intricacies of the feminine oedipal conflict*" (italics mine, p. 392). After this statement of limitation, his argument re-conflates the combined male-and-female scenario. The embodied female is thus ignored by assumption of male dominance. He states that for a human psyche to develop toward maturity, everyone needs psychologically to murder both parents ("commit parricide") to achieve autonomy. I have argued before with clinical evidence that this radical death of an internal mother is incorrect about female development. A woman comes into her biological maturity in pregnancy and with birthing experience in an average, expectable fashion. In these dramas, she often has need of her, by then, menopausal mother (or other close woman, such as a doula, as a displacement) in a lived, animated, present-tense and novel way. Premature "parricide" of the vitality of her female imago would have paralyzed or short-changed this necessary mentalized process of the development of "maternal eroticism" (Kristeva, 2014). Moreover, to me, this demand for "parricide" seems at odds with some of the main tenets of Loewaldian theory. Perhaps the father of a female is more likely to be subject to "parricide" in heterosexual patterning. Perhaps it is the mother of a male who is more subject to parricide in heterosexual development? There are likely different fates for the internalized incestuous objects, contributing to different outcomes. No single way can suffice. In the case of female body development into a baby-making biological maturity and thus motherhood, I am convinced that the old mother or her midwifely substitute takes on a new role for internalization at that juncture in relation to the pregnant daughter, the vulnerability and new openness due to the shared bodily sensual knowledge of pregnancy. The libidinal charge for the resultant internalization, I believe, is the "maternal eroticism" described by Kristeva (2014). The psychic process is an active, here-and-now event full of vitality, assertion, difference, separation and re-joining, aloneness and togetherness, psychologically akin to the anlage of the reciprocity of the earliest maternal activities with her girl infant. Loewald's strong emphasis on a necessary "parricide" of incestuous objects in his 1979 paper has, however, been touted by many modern psychoanalytic writers and is often explicated favorably (see in this volume, for example, Chodorow, Whitebook and Levenson, and also Ogden, 2006, as very thoughtful examples). The lack of debate, though, about the general applicability of matricide on the road to female independence and the blurring of the two sexes, dare I say, may be an ongoing symptom of the ease of shared unconscious phallocentrism in our field, in spite of sophistication. One form of expression is the frequent interpretation offered in case conferences that judge women as "too close" to their mothers as adults and too readily subject to "preoedipal" fixations with automatic limitations against implied "oedipal") maturity.

3)   The third gender pointers in Loewald's work are passages in "Man as Moral Agent" (1978), where he writes that the task of maturation is also to preserve psychically our original rootedness within our objects while allowing transformational psychic acts to interact and carry us forward in a full way into the present. In the beginning, he re-emphasizes "the primordial infant-mother psychic unit, as a living mirror in which the infant gradually begins to recognize, to know himself, by being recognized by the mother...mediated to the infant and growing child by...activities and interactions with the child's bodily and instinctual life" (pp. 538, 539). He notes that "The *con* in *conscire*-- the root verb for the words conscious and

conscience—expresses the belonging-together of, and internal encounter between 'raw' experience and its reflecting recognition by the other in oneself" (p. 540). Peopling the superego, Loewald writes, "The superego…is brought about by the internalization of the parents' acts of envisioning future development and exemplifying it. At the same time, Freud stressed the intimate relation of the superego to the id" (1978, p. 547). Quoting from Freud and Goethe, he asserts, "'What thou hast inherited from thy fathers, acquire it to make it thine'. The past comprises the inherited, innate potential of our genes, the historical, cultural moral tradition transmitted to us by our elders" and "…the contents of our lives that are experiences in this primordial form at the earliest level" (1978, p. 547). This speaks to the development of the sexed and gendered body with all its encoded emotional and bodily interactions that fill our minds and beings.

4) The fourth gender indicator is in the final passages of his 1988 book on "Sublimation," where he has suggested richly that we, as sentient beings, emerge – struggle from – the natural universe in which we exist, and we evolve in different iterations by keeping returning to the fountains of our origins, pushing to re-emerge and re-form against our own resistance to return to the womb – as a metaphor for the creative womb of the universe – into more separated levels suited to individual transactions. The sexed universe of the human body and the processes of conception, embedded growth and creativity, as well as the powerful ferocity of birthing and the violence of separation, make the fecund female body central to these galaxies of a lived universe. This is the body and the conscious and unconscious communicable experience that help shape the mentalized genders in the offspring for the following generation.

1) "In the same breath, and the same sucking of milk…" (1960, p. 238)

This passage captures the experience of intense closeness for a mother who has given birth to a child and has the joy (or agitated confusion, anxiety, anger, misery, terror and excitement) of holding the little creature to her breast to feed it (or try to) and feel its warm life against her skin, knowing that its body has emerged – far outside of her control – from the depths of her own. Individually, birthing runs the gamut from delight to loathing, but the commonality is that these signals will be transmitted and absorbed by the infant in some form of reciprocity. And once born, the infant will call back with its own unbidden flood of emotional reactions from soothed contentment to inconsolable screeching. An awe of the primal force of life is present in this act of feeding. The child feeds from the birthing mother's body contents, and the mother participates in a power beyond her full control to deliver nurturance right into the infant's body. There is significant biological dominion in that act for the person feeding an infant – a magical and surreal forcefield – as the feeding person drifts into a boundaryless state with a gradually satiating and satiated baby. Freud knew this once but strayed from his own knowledge. Once he published "On the Sexual Theories of Children" in 1908, affirmed its findings in 1915 in a revised edition of the 1905 *Three Essays,* and enunciated once and for all that he was "obliged to recognize that the little girl is a little man" and that early vaginal sensations "cannot play a great part" (1933, p. 149), he more or less ended the field's sustained discoveries about women's development qua female. I note that

Very late in life he did acknowledge that a girl's desire for a baby precedes penis envy (Mack Brunswick 1940), but even then he regarded this desire as the result solely of her "male"-driven eroticism toward her mother—never, for Freud, as rooted in female merger or identification with her same-bodied mother!

(Balsam, 2017, p. 62)

Consider the possibilities for potential body memories for both participants in this scene. The breast and adult female flesh are soft, particularly close to parturition. Softness and smoothness will brush on the skin of the infant. Wet, warm milk will touch its sensitive lips and follow down its throat. The infant's uncontrolled but rhythmic reflex muscular mouth actions to pull in the milk are activated and felt. The mother's nipple is taut and sensitive to the pull as her milk "lets down" – another uncontrolled reflex sensation. Phallocentric-driven Freudian followers used to stress the orgasm of sexual intercourse as the prime physical achievement of "letting go," by which even emotional maturity or neurosis was measured. Julia Kristeva has fore-fronted the importance of "maternal reliance or eroticism" (2014). The female body's interactive stimulus of milk production would be an aspect of such erotics. It is as if Kristeva took a similar sense of Loewald's appreciation of the sensual interchange between mother and infant and took it further, articulating strongly the erotic adult female components. Laplanche (2015 in English translation) would consider these exchanges "enigmatic" messaging of eroticism from mother to infant, balanced toward the infant's standpoint. In Didier Anzieu's (1987/2016 in English translation) "skin ego" as a mode of grasping human subjectivity, the sensitivities of the body's surface become crucial constituents of the mind's structures and functions. The soft, smooth maternal skin touch, combined with the sweet anaclitic pleasures of satisfying hunger and being satisfied, become templates for building ego experiences of trust or mistrust. One woman, for example, recalled (or symbolized) and recoiled from her mother's skin and touched it "like sandpaper." In adulthood, she would never have her mother babysit her own children. In this family of ideas, Loewald's talk of "early shapes" refers to the most primitive elements of a burgeoning object for internalization. The scenario creates a packed sensory scene that will not only become an encoded self-object but also embryonically, unknowingly, gendered: "I-and-mother, caretaker/female." Had all the feeding occurred with a male, that firm muscular frame, strong arms and hairy chest would be encoded as "I-and-caretaker/father/male." Much later, after recognition of sameness or difference of sex, the body of the mothering person (if female) will be metabolized as closer to self (if a female child) or ultimately differentiable in a preliminary fashion as "other" (if a male child). Mother's excited or forced voice will add a bodily affirming, differentiating gender-influencing voice: "my darling girl" or "my precious boy." Or "my bonny-lass, my vixen-girl, my lion-man, my devil dog" – all words I've heard, all gendered and qualified. Her voice may curse the child's sex also. The voices and tonalities are absorbed by introjection, identification, projection and re-projection as if in a duet and gradually become part of the infant's own inner world.

Case Vignette of Mother and Son

Jon, a college sophomore whose psychoanalytically oriented psychotherapy case I supervised, said he had known since he was young that he was more interested sexually in boys. He was fascinated with how their "waterworks worked" and how he loved to watch their "big streams," admiring most the boy with the flashiest arc. He looked forward to gym class, seeing other boy bodies and feeling aroused and alive. He yearned to touch, hold, cradle and sexually excite a boy who was a close friend but who was straight. Jon was sure he could sexually interest his high-school pal if he only spent enough time on sleepovers and that his friend truly was more interested in him than in "stupid" girls. Jon's mother loved to hear his stories, often visited him at college, and was full of advice. She had him sit on her bed as he had as a child and tell it all, which he delighted in doing. His sister was despised by his mother for being "secretive" and failing to share her love life and love temptations so freely. Jon described his mother as a beautiful brunette, her soft brown eyes glistening with admiration for him – just the way she had looked at him in the bath when he was little; they'd giggle together, and she would stroke his "little man." In delight, they would watch "it" rise together. Many stories took place while Jon was in her bed or his, or while in the bath. To the supervisory listener, while engaged in free floating attention, the stories became intermingled with stories with which his mother had regaled Jon about her home birthing experience with him. She had had a warm water bath to sit in, for example. She luxuriated in describing the pains, the ebb and flow; the final appearance of his head; and then, OMG!…when his penis arrived in view! "So red and big I was shocked," she told him with intense excitement. She told the story often. He said dreamily that it was as if no one else in the world was there between them. It was clear she and he were enmeshed in a cocoon within these bodily giggles, shared excitements, mutual interplay of call and echo in response to erotic and sensual titillation.

The rhythms of lull and excitement induced in and reported to me by the (female) therapist while listening and responding seemed to echo Jon's body movements too – leaning forward, then backward, then with hands outreached, then with withdrawal, then with preoccupation, and finally with an overt blush of excitement with a bulge in his pants he later said was an erection. As supervisor, one step further removed from the action, I also felt absorbed in the form of the sessions. To use Kristeva's language, I believed that we were in the presence of the effects of the internalized mother-son's space of "chora" (the earliest flow of sensory experience into a chaotic communicative language), with its erotic semiotic function (Kristeva, 1974/1984). As such, we could imagine the vast depths of the pool of enmeshment which this young man was enacting. It would be a long, winding path for him to begin to appreciate how captivated and enraptured he was within the mesmerizing spell of his mother's profound, restlessly unsatisfiable maternal yearnings for his enclosure. Consonant with Kristeva's Lacanian understanding, this particular mother's subjectivity was inseparable from the "lack" that produced it and the metonymic desire (engaged with her son), which represented that unsatisfied endless quest for the lost and the impossible. She used her son to fill that space. In Loewaldian terms, the son was filled with the tender, erotic attentions of a mother who was perpetually engaged in a merger, having him as a part of herself, attuned to an early maternal infant state in this echoing, erotic closeness with her own body. By now this constellation had flourished into a frankly incestuous object relationship, where he was her passionate object of desire, whose love life was caught up in this cocoon with a mutual delight in their entanglement. His freedom for adolescent growth toward adulthood and more autonomy reached toward a body that she could never give to him because of her femaleness – the male body habitus – that he could be freer to explore himself and love, while enwrapping in his love, his yearning for ongoing maternal admiration.

The body eroticism and worship in the narcissistic sphere of development, conjured up in the mutuality of mother-baby enthrall, in Jon's case, is a self-identified sexed male. He is physically affirmed and supported in a male-cis-gendered identification, nurtured by this longing female who gave birth to him. He self-identifies as the object of her passion, not with her body's femaleness. The young man was strongly male-cis-gendered, with few doubts about his abilities and sexual attractiveness to either females or males. Jon loved his own body. The direction of his desire toward males as a sexual choice of partner encoded messages from his mother that males were supreme. Why shouldn't he, her prince, choose a fully admired person that allows enough separateness for an independent love life? His male companion is a narcissistic object choice at a primitive level, echoing maternal adoration, but this male partner holds more potential than a female sexual choice for Jon. His ego transformations may develop beyond early body love, with enough emotional closeness to this man to separate sufficiently from his mother, enter into tender attachment, and caretaking empathy through his non-incestuously less engulfing male-to-male sexual attachment.

Freud (1892): A Case of Breastfeeding

Loewald, while theorizing, was free to imagine the deep psychic impacts of people on other people as they lived their lives. Freud, too, when writing clinically about his patients, is lively about their impact on one another. For example, in 1892, in a case of success with his hypnosis treatment, he tells of a young woman in her mid-20s[2] whom he was able to "assist at an important moment of her existence" "…a case of a mother who was unable to feed her new-born baby till hypnotic suggestion intervened" (p. 117). His diagnosis was *hystérique d'occasion*. He stressed how healthy her mother, she and her sister were. He described her as having "capability…quiet common sense, and [with]naturalness." At her bedside, "I found her lying in bed with flushed cheeks and furious at her inability to feed the baby – an inability which increased at every attempt but against which she struggled with all her strength" (p. 119). He hypnotized her in three minutes, even though he said earlier that he "was obviously being received with bad grace and I could not count on the patient's having much confidence in me." Her husband, in fact, murmured that she might be damaged by this hypnosis. Freud used the hypnosis to "contradict all her fears and the feelings on which those fears were based." "Have no fear!" he declared. "You will make an excellent nurse and the baby will thrive." By the next day, the baby was feeding, the patient's vomiting troubles had gone and her appetite had returned. Freud reported that "I found it hard to understand…as well as annoying, that no reference was ever made to my remarkable achievement" (p. 120). I found this admission hilariously open and modern of Freud. Later, she and her husband told him that she was ashamed that an act like hypnosis could succeed where her own will had failed. She reminds me of a type of young mother who relishes control in her life and brings style to this new situation. After giving birth, she expects the baby to adapt to her. Raphael-Leff calls this style of mother a "regulator" (1986). This differs from a "facilitator," who will adapt herself to the baby's lead. When Freud starts to theorize formally about her psychic situation, working as he was in those days on the recognition of "the unconscious," his deductions and inferences lead to her mind's defenses. Due to fatigue, he offers, her "distressing antithetic ideas" had overcome her conscious intentions and were "put in motion" by her "counter-will," as in "I shall not succeed in carrying out my intention because this is too difficult for me and I am unfit to do it" (p. 121). A healthy person, he notes, will deal with "antithetic ideas" through "self-confidence of health" and suppress them. The fatigue, or exhaustion, after the young woman's first confinement, he identified as a predispositional foundation to the lack of the usual inhibition of the antithetical ideas.

Freud also writes in this case report with an interest, empathy and wisdom about women that one wishes he had been able to access later. This was missing by 1908, when beginning to compose formally his psychology of women. By contrast, in 1892, he notes that, "a first confinement is the greatest shock to which the female organism is subject, and as a result of it a woman will as a rule produce any neurotic symptoms that may be latent in her disposition" (p. 123). After this, alas, in his entire oeuvre, he mentions pregnancy seldom, and birthing never from the point of view of the woman (Balsam, 2017).

2) **Is "Parricide" Necessary in Maturing Female Triangulation, in the Waning of (her Version) of an "Oedipus Complex"?**

and

3) **What of the development of female independence, maturity, and the moral responsibility of autonomy?**

Loewald was unusually avid about the necessity for internal "parricide" in relation to the Oedipal complex. Like Freud, he actually stated that this was so for males and allowed uncertainty for females (for a full review of Freud's wavering on the same issue, see Balsam, 2015a). But also, like Freud, he stated his doubts but then proceeded to negate them by making his theory a general one, as if human bodies were one sex.

I first began to question the application of the Oedipal myth to female development due to my clinical experiences. I noticed that during pregnancy and delivery, and in their first experiences as new mothers, women's own mothers, often on the actual scene, loomed exceptionally large – like the harvest moon. As a medical student attending deliveries in Belfast, Northern Ireland, I noticed that women in the throes of birth often cried out to their mothers. Their mothers, or other women experienced in birthing children in the surrounding area, became ready models, judges and juries for the new mothers' doubts, anxieties, attitudes, and behaviors during delivery and beyond. Once the women began to get used to caring for these children of their own, their own mothers or these substitutes began to fade in the minds of these adult daughters as such active reference points. The mothers, or senior women, were perhaps actively involved with their grandchildren by then, and in that sense integrating generationally within the young family. This seemed contrary to the analytic literature's abstract insistence on the advisability of a more radical internal separation from both mother and father that supposedly promotes individual maturation. Hans's idea of "parricide" is one of the most dramatic insistences, but it is in a similar vein to others. My mother-involved patients theoretically, in those terms, should have been quite infantile even in their 30s and 40s, and perhaps confused about who was the caretaker of the babies. They would not qualify as "good-enough" mothers if we stuck to this picture of Oedipal evolution. However, dependent though they may have been in the exigencies of birthing, it seemed a productive dependency, and many seemed to proceed flexibly and *successfully* to individuate comfortably from their families of origin. Many were relatively at ease with having minds and lives of their own and had internalized these dependency experiences as resources to take over care-taking by themselves.

In contrast, many of those women who had "left" their mothers behind as internal beacons long before their pregnancies seemed suspicious of their adult ties to more senior women. They often suffered "haunting" from their ghostly mothers' internal presences with painful self-excoriating fantasies of not living up to excessively high standards as mothers (see Loewald, 1960, on the optimal separation process of turning ghosts into ancestors). Loewald would have pointed to such material as signs of limitation in a patient's negotiated maturity. One woman quoted her early repudiated mother as warning, "You will never get away from me when you wrong me. Even if I'm dead, I'll come back to scratch the soles of your feet when you're asleep." The patient would visibly shudder at the image. The voice of another mother in the head of her adult daughter, long after her rejection by the daughter who had moved a continent away, kept saying, "You'll kill me with all your complaints. I don't need to hear any of this." Another 60-year-old woman's mother, aged 98, regularly appeared in her dreams as a wraith, floating about unconcerned, while she felt compelled to be on her knees scrubbing mess off the floors. The fate of these mothers in their teenage daughters' psyches had been a Loewaldian matricidal parricide. It strikes me that it would be hard to "murder" such a key person and expect her spirit to become a leisurely ancestor! An active ghost would have been murdered in a rage. One thinks about the old comedian Stanley Holloway's dark song about Henry VIII's beheaded wife, Anne Boleyn:

> …She comes to haunt King Henry, she means giving him what-for,
> Gadzooks, she's going to tell him off for having spilled her gore,
> And just in case the headsman wants to give her an encore
> She has her head tucked underneath her arm.
> Chorus: With her head tucked underneath her arm
> She walks the bloody tower
> With her head tucked underneath her arm
> At the midnight hour….

Does a son need to axe a father's early erotic influence to gain autonomy? I am not sure. But Oedipus and his father's murder at the crossroads are inapplicable to females maturing in a route that involves their embodied motherhood. Murder would have made the old mothers inaccessible to the new mothers for new, bodily comparisons and shared intimate experiences of the toleration of birth contractions, Cesarean sections, forceps delivery, or how best to hold a slippery baby in the bathwater, or what squirrely behaviors go with producing a potty for a toddler. There are abundant opportunities there for the old mothers or doulas, or midwives and nannies to "lend their egos" at times in caretaking, relating body processes that, I believe, are not just old re-iterations, and promote active and necessary progressive internalization for the young mother's developmental road ahead.

Kulish and Holtzman, in 2008, also showed that the Oedipus myth is of limited value. They examine a pattern of a maturing female's developing sexuality in light of the myth of Persephone and Demeter as more apt. Hades, her uncle, steals her away to his underworld in a rape scenario before she is ready to leave her mother, and vice versa. She and her mother do regularly briefly reunite thereafter. In this myth, the man is an unwelcome intruder, but in some versions, eventually she loves him. Mother Demeter is left behind, bereft, on the earth. This tracks much more mother-and-daughter closeness than Freud imagined. But it does raise questions about how such a woman can mature beyond this unwelcome, rupturing encounter with a male. Might she have found other mother figures in the Underworld while her mother Demeter mourned for her in the earthly winter, awaiting her brief, uplifting visit in the Spring?

Daniel Stern, in his 1995 "Motherhood Constellation," sees a woman almost as becoming an entirely new person via the experience of motherhood. He sequesters the state off as special and focuses on the new relations that develop from the old familial ties. He recommends special attention by the therapy professionals. Stern does not think much about the internal continuities of this female development from childhood. The new state is thus characterized as differing from other mental organizations in altering the mother's sensibilities, fantasies and actions. He too notes a different mental engagement with her own mother, but stops with wonderment at its newness. Earlier writers, for example, like Bibring (1959) or Benedek (1970) and others, also captured the newness, and while stressing its normality for a female, they also sequestered. These two writers (among the few analysts who have focused their experience on women) did not consider their observations grounds to challenge Freud's developmental theory or female Oedipal dynamics for womanhood. Chodorow, who also proposed the Persephone and Demeter myths as relevant to female analytic developmental theory (Chodorow, 1994), had been one of the first scholars, if not the first, to take the closeness of modeling of daughter upon mother the key mental process in becoming a mother (Chodorow, 1978). She was a sociologist in those days, before she became a psychoanalyst in the 1990s. She used this theoretical psychoanalytic insight at that time, more for the feminist politics of the situation rather than its import for psychoanalysis, which was later appreciated. Julia Kristeva is another psychoanalyst with an academic background who, in her more recent work, is explicitly inclusive of women's experience of producing children and birthing. She has placed the female, alongside the male, right at the heart of psychic development by emphasizing the role of maternal eroticism and "reliance" for herself and her child (2014).

The maturation cycle toward female birthing takes far longer than Freud's stages of development, which speak to a child's earliest steps in procreation. His emphasis on babies stops with phallic issues and the achievement of heterosexual intimacy with a gradual tolerance for relations with both parents, with a diminution of the active male same-sex competition for love of mother and a growth of responsibility and conscience. By the time the male is in adolescence, the constellation emerges again for further working though. But the boy may not need much hands-on guidance from a father or anyone in an older generation, necessarily, to enable him to have sex with a female peer! He is usually much younger at the developmental point of first sexual intercourse than a female who is having her first baby. (Female first sex seems a minor way-station compared to the body dramas that await her later.) Not so males. Triangulation of object relationships for a female is then not sufficient to demark "maturity."

The *body* of a woman needs time to season, and her relationship with her own mother, long post-birthing, plays a slowly evolving role in that ultimate maturation. It is this rhythm of nature that I claim is normative and calls into question theories about how "preoedipal" women seem and implies that they are insufficiently mature. We do not need to posit "regression." The trajectory is simply different between males and females psychologically. I am not claiming either, like Freud and many of his followers, that baby-making is the sole path to female maturity. But there is one route that is viable, where that path is pursued. There are others.

Kulish and Holtzmann, 2008, wrote about replacing the Oedipal complex for women with "the Persephone Complex." At the time, welcoming this well-developed argument that advanced the field, in a recommendation on the back cover of their book, I said that their theories "ought necessarily to upset psychoanalysts' familiar, favorite but limiting tropes." Harold Blum, too, declared it

> a major revision of the theory of female development. Traditional concepts of the female Oedipus complex are replaced with a new model of the girls' triangular situation, the myth of Persephone instead of Oedipus. The female Persephone vividly depicts the cyclical female experience. ...Persephone balances loyalties and relationships to both parents, a rival for father's love, while retaining her mother's love and love of her mother.

It is surprising, however, how few writers have actually allowed this challenge to have much impact.

Having treated also women who did not wish to have children, the former slow, diminishing trajectory that I describe in the power of the actual mother can sometimes appear less marked. But it is nevertheless a gradually diminishing influence, compared to Hans's optimal vision of the necessary "murder" at the crossroads that precedes individuation. If this is "murder," as far as I am concerned, the experience internally is at most a very slow death by single drops of blood! Patricide may be more common than matricide internally for women. Love takes on a different form by mirroring shared female bodies and minds. I have concluded that the mother's slow exit off-stage is directly related to the fact that the onset of the test of female bodily maturity in pregnancy and birthing does not take place until usually the third decade of life.

There are other paths to maturity for women in terms of sufficiently comfortable separation from the original family to become their own people. Some females preferentially hold their fathers very close internally, even through their birthing experiences, and slowly detach from the father over subsequent decades. These women have been remarkably male-identified and share the slow-moving trajectory of being into the second, third or fourth decade of life, if using their bodies in this demanding and procreative fashion for the first time.

4) "Could sublimation be both a mourning of lost original oneness and a celebration of oneness regained?" (Loewald, 1988, p. 81.)

The last section of Loewald's 1988 book on sublimation, his late work, focuses on how we humans emerge from being blended into the natural surroundings as elements of nature and wrest the development of our egos from a struggle against a return to the womb of where we came from. This is a potentially profoundly archaically gendered inner world, if it is so. Julia Kristeva provides a graphic and more embodied sense of this scenario in her writing about the violence of separation in our wish to remain merged. Her imagery is of the ferocity of birthing and the power of this embodiment (Kristeva, 2014). Loewald's writing about separation, mourning, atonement and reunion is capacious, holding a vision of our very origins within nature. It is like the fruit of the James Webb telescope, as it unfolds our fragility and our origins within the vastness of the universe. Freud speaks of origins in the context of the child's pluripotential sexuality and his "Riddle of the Sphinx" (Freud, 1905, p. 194) as the abiding question of all humans, "Where do babies come from?" or his comment about the unconscious and "the navel of the dream" (Freud, 1900, p. 111). It is within these matrices that our bodies – polarized in their natal biology – become forces within our natural surroundings. We pick up cues, especially from those with similar bodies. Loewald's aim in theory-building about the psyche was to strengthen "symbolic links between the concrete and the abstract" (1988, p. 15). I thus feel encouraged to imagine the interchange of body language, sex and gender as being an integral element of our inter-communicative symbolic expressions toward each other. Are we loved? Admired? Desired? Companioned? Needed? Taunted? Excited? Soothed? Wrestled with? Hugged too close? Thrown out? Can we get breath? Is our breath squeezed out of us by the demands of the other? Who do we look to? Who do we want to be when we grow up? What are they doing that we want to do too? Can I imagine my own offspring? What are these sensations from within our own bodies, our own souls? What do we make of them? Who is a partner? Am I he, she, neither, both or they? Who is this sister? This brother? This aunt? This uncle? Why is she Nona? Or Zeda? What is a cousin once removed?

We grow. We become; we are sexed and gendered. How are we to live – as she, he and they? We will try to multiply ourselves in tune with our current planetary heritage – and how will we do this and nurture the surviving young so that they too can multiply to co-create the earthly illusion[3] of a foreseeable future.

A Dream[4]

At a recent meeting I heard this dream about origins. It was reported to be from the analysis of a male scientist who had a problem younger sister. Hans would have loved it. I can see him sitting across from me, thin legs crossed and tucked neatly; arms on the arm rests; bent slightly forward with a faint smile; hand drooped with his lit cigarette; listening intently; the blue smoke curling contentedly up to the ceiling; his eyes peaceful and far away.

"I was in a room, somewhat like the library stacks, full of old books, but also somewhat like my analyst's office. I seemed to be the only one in the room, but that was not exactly comforting. I wasn't sure I was *allowed* or should be allowed in the room alone, and almost worse, I wasn't completely sure I *was* actually alone. I *did* know that an intense curiosity was piqued. It was partly the books and their possible contents, ancient secrets. And it was also the vaguely threatening possibility of someone else's being in there without my knowing.

[My thoughts, listening…her female body is near, but is he alone? or is she there too? … a resonance with a being "one but not one" at one's beginnings, in the womb].

"About then in the dream, I noticed that there were several books missing from the eye-level shelf, leaving a square shaped opening through which I could see the next set of shelves in the darkened stacks, or perhaps I was seeing into another room. I was looking through this opening with curiosity and foreboding.

[My thoughts, listening: Is this a body memory of preparing for birth, going towards the birth canal, propelled and with "foreboding"?]

"I moved closer to the bookshelf until my face was maybe two feet from the opening when my sister's face suddenly appeared in the opening, as though she had suddenly popped into being behind the shelves."

[My thoughts, listening: She came out of that opening in the mother too...a sense of forced sharing of this tiny space, head first.]

This startled me, and in fear and a resulting burst of aggression, I tried to will her out of existence. I thought of grabbing a pencil or a ruler and trying to push her away from the opening, but I feared that I would hurt her or somehow come to grief myself in the whole business. Instead, as I furiously tried to will her back whence she came,

[My thoughts, listening: He ferociously wants to shove her out. He is possessive of this enclosure. It is *his* way out – and *she's* blocking the way by being there. He desperately is controlling his expelling rage and turning it to mental power – to "will" her away – to use magic and mentalized power and phallic objects urgently to get rid of this female. Perhaps this is also the threat of his own desire to *be* her, to be female. He can overcome this by will power].

I succeeded in waking up. It seemed that it was the startle that had given rise to my fear and the impulse to repel her. When I woke up, I felt oddly soothed, though, that it had only been my sister in the room and that no harm had come to anyone.

[My thoughts, listening: He got rid of the impingement of femaleness. He is "soothed." He does not have to be a woman, give birth, have a child struggling out of him, expel a baby if he is aware he is equipped only with "a ruler." He has not harmed his male selfhood. He is safe from these experiences, in charge of and pleased to be reunited with his ruler. He can stay in the womb if he wants or get out. She never managed to get back in and compete for space. He creates his "rule" with his mind and his library, without needing the use of undue deadly force. The scientist can sublimate and create his world also for the participation of others.]

As Loewald concluded about the "psychoanalytic work that analyst and patient do together," in the Epilogue to his Sublimation book, we are engaged in "[S]ublimation in action" (1988, p. 519).

Notes

1 Gerald Fogel (personal communication, and letter, circa 1991 or 2, in the Loewald archive at Yale) introduced Loewald to Laplanche and his writing. They then had a brief exchange of letters, with HL sending a paper and reading a book by JL.
2 Some say this patient was Freud's wife, Martha (Skues, 2017).

3 Loewald writes that "being deceived about the reality of something is central to illusion" (1988, p. 70).
4 With thanks to my colleague, Oscar Hills, MD.

References

Anzieu, D. (1987/2016). *The Skin-Ego: A New Translation by Naomi Segal.* London and New York: Routledge.

Balsam, R.H. (2012). *Women's Bodies in Psychoanalysis.* London and New York: Routledge.

Balsam, R.H. (2015a). Oedipus rex: Where are we going, especially with women? *Psychoanalytic Quarterly* 84: 555–588.

Balsam, R.H. (2015b). The war on women in psychoanalytic theory building: Past to present. *Psychoanalalytic Study of the Child* 69: 83–107.

Balsam, R.H. (2017). Freud, the birthing body and modern life. *Journal of the American Psychoanalytic Association* 65: 61–90.

Balsam, R.H. (2018). Response to John Steiner's "overcoming obstacles in analysis: Is it possible to relinquish omnipotence and accept receptive femininity?" *The Psychoanalytic Quarterly* 87(1): 21–31.

Benedek, T. (1970). The psychology of pregnancy. In *Parenthood*, eds. J. Anthony & T. Benedek. Boston, MA: Little, Brown, 137–151.

Bibring, G. (1959). Some considerations of the psychological process in pregnancy. *The Psychoanalytic Study of the Child* 14: 113–121.

Brunswick, R.M. (1940). The pre oedipal phase of libido development. *Psychoanalytic Quarterly* 9: 293–319.

Chodorow, N. (1994). *Femininities, Masculinities, Sexualities: Freud and Beyond.* Lexington: The University of Kentucky Press and London: Free Association Books.

Chodorow, N. (1978) *The Reproduction of Mothering: Psychoanalysis and the Sociology of Gender.* Oakland, New York: U of Cal Press.

Chodorow, N. (2011). *Individualiizing Sexuality and Gender: Practice and Theory* (the Relational Series). London: Routledge.

Freud, S. (1892–1893). *A Case of Successful Treatment by Hypnotism.* Standard Edition, London: Hogarth Press, vol. 1, 115–131.

Freud, S. (1900). *The Interpretation of Dreams.* Part 1. Standard Edition, London: Hogarth Press, vol. 4, 1–338.

Freud, S. (1905). *Three Essays on the Theory of Sexuality.* Standard Edition, London: Hogarth Press, vol. 7, 123–246.

Freud, S. (1908). *On the Sexual Theories of Children.* Standard Edition, London: Hogarth Press, vol. 9, 205–226.

Freud, S. (1933). *Femininity.* Standard Edition, London: Hogarth Press, vol. 22, 112–135.

Kristeva, J. (1974/1984). (Translated into English) *Revolution in Poetic Language* (European Perspectives Series) Margaret Waller (Translator), Leon S. Roudiez (Introduction). New York: Columbia University Press.

Kristeva, J. (2014). Reliance, or maternal eroticism. *Journal of the American Psychoanalytic Association* 62(1): 69–85.

Kulish, N. and Holtzman, D. (2008). *A Story of Her Own: The Female Oedipus Complex Reexamined and Renamed.* Northvale, NJ: Jason Aronson.

Laplanche, J. (2015). *Between Seduction and Inspiration: Man Translated and with an Introduction by Jeffrey Mehlman.* New York: The Unconscious in Translation.

Lee, B. and Weston, R. (1934). "With H\er Head Tucked Underneath her Arm." https://genius.com/Stanley-holloway-with-her-head-tucked-under-her-arm-lyrics (accessed October 3, 2022).

Loewald, H. (1960). On the therapeutic action in psychoanalysis. *International Journal of Psychoanalysis* 41: 16–33.

Loewald, H. (1978). *Psychoanalysis and the History of the Individual*. New Haven, CT and London: Yale University Press.

Loewald, H. (1979). The waning of the oedipus complex. *Journal of the American Psychoanalytic Association* 27: 751–775.

Loewald, H. (1988). *Sublimation: Inquiries into Theoretical Psychoanalysis*. New Haven, CT: Yale University Press.

Ogden, T. (2006). Reading Loewald: Oedipus reconceived. *International Journal of Psychoanalysis* 87(Pt 3): 651–666.

Raphael-Leff, J. (1986) Facilitators and regulators: Conscious and unconscious processes in pregnancy and early motherhood. *British Journal of Medical Psychology* 59(Pt 1): 43–55.

Skues, R. (2017). Who was the 'Heroine' of Freud's first case history? Problems and issues in the identification of Freud's patients. *Psychoanalysis and History* 19: 7–54.

Stern, D. (1995). *The Motherhood Constellation: A Unified View of Parent–Infant Psychotherapy*. New York: Basic Books.

Chapter 10

Why Mourn?

Lawrence Levenson

Introduction

"He wonders if this is the most important book he's ever written. Not because it will make his fortune. But because it will save his life." Helen MacDonald is referring to the British writer T.H. White and an obscure book about training a hawk that he wrote many years before his famous King Arthur novels. But the reader of MacDonald's memoir *H is for Hawk*, coming to these sentences (MacDonald 2014, p.123), knows that MacDonald is thinking of herself and her book as well. Deep in grief over her father's sudden death, her life in ruins, she follows White's lead and acquires a hawk to train. In describing her improbable relationship with her hawk, she writes her way into and through her grief over the loss of her father. Her remarkable book brings to life important psychoanalytic insights about mourning that were developed in another remarkable book, Hans Loewald's *Papers on Psychoanalysis*. Observations about loss and mourning in these two books are the subject of this chapter.

Loss

Helen MacDonald's memoir, *H is for Hawk* (MacDonald 2014), opens with Mac-Donald, a single woman in her thirties, standing in a forest early one morning, binoculars in hand, hoping to spot hawks. She waits patiently, and eventually two hawks appear, a male and a female, soaring, dipping, and carving arcs in the vast space above her. After they fly off, MacDonald, tired and content, sits down in the woods and loses herself in a memory of looking for hawks with her father when she was nine years old. Waiting for the birds to come had been hard for a 9-year-old, and she had squirmed and fidgeted. She remembered that her father had then told her about patience.

> He said it was the most important thing of all to remember, this: that when you wanted to see something very badly, sometimes you had to stay still, stay in the same place, remember how much you wanted to see it, and be patient.
>
> (MacDonald 2014, p.10)

DOI: 10.4324/9781003328230-13

MacDonald gets up to leave the woods and notices that she is holding a small clump of reindeer moss. Reindeer moss, she tells the reader, "is patience made manifest. Keep reindeer moss in the dark, freeze it, dry it to a crisp, it won't die. It goes dormant and waits for things to improve. Impressive stuff" (p.11).

Three weeks later, Macdonald is staring at the piece of reindeer moss on her bookshelf when her mother phones her with the news that her father is dead. Macdonald's legs break and buckle, and she is on the floor, listening to her mother explain that there was nothing they could do for him at the hospital, that it was his heart and nothing could be done; and as Macdonald listens to the news that the world she knew is gone for good, she looks at the little ball of reindeer moss, "impossibly light, a buoyant tangle of hard grey stems with sharp, dusty tips and quiet spaces that were air in between them" (p.12).

MacDonald is a published poet, an academic and a naturalist. Her book is an utterly original work that brilliantly braids together many seemingly disparate subjects, but the central and essential subject is loss. Macdonald is deeply attuned to her emotional experiences, and references to Freud, Winnicott, and Klein indicate that she has some familiarity with psychoanalysis. But her book is not an academic treatise on loss and mourning but mourning itself, or, rather, that stage of mourning when a mourner tries to find words, form, and narrative to give coherence to an experience that for a long time is mostly shock and disorientation at the end of language.

MacDonald suffers a great loss when her father dies. Most of us have suffered or will suffer our own great losses. She comes subtly unhinged – most of us do after a great loss. Time passes, and she slowly regains her bearings – again, as most of us do. We know that after a devastating loss, most people do return to the flow of life. But psychoanalysts have yet to spell out very satisfactorily the psychic processes that go into mourning and recovery from object loss and how and why some individuals go on better than others. Loss is fundamental to psychic life, but despite a sizable psychoanalytic literature on the subject, we still have much to clarify about what happens intra-psychically that enables a person, after experiencing a great loss, to return to living a good and rewarding life. MacDonald's memoir is a moving, evocative, exquisitely written, and self-aware account of coming through a painful loss and thus offers a valuable autobiographical record to consider in investigating the internal dynamics in the move from loss to mourning, from despair to acceptance, and from privation to maturation.

MacDonald's father had been a kind man and a good father, and MacDonald had been very close to him. They were similar in many ways. Both preferred watching to doing. Her father had been a photographer for several London newspapers, and MacDonald thinks that having a lens between himself and difficulties in the world had suited his predilection for detachment from the world around him. Both had liked looking up at the sky to spot objects in flight. The father had tracked planes flying over the countryside when he was a boy, and MacDonald loved watching for birds, hawks especially. The connection between them had been very deep, and after his death, MacDonald is unsure who she is without him. She recalls an experiment with chaffinches (p.64). The experiment found that there is a short window of time in which isolated chicks need to hear the elaborate trills of adult chaffinch song. If that window is missed, the chaffinches never manage to produce the birdsong themselves. What makes a chaffinch a chaffinch, MacDonald wonders? Is a chaffinch still a chaffinch if it doesn't produce a chaffinch song? If it is exposed to different adult bird songs and produces that song instead, how do you become who you are? What does it mean to change who you are? MacDonald has heard her father's song, and she has become a lot like him. Who is she now that he is gone? And who will she become? Can allegiances be changed? Would one want to change them?

Anyone who has lost a loved one can relate to such questions and to the ways in which MacDonald feels utterly at sea after her father dies. MacDonald told an interviewer that the title of her book, *H is for Hawk*, refers to learning the alphabet again because, after her father died, she felt as if she had to learn about the world from scratch. She was a chaffinch deeply identified with her father chaffinch, and she suddenly was at a loss about who she was and how to be in a world that, without him, was an entirely unfamiliar world to her. Most survivors of loss can relate as well to the excruciating physical pain of grief that Macdonald vividly describes as "pain worming around my chest like a thing with a million tiny teeth and claws" (p.172). The bereaved can relate, too, to the unbearable presence of absence that Macdonald experiences on a visit to her parents' house (that, she realizes, is her mother's house now): "We sat in chairs that Dad should be sitting in, drank from cups he had drunk from, and when I saw his careful handwriting on a note pinned by the back door it got too much" (p.172). And every grieving person knows the constant ache of forlorn yearning. "I felt a great and simple sadness," Macdonald tells us. "I missed my father. I missed him very much" (p.150).

And most of us who have experienced loss understand making off-kilter decisions that in the moment seem to be exactly what one must do, such as MacDonald's decision to acquire and train a goshawk, the same species of hawk that she had gone to look for in the sky with her father when she was a young girl, and again three weeks before he died of the heart attack. After her father's death, she had had a recurring dream about a hawk that she once cared for at a bird of prey treatment center. When she had taken the hawk outside to release it, the bird had disappeared in seconds, as if it had found a rent in the air and slipped through it. Sometime after acquiring a hawk, MacDonald realizes that she had wanted the hawk because of the fantasy, represented in the dream, that she would be able to fly with a hawk through rents in reality to be reunited with her father. But when she obtains the hawk, she isn't thinking about her motivations. She isn't really thinking; she is trying to see her way forward in a world suddenly made unfamiliar and to cope with a terrible void.

A vast void in one's object world, a self in disarray: "I was in ruins," MacDonald writes (p.85). This is the crisis of grief, and MacDonald's attempt to end the crisis by finding a substitute for the lost object, in Macdonald's case, a hawk, is a common response to the disappearance of someone who has been a central constituent of how one knew oneself and one's world. For a time, a survivor may feel that he or she has brought the lost object back to life in the form of a substitute object. Impotence flips over into omnipotence, despair into giddy hypomania, over the sense that one has found a way to resurrect and restore the lost loved one. Love has transcended reality. MacDonald acquires a hawk, names her Mabel, and falls madly, head over heels, in love with her. Her love for the hawk is passionate and compulsive, fueled by her belief that it has restored and therefore undone the loss of her father. MacDonald disengages from her teaching and scholarly work at Cambridge and shuns social engagements to give herself fully to the bird. She enters a state akin to Winnicott's primary maternal preoccupation, in which her every thought links her with the hawk – what and how much to feed Mabel, what weight to maintain her at, when to hood the bird for naps and night sleep. She is enthralled by the relationship that develops between the two of them. One day, MacDonald playfully tosses a piece of crumbled paper in Mabel's direction, and the hawk, using her beak, tosses it back. The two of them begin to play catch. This is enchanting to MacDonald, all the more so because goshawks like Mabel are notorious for being surly and antisocial.

H is for Hawk is not a book that one would automatically file on the shelf for grief memoirs. While the loss of her father sits at its center, MacDonald's book is also a naturalist's guide to hawks and falconry and a condensed literary biography of the novelist T.H. White, himself a falconer, who in the 1930s wrote a classic account of his feckless efforts to train a goshawk. MacDonald is artful in weaving together her grief for her father, her passion for falconry, and her fascination with White in such a way that each part enhances the others, resulting in a reading experience that is unique and powerful. I suspect that many readers are surprised to find themselves taking an interest in the arcane science of falconry and the tortured, closeted homosexual back story of T.H. White, the now largely disregarded author of *The Once and Future King* and *The Sword in the Stone*. One cares because both subjects, as well as MacDonald's occasional forays into British history and geography, evoke the timelessness of alienation and loss. It seems to be consoling to MacDonald and, in turn, to the reader to recognize that death and loss have always been part of the world.

Still, the reader worries for MacDonald as she prepares Mabel to fly without the long leashes that until then had kept the hawk tied to her while flying. She has always made sure that the leather straps, called creances, that tether her to the hawk were sturdy and secure. When she allows Mabel to fly without the creances, she is testing the emotional lines that have been forming between them. These are, MacDonald writes, "palpable lines, not physical ones: lines of habit, of hunger, of partnership, of familiarity. Of something the old falconers call love" (p.158). She knows this is freighted with symbolism, that the invisible lines to Mabel are lines to her father as well. She thinks of Winnicott's string boy, for whom strings represented a denial of separation, a way of holding tightly to others. MacDonald is relieved and elated, as are we, when Mabel begins to fly without the cords to the tops of tall trees, to distant fields, and to hunt down quarry, faithfully returning to MacDonald's fist. "The hawk flew to me as if I were home," she writes. "It was always a miracle. I choose to be here, it meant. I eschew the air, the woods, the fields. There was nothing that was such a salve to my grieving heart as the hawk returning" (p.135). This indicates to MacDonald that the hold between them is real and alive; and similarly, just beneath the surface, is MacDonald's hold in fantasy for her dead father.

Boundaries disappear for MacDonald. She feels incomplete unless the hawk is in her fist. White had written that for a falconer, the hawk returning to the fist is like a lame man putting on his accustomed wooden leg after it had been lost. MacDonald feels that way, too: "When the hawk was on my fist I knew who I was," she writes. "I'd turned myself into a hawk... I was nervous, high strung, paranoid, prone to fits and terror and rage. I ate greedily or didn't eat at all; I fled from society; hid everything" (p.211). The fusion with Mabel brings her the thrill of archaic, undifferentiated intimacy and the excitement over satisfying primitive bloodthirsty aggression. When she and Mabel go hunting, she feels herself fully with Mabel – of Mabel – as the hawk tears into and consumes the flesh of rabbits, pheasants, and chickens. "By skillfully training a hunting animal, by closely associating with it," Macdonald writes, "you might be allowed to experience all your vital, sincere desires, even your bloodthirsty ones, in total innocence."

But gradually, there is a turn in MacDonald's relationship with the hawk. The magic of merger wears off, and the high gives way to depression. The days spent hunting animals with Mabel while avoiding contact with people became dark for her. She has no partner, no child, and no career prospects. She goes to a psychiatrist, who comforts her and prescribes medication, and soon she is feeling better. She wants to be with people again: "Hands are meant to hold other hands" (p.218). Hands are not meant only as perches for hawks. She had reached out a hand to the psychiatrist, and he had extended a hand back.

A different perspective on her relationship with Mabel begins to take shape for Macdonald. One day, after she and Mabel have hunted down a rabbit, MacDonald, disturbed by the rabbit's suffering, thinks, "The borders between life and death are somewhere in the taking of a meal. I couldn't let that suffering happen. Hunting makes you animal, but the death of an animal makes you human" (p.196). Unlike a hawk, which is all animal desire, a human is more than just desire. A human has a conscience. Borders now begin to come into view for MacDonald: between animal need and conscience, hawks and humans, death and life, her father, and herself. For psychoanalysts tracking MacDonald's evolving psychological state, another border begins to come into view as well: the border between loss and internalization.

Mourning and Internalization

No psychoanalyst mined the border between loss and internalization more searchingly than Hans Loewald (Loewald 1980). For Loewald, on one side of the border, the side of loss, was privation, depression, and the urge to deny the loss by seeking out substitute objects; on the other side, the side of internalization, lay acceptance of loss, responsibility for the self and novel object relations: more life. And the activity that established the boundary between loss and internalization was mourning.

Loewald never wrote a paper specifically on mourning. One could fairly say that instead he contributed an entire corpus on the subject – an entire psychology even – inasmuch as he viewed mourning as a driving force in psychic development. In his paper, "On Internalization," he spoke of "an inner life.... made necessary by the loss of objects" (1980, p.70), and throughout his writings, he posited that an inner life with structures and secondary process mentation and a differentiated self in relation to differentiated objects come about from loss, mourning, and internalization. Development throughout the life cycle is a story of loss, mourning, and internalization; fixations in development occur when conflict interferes with mourning and internalization.

Loewald's writings about the Oedipus complex constitute his most extensive consideration of the centrality of mourning and internalization for psychic development. The Oedipus complex is about love and hate and their vicissitudes, but it is also very much about loss. The incestuous object that the child has come to love must be given up, and how the child responds to this loss will have significant implications for the child's psychological situation going forward. Will the child repress the loss or mourn it? If he represses the loss, then the child will not have made use of the loss, instead remaining unconsciously bound to and burdened by the lost object. When he forms libidinal attachments to other objects, they will not be truly new objects but substitutes for the repressed incestuous object. His object relations will be haunted by the ghosts of unmourned, unconscious infantile relations.

If, on the other hand, the child accepts the loss, he can mourn the object, opening the way for internalization of the object relationship. Loss of the object is then made up for in gain in structure through internalization, which reduces the sense of painful external deprivation. Internalization is a part of mourning and, as such, a healthy alternative to repression in dealing with the pain of object loss. Internalization, like identification, begins as a defense against object loss. But with object loss, as with so much else in psychic life, there is the thinnest of lines between defense and growth, and internalization undergoes a change of function, becoming a positive achievement, an activity of advancement and expansion for the psyche, rather than defensively restrictive of psychic development. Internalization of mourned objects is how the mind becomes a more autonomous mind, how it acquires structure and higher organization, and how it may be continually enriched throughout life.

For the Oedipal child to mourn the object, he must sense, however obscurely, that the separation from his love object, while a deprivation, also carries the potential of emancipation and growth. Then the child will experience the separation not only as a heartbreaking defeat – the loss of the object because of the boundary against incestuous relations – but also as a gain in beginning to assemble a structured, autonomous self. His grief over the loss will be mitigated by his sense that he is coming into being as an individual. He is coming into being because, as he separates from objects, he is bringing elements of the objects into himself.

There is nothing simple or benign about mourning and internalization. In writing about the Oedipus Complex, Loewald observed that during the Oedipal struggle, "... significant emotional ties with the parents are severed. They are not simply renounced by force of circumstance, castration threats, etc. they are also actively rejected, fought against, destroyed" (1980, p.388). And, he goes on:

> ...it is no exaggeration to say that the assumption of responsibility for one's own life and its conduct is in psychic reality tantamount to the murder of the parents, to the crime of parricide, and involves dealing with the guilt incurred thereby.
>
> (p.389)

A page later:

> In an important sense, by evolving our own autonomy, our own superego, and by engaging in non-incestuous object relations we are killing our parents. We are usurping their power, their competence, their responsibility for us, and we are abnegating, rejecting them as libidinal objects.
>
> (p.390)

Oedipal defeat makes possible, if things go well, the movement towards Oedipal emancipation.

Mourning, then, draws upon aggressive energy. When an object is internalized, it loses its character as an object in becoming part of the subject's ego. The child who rejects/fights against/destroys/kills/murders/usurps the parental objects is doing so because he has been able to grasp that in the separation of loss is also separateness of self, the beginning of responsibility for oneself, and a move towards a more structured, differentiated self. His cathexis of his objects is made over into the cathexis of his developing self: object cathexis into narcissistic cathexis. Loewald compares the fate of the object in internalization to non-objective art, "where there is a destruction of the object and of ordinary relations and a reconstruction following new principles of structures" (p.70). This transformation of object into ego results in further ego differentiation and richer self-organization. In internalization, "the ego opens itself up, loosens its current organization to allow for its own further growth" (p.75). Internalization is structure-building. Mourning, we might say, is an act of creative destruction.

Internalization is at once an act of destruction of the object, qua object, and an act of mastering the guilt over the act of destruction by taking elements of the object into the ego and superego. Mastery of guilt is achieved not by repression and self-punishment but by a reconciliation of conflicting strivings – the striving for emancipation and the striving for merger with the object – in the one and same act of internalization. This mastery of guilt and of the aggression that incurs guilt is the active side of internalization. Acceptance of the loss of the object and acceptance of the object into the self as a constituent of the self are the passive sides of internalization. Passive-receptive, incorporative instinctual processes are probably involved here and perhaps account for the moments of elation that, oddly, are part of mourning. Internalization as the essential process in intrapsychic formation may be a sign, Loewald suggests, of man's affirmative acceptance of "femininity" in that the ego opens itself up to allow for its own further growth. In internalization, an individual is both responsive to the loss of objects and responsible for the increasingly autonomous self that is the result. "The self, in its autonomy is an atonement structure, a structure of reconciliation," Loewald declares, "and as such a supreme achievement" (p.394).

The mourning of the Oedipus complex is the prototype for the mourning that occurs throughout the course of life. In developmental mourning, beginning with Oedipal mourning, the external object being mourned is often present and can play a helpful role in the child's mourning process. The adolescent child's mourning, for example, is facilitated if the parent accepts being rejected and diminished because the parent understands the developmental importance of separation for the child. Grief and guilt will be mitigated and thus bearable for the child who discovers that the external objects being mourned – as incestuous objects, as parental authority – have not only not resisted being mourned but are now available to enter into new object relations with the child. "What will be left if things go well," Loewald says, "is tenderness, mutual trust, and respect, the signs of equality" (p.390).

With the death of a love object, the external object relationship is lost permanently. The external love object is not present to assist in the mourning or available to enter into new object relations with the survivor. In the early stages of bereavement, the survivor may feel a heightened awareness of and attachment to the internal object, reflecting an internal denial that the object is gone. This heightened attachment to the internal object jarringly co-exists with the survivor's awareness that the external object is gone. The contradiction between the hyper-cathexis of the internal object and the absence of the object in external reality may account for the visual and auditory hallucinations of the external object that are common occurrences in the weeks and months after a loss. It may also explain why, for a long time after a death, a survivor has difficulty believing that the love object actually is gone and why many mourners, Joan Didion in her excellent book *The Year of Magical Thinking*, among them, describe grief as a form of psychosis (Didion 2007).

Grieving becomes mourning when the survivor begins the psychological work of mourning the internal object. When mourning is resisted, the survivor holds onto the internal relationship in a melancholy way – melancholy because the relationship is deadened now that there is no longer any sensory contact with the external object to refresh, enliven, and move the internal relationship. As painful as melancholia is, it is the path chosen by a survivor when the alternative, giving up the internal relationship in the act of mourning, is felt to be more than the survivor can bear. There is probably always a mix of melancholia, holding on to the object relationship, and mourning, relinquishing the internal object and bringing it into the structure of the self through internalizing processes, in the response to loss; which of the two predominates, melancholy or mourning, will determine how a survivor comes through the loss.

Conflict and resistance are inevitable in the mourning process given that instinctual energies, object-destroying aggression and object-accepting incorporative receptivity, are activated; given that despair over object loss is the primary affect state for long stretches; and given that self as well as object is lost in the re-constitution of self that mourning brings about (no one is ever the same after a great loss). The question, then, is not whether there will be conflict and resistance in mourning, but whether and how the mourner will go about the work of mourning in such a way that conflict and resistance can be recognized and dealt with. In this respect, mourning is no different from every other intra-psychic activity.

Even absent conflict, it is not self-evident that a person would choose mourning over melancholia, or even over madness. This is the mourner's dilemma: why mourn? Why let go of an object to which one has formed deep instinctual and loving attachments, often so deep that much of one's love life and instinctual life have come to seem inextricably tied to that person, often so deep that self and object have become an indivisible unit? I think many mourners at some point do ask themselves how they are managing to go on without their beloved, how they are not merely staying alive but living again, and how it could happen that side by side with a vast void they also feel in some ways more than they were before the loss. Mourning is a terrible, deeply painful affliction, but it is also an aptitude, and a puzzling aptitude at that. It isn't that the survivor is puzzled by lack of guilt, for he may still have guilt, or by no longer yearning for the beloved, for he may still have yearning; he is puzzled that guilty or not, yearning or not, he does want life and is able to mourn to have more life. These are questions about what drives us to go on, what urges mourning to go forward, and what enables us to release a loved one who has become as essential to us as our beating hearts. The answer must lie in Freud's late conceptualization of Eros as a fundamental instinctual force, which Loewald helpfully clarified was a force for integration, for binding together, for internalization – a force for more and richer life.

MacDonald's story points to an important ally in this difficult work of mourning, and that ally is transference. Loewald stated that the resolution of the Oedipal mourning, and the structuralization that ensues, enables the individual to mourn objects in later life without the involvement of the external objects being mourned. But interaction with other cathected external objects is helpful, and arguably essential, for mourning to go forward. After the death of a love object, the corresponding internal object relationship for the survivor is under duress. And under duress, it becomes an "active" internal relationship and tends to be displaced into other contexts and other object relationships as transferences. If the individual is in therapy, the work of mourning can be lived through in the transference relationship with the therapist. Or the internal object relationship with the deceased can emerge in other relational contexts, in a relationship with other family members, close friends, mentors, authority figures, or, even, with non-human objects such as a hawk, where, if circumstances are propitious and the individual is emotionally aware enough, the work of mourning can proceed.

Reading MacDonald's story, one gets the feeling that the fact that the transference object was a hawk – not another human, not another mammal even – gave MacDonald the license to go all the way, go wild, in her grieving. There is a quality of the wild archaic in her identificatory merger with the hawk and in the primitive oral sadism of hunting with it. Merging with Mabel actualized Macdonald's wish to merge with and thus hold onto her father; hunting with her provided an arena for expressing in action the oral aggression that is the instinctual component of internalization Where she most wants to go is to her father, expressed in the fantasy that if she identifies enough with the hawk, she will magically acquire hawk's mythic ability to slip through the rents in this world and fly to the otherworld to reunite with him.

But then there is that turn in her transference to Mabel that signals a turn from melancholia to mourning in her relations with her father. Mabel has not left her after she was allowed to fly free; if she had, it would have been a catastrophic repetition of her father leaving her. Instead, the relationship that has formed between them constitutes tight and dependable lines that keep MacDonald and Hawk bound together. And as that alliance makes sudden, re-traumatizing loss less of a concern, MacDonald is able to feel the melancholy in the invisible lines that are tying her to a bloodthirsty raptor and to a dead father. They are lines of love, but even lines of love, especially lines of love, may hold a person captive and must be reconciled with the press for separateness and individuation. In her melancholy, Macdonald goes to a psychiatrist, who prescribes medicine, and the melancholy lifts. In asking for and receiving help from a person instead of continuing to rely on her entwined, exclusive attachment to the hawk – to her father – MacDonald chooses light over darkness, life over death, and mourning over melancholia. She has formed a relationship with Mabel that, as psychoanalysts, we recognize as a transference relationship in which the dynamics of mourning for her father have been lived out and, in time, reflected upon and worked through. As MacDonald loosens her tie to Mabel and begins to develop relationships with people again, she also loosens her tight hold on her father (and his hold on her) and can now mourn him. MacDonald's capacity to create and use transference in order to live out and work through her mourning for her father reminds us that transference, far from being a manifestation of pathology, is a vital ego function in which the ego constructs an externalized relational context for growth and conflict resolution (Bird 1972). Transference, like any ego function, may become distorted by pathology, and loudly express pathology, but transference is also a powerful force for change and growth.

Mature Object Relations: A Differentiated Union

Mourning and the internalization processes central to it establish borders between oneself and one's objects. Mourning and internalization are boundary-making and differentiating processes that result in enhanced separateness between self and other. Archaic states of merged, undifferentiated object relations, such as MacDonald had with her hawk, are always present to some degree as a dimension of object relations but are generally overshadowed and checked by more mature levels of relating. Loewald observed that with separations from love objects, "we may feel that we have received a wound, as though part of oneself has been torn off, a part that was strongly cathected with a kind of cathexis similar to the investment in our own body parts..." (p.82). In an emotional crisis, like the death of a loved one, archaic merger states with substitute objects offer the magic of a reunion with the lost object, and in the throes of terrible, devastating loss, such magic has a strong allure. But at some point, the survivor is faced with the illusory nature of a magical reunion, and when that occurs, deep depression can ensue – or the beginning of true mourning. Indeed, recognizing that one has been under the spell of the magic of reunion with the lost beloved may mark the beginning of true mourning. "I'd wanted to follow [the hawk], fly with it, and disappear," MacDonald writes.

> I had thought for a long while that I was the hawk – one of those sulky goshawks able to vanish into another world, getting high in the winter trees. But I was not the hawk, no matter how much I pared myself away, no matter how many times I lost myself in blood and leaves and fields. I was the figure standing underneath the tree at nightfall, collar upturned against the damp, waiting patiently for the hawk to return.
>
> (p.219)

And a few pages later:

> I'd wanted to slip across the borders of this world into that wood...Some part of me that was very small and old had known this, some part of me that didn't work according to the everyday rules of the world but with the logic of myths and dreams. And that part of me had hoped, too, that somewhere in that other world was my father.
>
> (p.220)

We hear in these sentences that MacDonald is beginning to understand the extent to which she had been ruled by primary process and wishful fantasy – the fantasy that fusion with the hawk would mean reunion with her father – in order to resist the arduous, painful task of mourning. Recognizing the fantasy begins the process of differentiation from the hawk (she is not the hawk but the figure standing underneath the tree at nightfall, collar upturned) that is also the beginning of differentiation from her father, a differentiation that is the mark of a mourning process.

MacDonald's awareness of her separateness from the hawk continues. "I see...that her (Mabel's) world and my world are not the same, and some part of me is amazed that I ever thought they were" (p.234). After having been inseparable from the hawk for much of the year, MacDonald goes to the US to be with friends for Christmas and leaves Mabel in the care of other friends in the United Kingdom. As her memoir comes to its conclusion, MacDonald installs Mabel at an aviary to be tended to during the molting season. She will drop all her feathers, one by one, and grow new ones. When they see each other in three months, she knows that the hawk will have forgotten her. They will need to build their relationship anew. "Everything changes. Everything moves," MacDonald writes (p.279). But now, for MacDonald, this is an enlivening and not a melancholy prospect. She has a more developed love for Mabel in recognizing Mabel as a hawk with its own hawk reality and nature and fate. MacDonald has made a hawk into her Mabel and will continue to do so, but she also celebrates the hawk's independent existence outside of MacDonald's omnipotent-magical control. "Now," MacDonald says of her relationship with Mabel at the end of her memoir, "...we share our lives happily in all their separation" (p.275).

Sharing lives happily in all their separation: Loewald lamented the inadequacy of the psychoanalytic theory of mature object relations even as he contributed some important ideas on the subject. If one is able to mourn lost objects, Loewald argued, the internalization of elements of the lost object relationships transforms not only the self in the direction of further internal differentiation and higher organization, it also raises object relations to a new level, a level characterized by enhanced differentiation between self and other in which there is separateness but with higher, more mature intimacy in the separateness. Union in differentiation, he called it. Sharing lives happily in all their separation, MacDonald calls it. That's what mourning and internalization bring: an enriched self and enriching object relations, not only in permanent separations like death but also in the separations and losses that occur with our objects all through life.

All of these gains from internalization are born of the loss of a beloved person, and as compelling as it is to think of the self as an atonement structure, a structure of reconciliation, as consoling as it is to think of internalizing elements of the lost object as enhancing of our selves and our future relations – after all, what could give greater comfort to a survivor than to see his future flourishing as memorial activity for his lost beloved – there is no evading the brute fact of the loss of someone deeply loved. And perhaps the hardest part of all is that we fear that by letting the object go, not only are we losing them, we are allowing the dead to lose us as the ones who have been keeping them alive. The only way they remain alive, we believe, is by remaining alive to us. In the most famous passage in the Loewald canon, Loewald writes:

> The transference neurosis, in the technical sense of the establishment and resolution of it in the analytic process, is due to the blood of recognition, which the patient's unconscious is given to taste so that the old ghosts may reawaken to life. Those who know ghosts tell us that they long to be released from their ghost life and led to rest as ancestors. As ancestors they live forth in the present generation, while as ghosts they are compelled to haunt the present generation with their shadow life. Transference is pathological insofar as the unconscious is a crowd of ghosts, and this is the beginning of the transference neurosis in analysis; ghosts of the unconscious, imprisoned by defenses but haunting the patient in the dark of his defenses, are allowed to taste blood, are let loose. In the daylight of analysis the ghosts of the unconscious are laid and led to rest as ancestors whose power is

taken over and transformed into the newer intensity of present life, of the secondary process and contemporary objects.

(p.248)

This passage is in The Therapeutic Action of Psychoanalysis, a brilliant, long, and demanding paper, but at the beginning of this paragraph, the tone for just a moment turns slightly playful and comforting. Loewald speaks of ghosts as if they really exist and as if some people really know them: "Those who know ghosts..." And why is he telling us that our ghosts yearn to be released by us from their ghost life? A guess is that Loewald, understanding that perhaps our greatest dread when it comes to mourning is that if we let go of our loved ones, we are abandoning them to oblivion, adopts a kindly, reassuring tone here to help us over that hurdle in mourning our objects. The fact that ghosts turn into ancestors has become one of the best-known metaphors in psychoanalysis, suggesting that Loewald captured something deep and important about mourning in this passage.

When we successfully mourn objects, we release them but do not lose them. We release them from the grip of our fantasies about them that had held them tightly to us – tightly, but as need satisfying internal fantasy objects, as ghosts. In releasing our lost objects, we are able to see them, perhaps for the first time since they became our love objects, as individuals who all along had been someone else and something more than one of our objects. We release them from their shadow lives as our fantasy objects, as our ghosts, and give back to them the integrity of their status as individuals separate from us. As we individuate our mourned objects, we are individuated from them, in a reciprocal process that is the thrust of mourning. Mourning is a process that releases the object; otherwise, the object is lost but not relinquished, a ghost continuing to haunt the survivor. With mourning and the release of the object, the mourner enters into a new relationship with his lost object in which the object is remembered and loved, remembered as a singular person who entered and enriched the life of the mourner, and loved as a singular person who loved the mourner in his singularity.

Conclusion

In a postscript, MacDonald tells of a visit she made after finishing the book to the cottage where White wrote his book, The Goshawk, in the 1930s. There, she sees White. He is planting his beloved geraniums in the garden. She sees him for just a second and then comes back to reality and to secondary process thinking and sees a man, a stranger, in a white shirt bowed over the ground, probably the gardener for the cottage. "For a moment," MacDonald writes,

that old desire to cross over and bring someone back flared up bright as flame.... But then I put that thought aside. I put it down, and the relief was immense, as if I had dragged a half-tonne weight from myself and cast it by the grassy road.

(p.283)

For a moment, she has swayed over to conjuring her lost object – White, her father, her younger self – just for a moment and then she is back on this side of reality and immensely relieved. But in all likelihood, for the rest of her life, there will be such moments of haunting that will be very hard yet in their way also very tender.

Our deceased objects don't come back to us. And there is no flying to them, either. But they are with us always in our mourning for them. Unmourned, they are lost, dead objects that we are trying futilely to resuscitate in a melancholy way. When we are able to mourn them, we mourn them forever and sorrowfully, but not in a melancholy way, rather in a way that animates, even if sorrowfully, our tie to them and fills us with gratitude and enduring love for him or her, even if, always, sorrowfully.

When she was 9, MacDonald's dad had explained patience.

> He said it was the most important thing of all to remember, this: that when you wanted to see something very badly, sometimes you had to stay still, stay in the same place, remember how much you wanted to see it, and be patient.
>
> (p.10)

At the book's end, she reflects, "My father's talk of patience had held within it all the magic that is waiting and looking up at the morning sky" (p.267). Looking patiently into the morning sky as a 9-year old, MacDonald saw amazing birds, planes, and all sorts of magical wonders. MacDonald comes back to patience at the end of her story because she has discovered that there is magic if one is patient in the face of shattering loss as well.

Late one night, MacDonald is looking through notebooks her father kept as a boy during World War II, where he carefully recorded the names and numbers of planes that he had spotted in the sky. The records remind MacDonald of her childhood obsession with hawks, and suddenly her father seems very close to her. When she puts the notebook back on the shelf, she notices a piece of brown cardboard. Turning it over, she notices a silver door key taped to the cardboard and these words written in pencil: Key to flat. Love, Dad. It is a copy of the key to his flat that he had made for her. MacDonald holds the cardboard and feels its scissor-cut edge. "And," MacDonald writes,

> for the first time I understood the shape of my grief. I could feel exactly how big it was. It was the strangest feeling, like holding something the size of a mountain in my arms. You have to be patient, he had said. If you want to see something very much, you just have to be patient and wait. There was no patience in my waiting, but time had passed all the same, and worked its careful magic. And now, holding the card in my hands and feeling its edges, all the grief had turned into something different. It was simply love. I tucked the card back into the bookshelf. 'Love you too, Dad,' I whispered.
>
> (p.268)

References

Bird, B. (1972). Notes on Transference: Universal Phenomenon and Hardest Part of Analysis. *Journal of the American Psychoanalytic Association* 20: 267–230.

Didion, J. (2007). *The Year of Magical Thinking.* New York: Vintage Books.

Loewald, H. (1980). *Papers on Psychoanalysis.* New Haven: Yale University Press.

MacDonald, H. (2014). *H Is for Hawk.* New York: Grove Press.

Chapter 11

When the World Looms Large

The Drive to Develop in Adolescence and Analysis[1,2]

Matthew Shaw

When the World Looms Large: The Drive to Develop in Adolescence and Analysis

During the first summer of the pandemic, the parents of a 13-year-old I'll call Lulu contacted me. They described a bright, previously well-behaved teenager who "has disappeared emotionally." Her parents said, "It's like the whole world fell away. All she has is her bedroom and whatever goes on in there." Lulu had become anxious and avoidant, irritable and withdrawn, barely ate, and stopped studying. She avoided school as the pandemic emerged and, over time, completely refused to attend classes. With the start of the new school year weeks away, Lulu cut herself on her arm with the blade from a pencil sharpener. Lulu and her parents, like so many families during the pandemic, were in crisis.

The entirety of Lulu's analysis occurred during COVID. Although pandemic pressures have spared no one, they have impacted adolescents in a particularly pervasive manner. With one foot in home life and one in the larger world, adolescents have felt the tension in both realms and the ruptures that arise between the two. The broader world they are entering seems strained and threatening. Lulu regularly spoke about the pandemic, the racial strife and economic disparities it exacerbates, and climate crises and authoritarian surges that led her to worry about what comes next. At a stage when a secure and flexible family life enables explorations beyond the home, Lulu described her immigrant parents scrambling to home-school her two younger siblings, worrying about salaries and recessions, and fearing for their health. Neither home nor the outside world seemed sturdy to her.

Perhaps most consequential to adolescents like Lulu, the movement from home into the world and back again has often been restricted and regulated during the pandemic. Masks, rapid and not-so-rapid tests, and mandated isolation periods rigidify these movements. Teens' attempts to play with different identities, explore outside relationships, and search for liveliness and cohesion beyond their families have often been fraught. An elder in Lulu's parish was infected with COVID, hospitalized, and died. Members of the congregation worried that she contracted the virus interacting with the church's youth group. Life with others could be lethal.

DOI: 10.4324/9781003328230-14

From one vantage point, the pandemic, recent social strife, and accumulating climate crises represent a categorically different context for today's teens, profoundly altering the broader world into which they are entering and restricting the flexibility and freedom by which they transition between the two. On the other hand, threatening historical eras are far from rare. The present circumstances highlight a more common aspect of adolescence that transcends the contemporary context.

Throughout her analysis, Lulu has shown me that she is not simply navigating an individual identity crisis. She is not questioning merely, *Who am I?* She also urgently asks, *What kind of world is this? What is my world?* Her answers shift and slide, deepen and flatten moment to moment. I have searched for ways to think about Lulu's relationships to her broader world of objects and what they reveal generally about adolescence. In so doing, I have returned repeatedly to Hans Loewald's writings. Although numerous contemporary psychoanalysts address similar concerns, Loewald does so with a rigor, clarity, and delight that I find particularly orienting. In this chapter, I will describe his developmental theory, provide vignettes from my work with Lulu, and argue for a developmental sense of the world of objects that is particularly prominent during adolescence and has been acutely impacted by the pandemic.

Before training as a psychoanalyst, Loewald studied intensely with the philosopher Martin Heidegger, and although Heidegger's affiliation with the Nazis ended their relationship, his thinking shaped Loewald's approach to the evolution of concepts and phenomena for the rest of his life (Lear, 2000, Preface, xlii–xliii). Loewald sees the individual's evolving relationship to reality, the psychological composition of reality itself, as central to development (Chodorow, 2003, 898). As the subject grows into a more differentiated and complex entity, so does her relationship to her world of objects. Reality is not merely a fixed given to which the self adapts and masters. Rather, subject and object, self and world, evolve in tandem (Lear, 2012, 7). For Loewald, the infant's mind originally emerges from a primal density he calls the maternal-infant matrix. Although Bion, Winnicott, and others have emphasized the movement from undifferentiated to differentiated states, Loewald does so with the greatest conceptual precision I have read.

In describing why Loewald is his favorite analyst to read, Stephen Mitchell uses the Big Bang to discuss the maternal-infant matrix:

> Like contemporary cosmology, it begins with a primal density in which all of the features of our everyday world, which we take to be separate, bounded elements, are collapsed in on one another. We begin…with experience in which there is no differentiation between inside and outside, self and other, actuality and fantasy, past and present. All these dichotomies, which we come to think of as givens, as basic features of the way the world simply is, are…complex constructions.
>
> (Mitchell, 1998, 825)

These structures emerge over time slowly and provide parallel forms of arranging experience. Each layer endures. The early condensed configurations provide vitality to the more differentiated, intricate structures superseding them. An increasingly complex psychic cosmos expands and develops and yet somehow holds together. Mitchell continues:

> That original and continuing primal density...operates as "hidden matter," tying together dimensions of experience that only appear to be fully separate, bounded, and disconnected. In fact...psychopathology, most broadly conceived, represents an imbalance between the centrifugal and centripetal forces of mind.
>
> (Mitchell, 1998, 825)

For Loewald, psychosis represents the excessive pull of the primal density such that the distinctions between self and other, inside and outside, actuality and fantasy are lost. Psychosis is not so much a withdrawal of cathexis from the world, as Freud originally claimed, as it is a regression of both self and other, a contraction in which boundaries dissolve and normative distinctions disappear. At the other extreme, in neurosis, centrifugal forces separate and isolate these dimensions of the mind. They grow too far apart. Self and other lose access to one another. Inside and outside disconnect, and actuality disengages from fantasy. Loewald thought our technoscientific culture overvalues rationality and independence and in so doing colludes with obsessive, schizoid approaches to the world. He believed this neurotic stance renders the self lifeless and the world meaningless (Loewald, 1952, 30).

Loewald did not discuss in detail the attacks on linking or other means by which psychopathologies arise. For vivid accounts of such ruptures and rigidities, Bion, Klein, and LaPlanche are more helpful. But Loewald wrote vividly about the means by which individuals grow in and out of analysis:

> The less mother and child are one, the more they become separate entities, the more will there be a dynamic interplay of forces between these two 'systems.' As the mother becomes 'outside,' and hand in hand with this, the child an 'inside,' there arises a tension system between the two.
>
> (Loewald, Ego and Reality, 11)

In separating from one another, infant and caregiver turn a primal density into an erotic field. Within this field, each subject has, as Jonathan Lear describes, "an inner potential to develop; and development consists in becoming more complex as it establishes more complicated relations to reality" (Lear, 1996, 680). He goes on to say that "For Loewald, this development should be understood as the reestablishment, at a higher level of organization, of the lost unity of the mother-child dyad" (Lear, 1996, 681).

The process Loewald describes is thoroughly interactive. Using traditional ego psychological language, he says that all levels of the child's and caregiver's minds – Id, Ego, and Superego – are available for interaction and modification (Loewald, 1970, 49). Drives are not constitutionally fixed. The Id is not considered inaccessible to influence. The child becomes a subject through interaction with the more highly differentiated other:

> The child...internalizes the parent's image of the child—an image that is mediated...in the thousand different ways of being handled, bodily and emotionally... as seen, felt, smelled, heard, touched by the mother...The child begins to experience himself as a centered unit by being centered upon.
>
> (Loewald, Therapeutic Action of Psychoanalysis, 19–20)

Loewald describes what he envisions to be the elemental dynamics of development: the formation of a mind through primary internalizations and the early growth that then ensues. These processes extend into adolescence but at much higher levels of complexity, thereby reposing the questions: Who is centering on the teen? What image of the adolescent is being internalized through these interactions, and how do they map onto early configurations?

Anticipating non-linear dynamic systems theory, Loewald envisions the fluctuations that unfold as not only tolerable but also essential to cultivating complexity and coherence (Knight, 2017, 79). The mind expands and contracts with varying degrees of dynamism. Too much intensity, and one surges toward the psychotic core. Too little, and one drifts toward the deadened, neurotic periphery. For Loewald, we are driven by Eros to develop into more intricate entities with ever more complex relations to the world around us.

He argues that the dynamic potential of this erotic field is harnessed in analysis (Brett, 2018, 217). The "psychoanalytic situation and process involves a re-enactment, a dramatization of the patient's life history, created and staged in conjunction with, and directed by, the analyst" (Loewald, 1975, 279), in which both "patient and analyst—each in his own way and on his own mental level—become both artist and medium for each other" (297). He uses the metaphor of the play and sees the transference-countertransference as the stage upon which it is performed. The analyst has many roles, but she manages the actors "not by telling them what to do or how to act, but by bringing out in them what they often manage to express only fleetingly, defensively, haltingly, in inhibited or distorted fashion" (Loewald, 1975, 280). Loewald asserts that transference neurosis is an ideal construct and that therapeutic enactments are partial and shifting but nonetheless cumulative. Within this erotic field, through the analysis of the re-enactment, the mind regains liveliness, complexity, and cohesion.

Loewald recognizes adolescence as a particularly vital stage of development and the one most closely resembling the analytic situation (Loewald, 1975, 283 and 284; Loewald, 1988, 7). Given the emphasis on revisiting and reworking early experiences, the unmistakable dynamism, and the demand to break apart and restore coherence, the adolescent vividly exemplifies the risks, limitations, and possibilities in analysis and development more broadly. I will now return to Lulu and her analysis and eventually describe in some detail two sessions surrounding her Quinceañera, her 15th birthday party. This rite of passage, delayed and altered by the pandemic, became a focal point of the psychic drama unfolding within and around her.

Lulu

Before I met Lulu, her parents told me about the world into which she was born, or as Heidegger would call it, thrown (Heidegger, 2008). Her parents were raised in the same South American country, though they occupied vastly different sociopolitical spheres. Mr. F was wealthier, attended private schools, came from a more cosmopolitan background, and had lighter skin. Mrs. F grew up in a rural, indigenous community, experienced more instability and violence, and has darker skin. Mr. F was thoughtful and kind but could veer into abstract realms when conflict arose. He had relied heavily on his intellect throughout his life. When he and his wife disagreed about some aspect of their home country, he talked about the macroeconomic history of the region. Mrs. F, however, spoke directly and with emotional intensity and responded to his lessons by waving her hand and saying, "No more lectures. Talk!"

The two met at university, began dating, and then Mrs. F dropped out once she became pregnant. Mr. F said his family did not support their marriage because they are "affluent racists who try to hide their prejudices but can't get rid of the smell." His mother refused to throw the customary large, public event and was "silently hostile" during their small, courthouse wedding.

The parents reported that Lulu met all developmental milestones and was verbally precocious. Mrs. F described feeling contented after Lulu's birth; however, she became "darker and darker over time." She ruminated about slights and resentments and became increasingly angry. While preparing dinner one night, she suddenly threw the food and plates across the room.

The family moved to the United States when Mrs. F became pregnant with Lulu's younger sister. Lulu was 4 years old. They found themselves largely alone here. Mr. F worked very long hours, and Mrs. F had multiple depressive episodes. She took to her bed for days and became volatile. She went from vacant to explosive without warning. She suffered deeply, and Lulu quieted, retreated, and hummed to herself.

When Lulu was 7 years old, her younger brother was born. By this time, the family was deeply involved in a local church community and had more support. Mrs. F started psychotherapy at a local Spanish-speaking clinic and began taking an antidepressant. She discussed a series of traumas that she thought explained her "anger, nerves, and dark spells," and she improved considerably. Lulu excelled at their church and in school by being good.

Lulu remains attached to her paternal family in their home country. She stays with relatives without her siblings and parents and calls them regularly. She is particularly attached to her erudite, warm paternal grandfather. They play correspondence chess, form a two-person book club, and exchange letters.

When I first spoke with Lulu via video, I saw a thin, anxious, lighter-skinned girl. She had the same coloring and facial shape as her father, though her nose resembled her mother's. She averted her eyes when speaking. When I asked her why she thought her parents contacted me, she looked away, pulled back her shirt sleeve, and held up her arm. I asked, "What am I seeing?" She described cutting herself, immediately showing a friend, and eventually her mother finding out. I said that I wondered what she was thinking or feeling throughout it all. She shrugged and looked away from the screen, but she seemed to want to talk more openly.

We met four times that first week, and I recommended a five-times-per-week analysis. Her parents seemed immensely relieved for me to focus on Lulu while they managed their packed, pandemic lives: homeschooling; working remotely; and five people "always breathing the same air." It was clear they loved Lulu deeply and were intensely concerned about her.

Lulu immediately took charge once the analysis started. She directed us toward various projects and interacted with me like I was a loving, supportive presence. She taught me how to play correspondence chess. We set up boards in our separate rooms and called moves to one another. I thought she was replicating the feel of her interactions with her grandfather. As we played, she talked about her annoyance with her siblings, her boredom with her summer reading book, and mostly her thoughts about her favorite TV show, High School Musical: The Musical: The Series. The show is a faux documentary about teenagers staging a production of a musical. It centers on a teenager named Nini.

Lulu played chess and talked about Nini throughout the initial two months. She often thought about how Nini doubted herself, felt anxious and uncertain, but worked to be brave. Nini sounded passionate to me. I heard nothing directly about Lulu's school year beginning, her anxieties about attending, or how the transition was going. I linked Nini to Lulu's inner life and our relationship, but not directly to her anxieties about school. One session, I said, "Nini feels so much. When you talk about her, you're reminding me how much you're feeling." She responded, "When Nini's feeling something, she belts out these songs. Powerful songs. When I'm feeling, I go into my room." I said, "Just because you're quiet doesn't mean you lack feelings. I think you have your own powerful feelings." She smiled.

Lulu attended school without absence for the first few months. Her parents were elated but also questioned whether she needed to continue treatment. A counselor from the school asked why they would end something that was working so well.

As Lulu settled into the school year and her analysis, she opened to a larger world. Our cozy retreat began to include others. She and her peers regularly discussed race, gender, class, and sexual identities and interwove these conversations with talk about DJs and clothes. As the presidential election approached, however, these discussions erupted. Whereas the initial months had seemed like reassurance in a world in crisis, this period was markedly more fractious. She called Trump "a racist who hates black and brown people." She said that she cannot even look at his "puffy, red face" and finds his adoring, cheering mobs terrifying. During these moments, she alternated between panic and rage and readily associated to COVID deaths, climate extinction, and racial hatred. It was as if opening to the world led everything to shatter.

I struggled during this period with her as I was in quite a mobilized, anxious state of my own about the election, COVID, and my racial identity. I struggled to hear transference communications amidst the blare of the threatening external world. I tried to stay close to the specific dynamics displayed moment by moment but had trouble experiencing any space in my mind. I consulted with a colleague twice.

In late October, Lulu reported a recent discussion with a Black American classmate who questioned whether White Americans could understand how threatening Trump and his followers are. I said that I wondered if Lulu questioned how much of her experience *I* could understand. She said this classmate asked if I was "one of those White savior people." I said sometimes friends speak our own thoughts. She said she knew I was charging her parents less than usual for her sessions and that Mr. Reynolds (who is also White) helped finance her treatment, and that she was very grateful for the help. I added, "Feeling grateful could make it hard to express other feelings too."

After the election and the jubilation and strife that followed, Lulu mentioned that her darker skinned friend had called her "Blanquita" (*little white girl* in Spanish) when Lulu talked effusively about a soaring love song she liked. Lulu felt ashamed. She discussed being lighter skinned than her siblings and mom, and she said that her mom treated her differently. As Lulu talked about these interactions, I stayed with each one without prematurely generalizing or synthesizing anything; sometimes she emphasized her brownness, sometimes her whiteness. I thought this was an important time for her to play with various identifications.

In mid-February, on a Monday, Lulu talked about missing classes last spring. She revealed a level of panic and misery previously concealed. Tuesday morning, she told her parents that she felt sick and skipped school and her session with me. She did the same the following two days. She then asked me to speak with her parents. They called and expressed concern that she did not seem physically ill and was once again disappearing. I tried to demonstrate that I heard their worries, and I encouraged them to tell Lulu that I thought she was experiencing something important and that she could tell me when she was ready. The parents seemed understandably terrified and furious. I, too, worried that Lulu would keep spiraling and become self-harming, but I also wanted to advocate for space rather than anxiously leaping into action.

During the session that followed, Lulu evoked images of suicide and mental breakdown. She portrayed a fractured, violent inner world in which no caring presence persisted. Lulu no longer treated me solely as a benevolent, grandfatherly figure. She now expressed anger, distrust, and yearning. In the weeks that followed, the actress who played Nini, Olivia Rodrigo, started her music career and released a hit called Driver's License. Lulu talked repeatedly about the emotional pain, anger, and defiance in it. In Lulu's rendering of the lyrics, it sounded like an oedipal ballad. The singer was seduced into believing that her lover would always be there, only to be betrayed as he left for a more mature, blond woman. The pre-Oedipal underpinnings of the annihilating threats of separation were also close at hand, though less obvious.

In May, midway through a session, Lulu tapped her fingers and sang to herself. I said, "You're singing." She responded, "Not really. Just humming." She then told me about Rodrigo's latest single, Déjà vu. She said it's also about heartbreak, and Rodrigo sings it with intensity. I said that I doubted Rodrigo just hummed it. Lulu shook her head and then to my surprise started singing. After a while, she stopped and said she could play the video for me. I said it was so powerful to hear it in her voice. She continued singing but looked away. At the end, I said, "So much feeling." She responded, "Olivia's incredible." She expressed her yearning, eroticism, and dependency on me. She both directed her longing toward me (like I was her beloved) and took great pleasure in being someone who feels deeply (like I was the audience for her passion).

A week later, Lulu looked in some boxes in her attic and found drawings she made over the previous few years. She developed a practice of drawing dense, busy scenes in which she could hide important details without people noticing. In one picture, she drew an elaborate forest with plants, animals, and trees and then hid a Colombian flag in one of the branches because she had a crush on a Columbian professional soccer player. In another drawing, she hid artifacts of her rage.

After Lulu turned 14 years old, her relationship with her parents exploded. Her mother wanted to throw Lulu a big, formal Quinceañera. Lulu explained that "Latin Americans, well, the rich ones," often give their daughters elaborate parties for their 15th birthdays to mark their passage from girlhood to womanhood. She compared them to debutante balls or bat mitzvahs.

The months that followed were tumultuous for Lulu and her parents. They fought over whether to have a Catholic Mass before the event, whether to have the traditional, gender-rigid customs, and where to hold it. Lulu's mother was deeply invested in every detail. She pressed to hold the Quince in a fancy country club and envisioned a grand celebration. Over time, it became clear to Lulu and me, and eventually her mother, that she was treating the Quinceañera as if it were the big, public wedding she was denied. Lulu initially resisted every suggestion her mother made and attacked every detail from a socio-political viewpoint. Lulu eventually expressed her own longing for a gathering that could bridge her South American roots and family connections, and she wished to have a queer-friendly, racially open, personal event. As the months unfolded, I was uncertain whether the Quince would even happen.

During the summer and fall, Lulu became more expressive, assertive, and started swearing and using slang. She often experienced me like she described her father: well-meaning, intellectual, and deferential to her mother. During particularly intense periods, she imagined I judged her a spoiled brat because of her socio-political activism. Occasionally, she wept, talking about how I'm the only person with whom she can talk about her "family side feelings and friend side feelings." Lurking beneath each of these relationships was an amorphous, vacant psychic constellation that only fleetingly and disturbingly emerged.

The vast majority of the analysis has been conducted via video. For three months over the summer and during the time surrounding her Quince, however, Lulu attended in person. The final planning came together surprisingly quickly, and Lulu and her parents collaborated closely. After months of turmoil, they suddenly made decisions and plans. Lulu was excited and nervous as the date approached, and in anticipation of her party, she brought me music to hear and food to taste.

The last session before Lulu's rite of passage was chaotic. She cloaked herself in a black hoody and only emerged to rage at me. She sent and received texts without telling me with whom she communicated and described an overwhelming world, full of harsh, threatening presences: her unreliable, abandoning friends; the morally condemning "pasty, wrinkly" priest; the attacking, racist relatives from Miami; and she alone carrying the massive burden of pacifying everyone. At the center of her worries, she described a mother who was so anxious and angry she could lash out at the people around her if not managed closely. Lulu was convinced the event would be a disaster and that I was not helping her. Staring directly into my eyes, she spoke of burning down the church and cutting her wrists so that the event would be cancelled. I interpreted her immense anxiety and rage in various ways and added that she so deeply wanted her Quinceañera to go well. Over the intervening weekend, I thought of her often and fantasized repeatedly about various calamities.

During the following Monday's session, she arrived in brightly colored clothes. She talked about the priest and her friends warmly, the messy delight in performing a flash-mob dance, and that her greatest complaint was that the empanadas were too dry. Although she listed numerous fears and mishaps, they seemed inconsequential. Her stories gained momentum as she re-immersed herself in the evening. She eventually took me vividly onto the dance floor with her as her friends and family removed their shoes, loosened their ties, and celebrated late into the night. Lulu described watching her mother open sensually to the music. She seemed intimately connected with her mom while also watching from a distance. I thought Lulu seemed both mournful that she was moving away from her parents and loving as she watched her mother bathe in the sounds, eyes closed and head tilted upward. Lulu talked about aching to arrange another Quince now that she knew how to do so. I imagined her planning her own daughter's rite of passage.

She then talked about the transformative arrival of a Bomba band that led everyone to join in rhythmic movement. She described people following the drummers around the tent as they sang and danced. She played with the sounds in session with me as she drummed on her legs and sang out: bomba-bomba-bombadabomba; bomba-bomba-bombadabadabadababomba! I felt as though I could hear the drumming and feel the pulsing in my chest. I silently recalled years ago her imitating a different tune her mother sang when she was young. Her mom had called her Bonbón and would playfully improvise rhymes around it. Lulu had initially remembered it with resentment because of the racial connotations of the dark chocolates and memories of the depressed version of her mother, but more recently she described it with warmth. I spoke the two sounds side by side, "Bomba. Bonbón. Bomba. Bonbón." Lulu delighted in the connection, recalled the childhood rhyme, and played with the sounds together: "Bomba. Bom-bom-bombón. Bomba. Bombadabón. Bombadabón." She again told me the story of her mother's childhood singing. She then surprised us both by bursting into tears as she talked about how important the Quince was for her parents and for her. Sharing this moment was also very important for us. She ended the session by telling me about a boy and their drumming on one another's legs, laughing so hard they nearly spit out their food.

Discussion

Lulu's adolescence started in many ways, like her early childhood. She was thrown into a time of tumult. When Lulu was born, her paternal extended family and mother hated one another. Broader racial, gender, and class antipathies primed them for conflict. Her father struggled to buffer the warring factions. Lulu's mother was intermittently depressed through Lulu's early years and suffered greatly. She struggled to center on Lulu in the way that she wished and Loewald describes as so important.

Lulu also was born into enough love and stability, however, to find her way to a largely neurotic stasis by latency. She became good. She was quiet, helpful, and excelled in church and school. She had little access to anger, yearning, and creativity but felt more stable. She rested on a tolerable but brittle developmental plateau. And so when she was thrown into adolescence, especially during a global pandemic and the vitriol surrounding the election, she retreated to her room and locked the door. As her body and mind changed rapidly, she felt overwhelmed by what arose within her and by a world that too closely resembled a depressed mother living in a bigoted society. When even her locked door failed to quiet her frenzied mind, she cut herself in a desperate attempt to bind the chaotic energy within her. Her parents then brought her to treatment.

With me, Lulu initially reconstructed a retreat in which we could hide, play chess, and interact. It resembled her neurotic solution. In the first act of Loewald's dramatic play, we were both good. After months, she opened to a broader world of objects, and her fragile stability fractured. Old structures crumbled and made way for new possibilities. She became terrified, enraged, and, at particularly intense moments, had greater access to something like psychotic intensity. I named new feelings and fantasies emerging, described the overall experience of shattering, but mostly helped her play the drama within her and between us. Even though I had ideas about what was unfolding, I largely tried to stay close to the disorganized intensity, help her dream her experience at her own pace, and resist the urge to seek premature reassurance through foreclosing formulations. Each in our own way, we felt uncertain, scared, and confused during these experiences and enjoyed the reconnecting and restoring that eventually followed.

Over the analysis, Lulu has endured numerous periods of disintegration: the initial fall when election tensions surged; her later withdrawal from school and treatment; and especially surrounding her Quinceañera. Lulu's Quince has been a nodal point for her and her family: the place where intergenerational, interpersonal, and intrapsychic dramas collided. Lulu's Quince was haunted by her experience of her parents' pasts, her mother's wish to reclaim herself through Lulu, and her father's emotional reserve. It was haunted by her early objects. It also became the stage upon which she played with essential questions of adolescence: *Who am I?* and *What is my world?* Each period of disintegration has been followed by a creative reconstituting at a higher level of complexity. Lulu's world of objects has expanded profoundly.

In the last session before the Quince, although Lulu felt overwhelmed, she did not retreat. Rather, she showed me her anger and yearning with intensity. She immersed me in her suffering and frightened me. She pulled us both from the neurotic periphery toward the vital psychotic core. Unlike the first act, in which we were both good, the second act has been livelier, less predictable, and essential to her (and my) growth.

In the session following the Quince, Lulu showed a more complex and layered psychic constellation. She had reconstituted herself, but now included a wider range of feelings and fantasies. From a more separate stance, she hinted at mourning leaving her parents (and me). I felt a deep, tender sadness as she described watching her mother dancing with her eyes closed, lost in the music. Lulu communicated a complex field of love, hate, hope, and loss.

In perhaps Loewald's most famous lines, he depicts analysis as the gradual transformation of ghosts into ancestors:

> The transference neurosis, in the technical sense of the establishment and resolution of it in the analytic process, is due to the blood of recognition, which the patient's unconscious is given to taste so that the old ghosts may reawaken to life. Those who know ghosts tell us that they long to be released from their ghost life and led to rest as ancestors. As ancestors they live forth in the present generation, while as ghosts they are compelled to haunt the present generation with their shadow life...In the daylight of analysis the ghosts of the unconscious are laid and led to rest as ancestors whose power is taken over and transformed into the newer intensity of present life, of the secondary process and contemporary objects.
>
> (Loewald, 1960, 29)

When Lulu linked the erotic, pulsing Bomba drumming to the early singing of her mother – Bomba and Bonbón – I thought she was doing just that: turning haunting voices into lifegiving rhythms. In so doing, for the first time, she described to me an erotic scene with a potential romantic interest: Stephen and she drumming on one another's legs. For a moment, when she expressed her wish to stage another Quinceañera, I pictured her dancing at *her* daughter's celebration. I imagined her as a lively, loving mother: her world of objects expanded and her openness to the world momentarily restored.

Conclusion

For Hans Loewald, development is dynamic, complex, and fueled by Eros. He does not see individuals simply moving through a linear sequence of psychosexual stages or managing an unfolding series of neurobiological phases. He advocates for the kind of close study that identifies patterns, investigates processes, and hopefully provides more differentiated understandings, but he resists the pull toward static structures and foreclosed systems.

For Loewald, self and other develop through interaction and in tandem. If all goes well, an erotic field arises out of a primal density, and in so doing, keeps the separating parts connected at ever greater distances and in ever more complex configurations. We can imagine this at the cosmological level of the Big Bang, the microscopic site of unicellular organisms becoming multicellular, and within our minds. He claims that there is a drive to develop in living organisms.

Loewald's emphasis on interaction and the centrality of not only the self but the other is particularly useful when considering adolescent development. At a time when individuals urgently ask not only, "Who am I?" but also, "What, who, is my world?" he provides a means for thinking about the world surrounding the teen, the world of objects alive within her, and the dynamic interaction between the two. His developmental approach empowers analysts to think about the complex ways in which race, class, and gender constructs develop, evolve, and impact individuals' growth and stagnancy (Chodorow, 2020, 249). Who is centering on the teen? What images of the world and herself is she internalizing?

For Loewald, a concept, culture, language, or individual is never simply what it is but also what it can and cannot be (Heidegger, 2008). Finding a patient emotionally in the present is also being able to imagine who that patient may grow to be, not in the prescriptive sense of suggestion but rather in an emergent sense of possibility. In using Loewald's notion of futurity, Saketopoulou (2018, 277) writes that the analyst's ability to tune into a child and imagine potential futures for her "has especially potent implications when it comes to trans children because their otherness can often make their futures seem especially tenuous." Loewald challenges analysts to remain creative and recognize the rigidities and failures of imagination that impede development in and out of treatments. In other words, the analyst must develop too.

Toward the end of Loewald's career, he published his last book, *Sublimation*. He begins as follows: "It is a sobering and strangely comforting thought that writing these investigations has been a sublimated way of cleaning and preening myself, like a cat after a meal, or after a frustrating hunt" (Loewald, 1988, ix). The humility in this introduction – that Loewald's career-culminating-writing is rooted in a kind of creatureliness – seems fitting. In order to be open to others, available to surprise, and able to grow, one must acknowledge the place from which one comes and the necessity of revitalizing creativity. To do otherwise is to stagnate and risk psychic deadness. It is to treat life "as a pastime" rather than the meaningful, lively drama it has the potential to be (Loewald, 1975, 281).

The links between this last book, in all its elaborated complexity, and his earliest writings are striking. There is an undeniable coherence. As he described the cycles of disintegration and integration that mark the psychic emergence of self and other decades earlier, he now writes that "sublimation is passion transformed" (Loewald,

1988, 9). Over 82 pages, he argues that sublimation is less of a higher-level defense mechanism than the transformative work by which individuals grow in complexity and coherence. He not only describes but vividly demonstrates the drive toward growth (Loewald, 1988, 12). In the last sentence before the Epilogue, he asks, "Could sublimation be both a mourning of lost original oneness and a celebration of oneness regained?" (Loewald, 1988, 81). The same could be asked of the adolescent navigating her way into adulthood, the analysand working her way through her analysis, and the analyst trying to remain creative and vital over time.

Notes

1 Portions of this chapter were presented for the Beata Rank Lecture at BPSI in November 2022.
2 Thanks to the following psychoanalysts who commented on sections of this chapter: Rosemary Balsam, MD; Elizabeth Brett, PhD; Lawrence Brown, PhD; James Herzog, MD; Lawrence Levenson, MD; Sidney Phillips, MD; and Judith Yanof, MD.

References

Brett, E. (2018). The Play's the Thing: Loewald's Metaphor of the Theater and the Force-Field. *Psychoanalytic Study of the Child*, 71:21–223.
Chodorow, N. (2003). The Psychoanalytic Vision of Hans Loewald. *International Journal of Psychoanalysis*, 84:897–913.
Chodorow, N. (2020). *The Psychoanalytic Ear and the Sociological Eye*. New York: Routledge, 290pp.
Heidegger, M. (2008). *Being and Time*. New York: Harper Collings, 608pp.
Knight, R. (2017). Emerging Adulthood and Nonlinear Dynamic Systems Theory. *The Psychoanalytic Study of the Child*, 70:74–81.
Lear, J. (1996). The Introduction of Eros: Reflections on the Work of Hans Loewald. *Journal of the American Psychoanalytic Association*, 44:673–698.
Lear, J. (Ed.) (2000). *The Essential Loewald: Collected Papers and Monographs*. Hagerstown, MD: University Publishing Group, 579pp.
Lear, J. (2012). The Thought of Hans W. Loewald. *The International Journal of Psychoanalysis*, 93(1):167–179.
Loewald, H. (1951). Ego and Reality. *The International Journal of Psychoanalysis*, 32:10–18.
Loewald, H. (1952). The Problem of Defense and the Neurotic Interpretation of Reality. In *Papers on Psychoanalysis*. New Haven: Yale University Press, 21–32.
Loewald, H. (1960). On the Therapeutic Action of Psycho-Analysis. *The International Journal of Psychoanalysis*, 41:16–33.
Loewald, H. (1970). Psychoanalytic Theory and the Psychoanalytic Process. *Psychoanalytic Study of the Child*, 25:45–68.
Loewald, H. (1975). Psychoanalysis as an Art and the Fantasy Character of the Psychoanalytic Situation. *Journal of the American Psychoanalytic Association*, 23:277–299.
Loewald, H. (1988). *Sublimation: Inquiries into Theoretical Psychoanalysis*. New Haven: Yale University Press, 89 pp.
Mitchell, S. (1998). From Ghosts to Ancestors: The Psychoanalytic Vision of Hans Loewald. *Psychoanalytic Dialogues*, 8:825–855.
Saketopoulou, A. (2018). Holding Futurity in Mind: Therapeutic Action in the Relational Treatment of a Transgender Girl. In: Bonovitz, C. & Harlem, A. eds. *Developmental Perspectives in Child Psychoanalysis and Psychotherapy*. New York: Routledge, 298pp.

Chapter 12

Loewald and Winnicott

Natasha Black and Gil Katz

Introduction

Hans Loewald's ideas are relevant to many of today's psychoanalytic theories and orientations—Winnicottian, Freudian, Relational, Kohutian, and Interpersonal. In his work, Loewald combined and *synthesized* classic drive-defense ego-psychology, object relations, and self-concepts—all developmentally grounded in the early mother-infant matrix.

In this chapter, the treatment of Charlie, presented in a Winnicottian framework by Natasha Black, PhD, is elaborated on and supplemented with the ideas and insights of Loewald's work, brought to it in a discussion by Gil Katz, PhD.

DOI: 10.4324/9781003328230-15

"Charlie"

Natasha Black, PhD

Prelude

Summer 2018. I am emailing my officemate, M, all but begging her to let me put a couch in our office so that I may start my first control case. Aware that my institute does not technically require couch work, I nonetheless found myself attached to providing what I deemed the most optimal conditions for analysis to occur. As it turns out, M is giving up the office and consigning the entire space to me, thereby enabling me not only to purchase my couch but also to rearrange the space, paint the lifeless walls, and bring in my own furnishings to create a consulting room home in anticipation of a particular patient—my analysand—in what I could only appreciate retrospectively as a form of *analytic primary maternal preoccupation*.

Session 1, January 2019. When I open the door to meet Charlie, I see a slender, spectacled man whose callow features betray his 34 years. He eagerly awaits with a wistful smile, his eyes twinkling with innocence. At first sight and without understanding, I am immediately drawn to him, filled with an otherworldly sense that we have been primordially linked in some way and are, at long last, now uniting.

Upon greeting him, Charlie cheerfully, albeit cautiously, rises and meekly steps toward my consulting room, his body hunched over and shrunken in, as if denying his towering stature. Glassy-eyed and palpably anxious, he begins to bemoan his recent breakup and legacy of failed relationships, his fear of vulnerability in the face of an Other that doesn't parasitically need him, and the resultant proclivity to placate others by matching their feeling states—"to create a fake me so that people like me."

Session 2: "I was curious about the couch," Charlie utters, crouching as far away as possible, clinging to his jacket with the fear-laden wonderment of a child. As we explore this option, he asks if he should lie down. I suggest that it's up to him, and almost as soon as the words leave my mouth, he plops into a supine position, his head landing on the footpad of my couch. Surprised at his immediacy, I worry if either one of us is ready for this—my own superego kicking into gear and demanding that I question the propriety of what is happening.

Nevertheless, trying to maintain my equanimity, I point to the pillow just beyond where Charlie's feet rest, and he immediately registers that he has positioned himself backwards—like a fetus ready for expulsion from the womb. Once he's repositioned, we begin. The room is saturated with vulnerability—Charlie anticipating the couch as a dive into the throes of his own mind, consisting of colliding tectonic plates that rest adjacent to one another yet remain disparate and unintegrated—and I, deluged with a sense of enormous responsibility in holding this vulnerable man lying on the couch, opening up about his constant struggle of feeling in the passenger seat of his own life.

Indeed, things just "happen" to Charlie, as if by destiny or at the behest of an old sage in the sky pointing his finger in the direction in which he should travel. Nothing feels real to Charlie—from his accomplishments as a brilliant artist to a sense of his own body—everything is just theoretical or lived through the eyes of a critical observer, controlling his thoughts and hampering his ability to actualize a future. It quickly thus becomes evident that Charlie longs to be told what to do, given the paucity of the psychic interiority needed for a capacity to imagine.

Behind the couch, my mind brims over with apprehensions afluttering when suddenly an image materializes of my own feet submerged in ocean water, the calmness of a halcyon current lulling me into a state of relaxation. Looking around, I see my supervisor and analyst further out in the ocean and recognize the safety net they have developed to keep me and Charlie out of dangerous waters. As the image fades into oblivion, I re-attune to Charlie's mind: He is discussing his family history, having grown up in an Evangelical household in the rural prairieland and becoming privy at an early age to his parents' fiery disputes over their financial precarity. He depicts an engulfing, behemoth mother who, beginning in early life, approached his mistakes in a critical, unsympathetic, and unreflective manner, demonstrating neither recognition nor concern for the workings of his mind. In consequence, her lack of attunement combined with an inattention to her own mercurial inner life would drive her to unprovoked, baleful explosions at Charlie—one time even threatening to shoot him for flunking a math test. Years of bearing his mother's reproachful fits of rage would result in a tendency for Charlie to freeze out of abject fear—his body paralyzing and his ability to think or speak stunned—and, in turn, the development of a psychic structure organized around protecting an inchoate ego against an overwhelming persecutory force that could cause an internal breakdown at any time.

Yet despite her petty cruelty, Charlie held his mother in deep affection, experiencing the good times with her as euphorically blissful. He derived particular enjoyment from making skin-to-skin contact with her, such as when he would sit on her lap and touch all her moles—early sensory experiences that would later be grafted onto the transference.

Charlie's father, by contrast, occupied a relatively benign role in his psychic economy, though he, too, had florid outbursts of rage—Charlie remembering as a child his father twice punching a hole in the wall after coming home in a drunken stupor. Given an environment of inadequate provision (Winnicott, 1971), Charlie learned to adapt by trying to anticipate his parents' desires and radically striving to please them, poignantly stating that at as early as age 3, he felt like he needed to be perfect or else he'd lose his parents' love.

As a result of a tempestuous caregiving milieu, Charlie's internal world teems with an intrusive, unreliable, hypercritical object, and attendant annihilation fears, warded off through a bulwark of faulty personas protecting a fragile core self—a process he likens to the healing of a scab. To protect himself from disappointing this internalized voice, he conscientiously complies with its demands, a compromise that devitalizes the ego and threatens the capacity to wish in the service of short-circuiting a complete ego death. What's left is a state of chronic pain and anxiety. Charlie's true self is constantly at risk for the anguish of raw exposure, captured well in an early dream wherein he is lying down on the street, kissing his ex-girlfriend, when suddenly a giant freight truck with 18 lights emerges from the darkness and strikes him down. Overwrought with impingements in his early life (i.e., 18 lights), Charlie's unmitigated annihilation anxieties impede spontaneity, severely delimit the ego's "sufficiency of 'going on being'" (Winnicott, 1956), and provoke a visceral shame response upon any threat of being seen as a self.

Further, poorly defined ego boundaries leave him feeling unreal, un-agentic, and unintegrated (Winnicott, 1945), and reliant on others to fill in the psychic lacunae born of a mind wrought with severe limitations on desire. Such insufficiencies leave the rigid, tenuously cohered subject lacking a robust sense of existence that can sacrifice spontaneity, or, as Winnicott (1956) puts it, a self that can afford to die. In turn, Charlie's survival strategy consists in binge drinking, chain smoking, and one-night stands—dissociative activities that keep reality sequestered and anesthetize the primitive agonies of a self under siege.

Spring 2019. Just weeks into treatment, Charlie has given up his penchant for self-destructive behaviors, banking on the analysis to offer him a future if he is able to show up for his own life. He has begun to reveal the full trappings of a ruthless, primitive superego and an extreme false self, assailing himself anytime he deviates from the diction of political correctness and recounting myriad experiences of dependence and radical accommodation, from allowing his mother to choose both his college and his graduate school to following doctors' orders to take an expensive drug for a problem he does not possess. Six weeks into analysis, Charlie dreams of being in a plantation home where slaves labor about the grounds. He descends into the basement, where he encounters a back-of-house laborer: a Black woman standing in a bathtub filled with water. She carefully oversees the home's operations, where a baby resides several floors up playing violent video games, confronting images of machine guns and skin-shearing shrapnel. He then hears a man's voice instructing him to come upstairs to perform front-of-house labor as a "cater waiter."

In his associations, Charlie superficially propounds his indignance at the racist subjugation he is witnessing, his guilt for being given a position of higher status on account of his lighter skin, and his ego dystonic obsequiousness to fulfill others' demands. In my private associations, the infant's videogame offers a direct window into Charlie's primitive mind, flooded with life-threatening mentations that foment precocious ego development. I am further taken with how the "Black woman standing in the bathtub" complements the early reverie experience of my feet submerged in water and how "back-of-house" labor could represent the watchful yet benign care of the "Black" analyst (i.e., Natasha Black) behind the couch. Finally, the distance between the infant battling a war upstairs and the woman downstairs foretells the deleterious consequences of a mother's inability to see her child's insides and thereby stimulates the process of psychic integration through responsiveness to the infant's body-needs and later, ego-needs. Instead, the infant suffers from delays in personalization, and the development of confidence that it can survive annihilation threats is thwarted.

Summer 2019. By summer, Charlie has grown more in touch with the torment of his aimlessness, in what he characterizes as a "fallow season," feeling that analysis is the only oar he has to propel him forward. He is struggling to finish his thesis and to find a job that can support his growing inclination to separate from his family and tend to the psychic lacerations born of pernicious objects relentlessly admonishing his thoughts. In one particularly disturbing dream, he is a teenager working for his mother at a pizza restaurant in a cliffside manor when she suddenly lunges at him from behind the counter with a kitchen knife, pinning him to the floor and screaming, "you're weak and stupid!" He then grabs the knife from her and stabs her repeatedly, only to find that she cannot be hurt. He then describes his mother's desire for him to be "**man**-ner," not weak, stupid, and small like an adolescent, spontaneously associating to a previous session in which he likened his life to that of Jim Carey's character in *The Truman Show*—a movie depicting a man unaware that he is living in a reality show that revolves around his day-to-day life, his every action captured through a foreboding camera built into the *trompe l'oeil* sky. This time, Charlie calls the movie *The True Man Show*, and as he descends further into his associative process, he observes that he's feeling hot, that his heart is racing, and that his throat is beginning to contract. I suggest that we share the room with the leviathan mother of his childhood, and he begins to calm down, remembering similar jolts of anxiety in his recent retail job that would render him speechless to his boss's innocuous questions about merchandising.

As the drama of Charlie's early life becomes ever more textured in analysis, I begin to intuitively respond to his need for a boundaried yet infinite space existing somewhere between reality and illusion, out of which the very possibility of subjectivity can emerge. Our intimate connection enables me to identify with him enough to closely experience the pain of impingement as though I am touching a *Mimosa pudica*, a delicate fern whose tiny comb-like leaves immediately curl up and close at the brush of a finger. I thus reflexively pull back in the micro-instances where Charlie recoils in shame, and over time, I understand that he needs not my words but my help to begin to see himself reflected through me to forge a sense of personhood authentically conceived from the inside.

Further, I begin to recognize that, like Charlie, I too must become vulnerable to the analytic process and trust that my unobtrusive holding—which I often experience as doing nothing—is helping to cultivate the transitional space required for the emergence of a self from desultory emptiness. In my quietude, I am striving to respect my own inner life, dominated by ineffable fantasies of Charlie's nascency. It is as if we are in a cocoon—a protective carapace woven of unconscious fiber that nurtures Charlie's increasingly articulable wish to "come to life" before he makes any further decisions. Within this psychic capsule, both patient and analyst relax into a mutually regressed state where merger experiences and primary processes predominate. At times I experience a deeply attuned rhythmic trance akin to a mother rocking her infant when I sit back, close my eyes, and take in Charlie's story-like narratives like a film being directly projected into the private theater of my mind.

Concurrently, Charlie undergoes a phase where early, unintegrated sensory experiences are enlivened in the transference, such as when he claims to have "smelled" his ex-girlfriend outside my office building and when he dreams of admiring a Klimt painting in his bedroom, enchanted with the artist's ability to capture the beauty of ordinary women's skin, replete with flawed splotches of green and yellow. I imagine an infant gazing at its mother's skin, its incipient cognition only able to grasp bits and pieces—"splotches"—of a terrain.

Fall 2019. In the fall, the transference quickly intensifies as Charlie's defensive rigidity gradually attenuates and he begins feeling ever more dependent on the analysis. He is now expediently working on his thesis and beginning to articulate a new goal to apply to an art academy. In one particularly eventful session, he regales me with a dream that he's in my office and has a sense that I am controlling the environment so that he can "realize" something when suddenly a gift bag appears on the floor. As he looks around, he notices other gift bags scattered about and wonders if it's my birthday. In session, he discusses with me his belief that I want him to know that it's my birthday and that I'm controlling the environment *for* him, the *control* patient—a term he encountered outside of analysis—in order to take "special care" of him. He then explains that when he actually entered my office that morning, he noticed that I had placed a magazine featuring Pete Buttigieg, then-Presidential hopeful, in the waiting room and wondered if I'm signaling to him that, like him, I too am a Democratic Socialist. Finally, he tells me that he's started a painting for his portfolio that depicts "someone who is in psychoanalyst—in psychoanalysis." As I attend to his slip, he bashfully indicates a growing comfort in a deepening "symbiotic" relationship with me, matched by a terror that he will become more distraught than ever as he makes more contact with himself. He laments feeling stuck at a crossroads between misery and possibility when, in a sudden moment of excitement, he intones, "Well, I feel like I'm stuck being exactly where I need to be."

We are working in Winnicott's (1971) *third area of potential space*, a timeless dimension where an adequacy of environmental provision enables *both* patient and analyst the sufficient freedom to engage in the serious work of play. This involves the process of us both abandoning our defensive rigidity in exchange for a position that accepts paradox and uncanniness and allows for the loosening of ego boundaries through which unconscious material can pass from one mind to another.

In the dream, Charlie is bemused by the gifts and wonders if it's my birthday, while in tandem, I wonder if it's *his* birthday, given his assertion of my desire to have him *real*ize—to birth his subjectivity, to be a True Man.

Simultaneously, I wonder if Charlie wants *me* to realize a message—a cautionary tale of the potentially noxious consequences of my controlling the environment—that if I go too far, I could fill up the space with my own subjectivity and leave him to orbit around my desires. Still, in the referential fantasy about the magazine, Charlie conveys his desire for us to share a mind—for him to be *someone in psychoanalyst*. I gather that without direct understanding, Charlie is representing the salubrious effects of a "controlled" environment where he can use me as a supportive buffer against the threats to his mind while providing himself the time and space necessary to "come to life."

Recognizing that the birthday dream is the first in which I directly appear, I wonder if Charlie's sudden plunge into the transference conveyed a shift—an accommodation, really—in response to my own development as an analyst. In retrospect, I realize that this session—which would mark the beginning of a series of momentous sessions—occurred precisely the week that I began intensifying the session frequency of my own analysis. Beginning to think more expansively myself, I muse upon the possibility that inner Charlie sensed my own growing capacity to receive and make room for his nascent mind and waited until I, too, was ready to bear a transference regression.

At this point in Charlie's analysis, I am now able to appreciate the significance of the months of email exchanges with M about the couch and my efforts to develop an optimal space for analysis to occur. Only vaguely conscious of it at the time, I was engaged in an important analytic process prior to initial contact with the patient, whereby gradually I directed internal (and external) resources to create a setting at the intersection of fantasy and reality, where physical and psychic space are intertwined and irreducible, and where the origins of subjectivity can safely germinate—with an intentionality that honors the significance of an analysis in a patient's life. It is this intentionality and "longing" for the patient that establishes a basic psychic foundation onto which the patient struggling with an amorphous selfhood can safely attach and reactivate deferred developmental processes. I was submerged in an *analytic primary maternal preoccupation* presupposing Charlie's treatment, enabling me to keenly adapt to his evolving needs and establish the environmental conditions necessary to reignite the process of integration. Within this "controlled" space, I could then rely heavily upon this remarkable patient's dreams and transference fantasies—his play—as well as my attentiveness to my own fantasy and sensory experiences, which together forged the Archimedean treatment lever through which the beginnings of a coherent self-hood became possible.

Concluding Note

On an ending note, we recently began discussing the upcoming transition back to my office, after 15 months of phone sessions given the COVID-19 pandemic. Despite my personal difficulties connecting without the bodily relatedness of in-person treatment, Charlie, by contrast, insists that analysis has been "fine" during our physical separation—perhaps a testament to his inveterate comfort with disembodied experience. A few days later, however, Charlie shares a dream in which he is entering my office and must input the pin code "0-0-0-0" to access the waiting room. Upon entering my consulting room, he notices a huge inflatable mattress rather than the analytic couch to which he is accustomed, and he sees my chair out of place, which he anxiously works to reposition. This prompts him to discuss with me the miserable convenience of air mattresses, exclaiming:

> Everybody thinks the air mattress is the solution to the problem: We can just blow up the mattress and have guests sleep comfortably—which is not true. No matter what brand, they are always uncomfortable. I always wake up on a deflated mattress.

He then notes that although phone sessions have been helpful, he wonders if he's been "locked out" of certain aspects of the analysis the way in which he's initially locked out of my suite and must input a code. He believes the code "0-0-0-0" must signify his emptiness and nullified personhood, immediately then associating to having been in love with his mother as a child. What he doesn't know at this point is that recently, my landlord had installed a keypad lock to enter the suite and that he would indeed soon be dialing a number to enter. I take the opportunity to inform him of this fact, and he marvels at the prescience of his own unconscious life, confirming for him our deep sense of connection. Finally, I ask him about the part of his dream where he's moving my chair, and he explains that my furniture should move rather than his, stating, "Well, I'm the analysand here, so it's kind of on *you* to accommodate *me*."

References

Winnicott, D. W. (1945). Primitive Emotional Development. *International Journal of Psychoanalysis*, 26, 137–143.

Winnicott, D. W. (1956). Primary Maternal Preoccupation. In *Through Paediatrics to Psycho-analysis* (pp. 300–305). New York, NY: Brunner/Mazel.

Winnicott, D. W. (1971). *Playing and Reality*. New York, NY: Routledge.

Loewald and the Treatment of "Charlie"

Gil Katz, Ph.D.

Natasha has provided us with an elegant, beautifully written description of the opening phase of her work with her patient "Charlie," which she conceptualizes largely within a Winnicottian framework. Why, you are surely asking yourselves, in a four-part series about applying *Loewald's* theoretical ideas to clinical work, are we talking about Winnicott? Well, because Loewald's ideas are relevant to many of today's psychoanalytic theories and orientations—Winnicottian, Freudian, Relational, Kohutian, and Interpersonal. Loewald did not see himself as creating a new theoretical school; he explicitly did not want there to be any "Loewaldians." In his work, Loewald combined and *synthesized* classic drive-defense ego psychology, object relations, and self-concepts—all developmentally grounded in the early mother-infant matrix.

Indeed, in addition to Winnicott, Loewald was also a kindred spirit with Mahler, Kohut, and others who were exploring early object relations in light of the ever-widening scope of analytic patients. He was invited to speak at a Margaret Mahler symposium, and he wrote a very favorable review of Kohut's *The Analysis of the Self* (not to mention a scathing one of Arlow and Brenner). This was an important paradigm shift away from the *exclusively* intrapsychic drive/defense posture of modern ego psychology toward a more developmentally based model of therapeutic action. Loewald's contribution to clinical work is not about any kind of change in technique or interpretive recommendations, but rather about a fuller understanding of the analytic relationship, modes of listening, and the therapeutic action of psychoanalysis.

As a *brief* historical sidenote, Loewald and Winnicott did *meet* once, very briefly, at the 1951 IPA Congress in London. Following the Congress, Loewald wrote a letter to Winnicott (this was pre-email days) asking for a reprint of his paper, "*Primitive Emotional Development.*" Winnicott wrote back that he had run out of reprints (!) and was ordering more. (Again, it was pre-internet, pre-PEP days. And, apparently, pre-Xerox days as well.) In his note, he also informed Loewald of the pamphlet he published that was based on his radio broadcast talks to mothers about infant development. Winnicott closed the letter, saying, "I remember with great pleasure our brief contact at the Congress dinner." I don't believe Winnicott ever referenced Loewald in his writings, although Loewald does discuss Winnicott in his *Sublimation Monograph*, finding commonality with Winnicott's ideas about play, thirdness, transitional space, and instinct.

Natasha's presentation affords us the opportunity to illustrate the relevance, indeed the wide appeal, of many of Loewald's ideas to contemporary clinicians. Equally welcome, we have the opportunity to discuss and enjoy Natasha's sensitive, developmentally grounded work with her patient Charlie.

So—Natasha and Charlie:

When analyst and patient meet in the consulting room for the first time, they are both "Newbies." Natasha is beginning her *psychoanalytic life*—undertaking her first control case in her analytic training. Charlie is starting his first venture into his internal world and the rawness of his psychic life that lay beneath the "scab," as he put it, of his defensive armor. When Charlie tries the couch, he lies backwards facing Natasha, perhaps fearful of letting his needed maternal object out of his sight at this vulnerable moment. With some chagrin, Natasha wonders if *either* of them is *really* ready to be on their own in their respective new worlds.

But then an image arises from Natasha's unconscious of a fetus ready for "expulsion" from the womb. Charlie's slip in a later session about his making a painting about "Someone who is *in* psychoanalyst"echos Natasha's fetus imagery. Just then, Natasha experiences an image of her own feet submerged in "calming ocean water." In this same image, her supervisor and her analyst—her analytic "birth parents," if you will—are further out in the ocean. They are not too far away and are creating a safety-net, protecting her and her patient from the dangerous waters that lie ahead. Natasha takes this image as a model for what she needs to provide Charlie in the analysis: an "*analytic* safety-net," a holding environment, so that her patient can also feel safe as he delves into his early history with, as Natasha puts it, his "critical, unsympathetic, engulfing behemoth of a mother"—a mother who is like that giant freight truck with 18 lights in another of Charlie's dreams that strikes him down on the road. He'll need this safety-net as he tries to deal with his murderous rage at this "leviathan" of a mother, as Natasha calls her, who cannot be wounded or killed even when—as in another dream—Charlie stabs her repeatedly with the kitchen knife that *she* brought to kill *him*.

So this was the "birth-day" of the analysis undertaken by Natasha and Charlie. Toward the end of the first year of the treatment, this "birth-day" metaphor becomes explicit in Charlie's dream about the birthday presents strewn throughout the office. Whose birthday is it? Is it Charlie's birthday? Is it Natasha's birthday?

Loewald and Winnicott on Holding

Before saying more about this question, a little more about the concept of analytic "holding."

Winnicott coined *his* concept of *holding* (1953, 1971) to describe the focused attention and concern that create the optimal therapeutic environment for "good enough" parenting and the good-enough analytic process. Natasha beautifully describes her own experience of the holding environment:

> It is as if we are in a cocoon—a protective carapace woven of unconscious fiber that nurtures Charlie's increasingly articulable wish to "come to life" before he makes any further decisions. Within this psychic capsule, both patient and analyst relax into a mutually regressed state where merger experiences and primary process predominate. At times I experience the deeply attuned rhythmic trance akin to a mother rocking her infant when I sit back, close my eyes, and take in Charlie's story-like narratives like a film being directly projected into the private theater of my mind.

Loewald used the concept of analytic holding in a related fashion. In his 1960 *Therapeutic Action*, paper he compares the work of the analyst to the work of a sculptor, whose subject *emerges* from the block of granite by chiseling away the parts that do not belong:

> In analysis, we bring out the true form by taking away the neurotic distortions. However, as in sculpture, we must have, if only in rudiments, an *image* of that

which needs to be brought into its own. The patient, by revealing himself to the analyst, provides rudiments of such an image through all the distortions—an image which the analyst has to focus in his mind, thus _holding it_ in safe keeping for the patient to whom it is mainly lost. It is this tenuous reciprocal tie which represents the germ of a new object-relationship.

Analytic holding fosters what Winnicott called a "transitional space"—an intermediate area of _experiencing_ to which inner reality and external life both contribute. It is neither internal nor external but rather a **potential** space, a realm that accepts paradox and the uncanny, a realm in which you never ask, as I did a few moments ago, "Whose birthday is it, Charlie's or Natasha's?" It is the realm of play, the realm in which subjectivity and true-self experience emerge.

Loewald called this area the _interpsychic realm_—a realm of analytic process in which there is joint functioning, and reciprocal influence, of two psyches. It has its origins in the developmental transitional area described by Winnicott, but it is not only an early developmental stage out of which self and other are formed. It is an _ongoing_, evolving realm of analytic process, a special psychological space into which individuals may enter from **any** developmental level. It is a realm in which the analytic dyad share, create, organize, and differentiate in the context of their common yet separate experience.

Let me further describe Loewald's concept of the interpsychic and _interpsychic communication_ in an analytic process. Inter-_psychic_ is not inter-_personal_ (interpersonal would refer to the conscious interactions between two **persons**—two **people** as opposed to two **psyches**); and _inter_-psychic is not _intra_-psychic, as _two_ psyches are involved. A lovely metaphor for interpsychic communication is Stefano Bolognini's metaphor (in his book _Secret Passages)_ of a cat-flap—the little swing-door near the bottom of the entry door to a house. Generally not paid attention to by the homeowner, it allows the house cat to come and go unobtrusively. Let's consider inside the house as one person and psyche, and outside the house an other person and psyche. _Interper-sonal_ interaction takes place through the front door proper, consciously and willingly. Inter**psychic** interactions are exchanges in analytic treatment that take place through the cat-flap, unnoticed or barely noticed preconscious/unconscious communication. And here I come to John Lennon. What does the late Beatles songwriter and singer have to say about enactments and their relationship to technique and the analytic process? There is a line in one of his songs that goes something like: life is what happens to you while you are doing other things. To paraphrase, interpsychic communication is what happens—to you and your patient—while you are both busily immersed in a psychoanalytic process. Part of analytic holding, in Loewald's view, involves providing a frame, an environment, that allows and optimizes both parties' ability to use the cat flap in the service of the analytic process.

Earlier, I mentioned that in the interpsychic realm, unconscious experience passes from one mind to another at _all_ levels of psychic development, both from more structured, higher-level subjective states where the distinction between self and other exists and from "pre-subjective" states where such distinction has not yet been made or made only fleetingly and in rudimentary form. To quote Loewald (1970, pp. 52–53):

> The psychoanalytic situation, in this regard, represents a novel interpsychic field in which more fully developed features of psychic fields, object relations, merge with or are strongly influenced by coexisting primitive features.

On the pre-subjective level, non-verbal unformulated experience and sensory-motor sensations may be transmitted and experienced by either or both parties—like Natasha *physically* feeling Charlie's recoil at an impingement.

Again, in Natasha's words:

> Our intimate connection enables me to identify with him enough to closely experience the ***pain*** of impingement as though I am touching a *mimosa pudica*, a delicate fern whose tiny comb-like leaves immediately curl up and close at the brush of a finger.

Interpsychic communication is also responsible for creating what feel like "uncanny" moments, as when Natasha and Charlie seem to have shared a similar or identical experience. For example, in Charlie's "plantation home" dream, the way the *Black* worker (Natasha Black), a "back-of-house laborer," is standing with her feet in a bathtub of water, echoing Natasha's image in the very first session of her own feet standing in the ocean. Or like when Natasha realizes that Charlie's deepening "plunge into the transference" occurred at the same time as her increasing the frequency in her *own* analysis—in Natasha's words, perhaps "inner Charlie sensed my own growing capacity to receive and make room for his nascent mind and waited until I, too, was ready to bear a transference regression."

The Dramatic Play, the Analytic Third, and the Enacted Dimension

So again, Loewald's concept of ***interpsychic* communication** is the pre-conscious/unconscious communication that takes place between the patient and analyst during the analytic work. The interpsychic realm is what many today call the "analytic third." In the interpsychic realm, unconscious fantasies, emotions, and sensations in both patient and analyst interpenetrate across and through the interpsychic "cat-flap," creating a third process that partakes of, but is different from, each of these. Again, in Natasha's words:

> Within this "controlled" space ["control" here referring to the control analysis], I could then rely heavily upon this remarkable patient's dreams and transference fantasies—his play—as well as my attentiveness to my own fantasy and sensory experiences, which together forged the Archimedean treatment lever through which the beginnings of a coherent selfhood became possible.

Natasha is here using the term "play" in the Winnicottian sense of psychotherapy as playing— the overlapping and interaction of two areas of playing, the patient's and the therapist's. Loewald, in one of my favorite of his papers, *Psychoanalysis as an Art and the Fantasy Character of the Analytic Situation* (1975), likened the development of transference-countertransference experience in analysis to the joint composition of a *play*, referring to play not only in the sense of children's play but also specifically to a play as a piece of dramatic art. In Loewald's words:

> Viewed as a dramatic play, the transference neurosis is a fantasy creation woven from memories and imaginative elaborations of present actuality, the present actuality being the psychoanalytic situation, the relationship of patient and analyst.
> (1975, p. 279)

The patient takes the lead in furnishing the material and the action of this fantasy creation, while the analyst takes the lead in coalescing, articulating, and explicating the action ... The patient experiences and acts without knowing at first that he is creating a play. Gradually he becomes more of an author aware of *being* an author, by virtue of the analyst's interventions which reflect back to the patient what he does and says, and by transference interpretations which reveal the relations between the play and the original action that the play imitates.

(279–280)

The dramatic play being created by Charlie and Natasha is being fashioned, as Natasha says, out of the "play" of Charlie's many rich dreams and the "play" of her own "fantasy and sensory experiences," along with her clarifying and interpretive comments. But another important aspect of this dramatic play is also evolving *unconsciously* in that intermediate space that Loewald called the interpsychic realm.

What is continuously evolving in this third area of analytic process, side by side and intertwined with what is taking place in the treatment's <u>verbal</u> dimension (what we typically refer to *the* analytic process), is what I have called the "**_enacted_** *dimension of analytic process*" (Katz, 2014). This dimension of analytic process is rooted in a number of Loewald's papers (1971, 1975, 1976), in which he distinguished between *representational memory* (memory encoded and represented in words) and *enactive memory* (memories encoded and represented in action). What we today call "Enactment" is not simply an unusual or atypical behavioral event, like the analyst's forgetting a session or "inadvertently" criticizing the patient in a similar way as the original object. Enactment is the underlying *unconscious* **_process_** between patient and analyst, the *interpsychic* process within the transference-countertransference matrix, that **creates** the atypical event. It is a process that may have been evolving unawares over a long stretch of time, perhaps even from the very outset of the treatment. In the enacted dimension, without awareness or intent, patient and analyst, for separate (but related) unconscious reasons of their own, will inevitably find themselves playing a part in, and thereby *actualizing*, the patient's (and to a lesser extent, the analyst's) unconscious object relationship or dissociated traumatic experience.

For example, as *this* treatment process evolves and unfolds, Natasha will inevitably *become* the old object—she and Charlie will inevitably create a new treatment version of Charlie's relationship with his mother. **In** this enacted process, the past will not simply be remembered; it will be *re-lived*—alive in the here-and-now of the analytic relationship, but in an attenuated, less traumatic form. In Loewald's metaphor of analysis as a "dramatic play," the enacted dimension is the unconscious "play **within** the play" (Katz, 2014). When the enacted process ultimately becomes consciously available to both Natasha and Charlie, it will form the basis—because it is so immediate and alive in the here-and-now—for <u>experientially</u> based interpretive work that will be able to create the kind of emotionally based <u>experiential</u> insight that produces meaningful psychoanalytic change.

Through the analytic work within this new treatment version, this "new edition," as Freud called it, of Charlie's early relationships with his primary object, Charlie will have the opportunity to *actively* master what, in childhood, with his original object, he had to endure *passively*. He will be able to have, in Loewald's words, a "new discovery of objects"—by which he meant a *new experience* with the *original internal object* now alive again in the transference-countertransference.

Let me spell this out a little more. The patient first has the experience of the analyst's <u>becoming</u> his or her old object (which the analyst inadvertently does to an extent), and then, via the symbolizing and interpretive functions of the analyst—which not only provide insight and understanding but are *themselves* new object-relational experiences—the analyst gradually becomes a new therapeutic object, less and less colored by transference. This will enable the patient, as Loewald says, to discover "new pathways" *to* the object, leading to new ways of understanding and experiencing himself and more adaptive and satisfying relationships with others. To again paraphrase Loewald, the "ghosts" of Charlie's past, now revivified and brought back to life in the treatment's enacted dimension, will finally be able to be "led and laid to rest as *ancestors*," freeing their power and energy for present-day living.

Concluding Remarks: Charlie's Final Dream and Therapeutic Action

I'd like to now return to the clinical material that Natasha presented, specifically to the three components of Charlie's last dream: The access code—0-0-0-0—needed to enter Natasha's office; the giant air mattress that is in the office in place of the couch; and Charlie's repositioning of the analyst's chair.

Charlie's association with 0-0-0-0 is the emptiness and nullified personhood he feels. Like the air mattress, his experience of self is easily "deflated" and flattened. Charlie's mother had deflated him all through his life. She made every major decision for him, even when he became an adult, not wanting or allowing him to become "man-er, or a "true-man."

But the 0-0-0-0 access code has another meaning: 0-0-0-0 may also refer to a re-set, like turning an odometer back to 0-0-0-0, a new beginning, or the re-birth of his subjectivity that Charlie is experiencing in the treatment. Natasha's holding in mind the image of who Charlie truly is and can become is, as Loewald tells us, the seed of a new object-relationship that can reactivate deferred developmental processes.

When Natasha tells Charlie that indeed there <u>will</u> soon be an access code for entry into the office, Charlie marvels at the prescience of his own psychic life, confirming for him the deep sense of connection he feels with his analyst. His experience on Natasha's couch has been quite different than his experience with his mother, which was like going to sleep on an uncomfortable air mattress only to awaken and to find it, and himself, on the floor, completely deflated.

Evidence that Charlie is starting to become more of an independent "agentic" self—perhaps beginning to "show up for his own life," as Natasha put it—comes in the last part of this dream, in which he repositions the analyst's chair. Why were you moving it? Natasha asks. "Well, I'm the analysand <u>here</u>," he says, "so it's kind of on *you*, to accommodate *me*." *I* give the orders now, he is saying, *you* have to take care of *me*. I'm tired of being a "cater-waiter," always catering to mother's needs for attention, always having to inflate *her*, always having to provide *her* with nourishment.

Charlie knows there is a difficult road ahead. As he says in an earlier session, he feels he is "at the crossroads of misery and possibility." And then, after a moment's reflection, in a sudden moment of excitement, she says, "Well, I feel like I'm stuck being <u>exactly</u> <u>where</u> <u>I need to be</u>."

References

Bolognini, S. (2011). *Secret Passages: The Theory and Technique of Interpsychic Relations* (Trans. G. Atkinson). London: Routledge.

Katz, G. (2014). *The Play within the Play: The Enacted Dimension of Psychoanalytic Practice.* London: Routledge.

Kohut, H. (1971). *The Analysis of the Self: A Systematic Approach to the Psychoanalytic Treatment of Narcissistic Personality Disorders.* New York, NY: International Universities Press.

Loewald, H. (1970). Psychoanalytic Theory and the Psychoanalytic Process. *Psychoanalytic Study of the Child*, 25: 45–68.

Loewald, H. (1971). Some Considerations on Repetition and Repetition Compulsion. *International Journal of Psycho-Analysis*, 52: 59–66.

Loewald, H. (1975). Psychoanalysis as an Art and the Fantasy Character of the Psychoanalytic Situation. *Journal of the American Psychoanalytic Association*, 23: 277–299.

Loewald, H. (1976). Perspectives on Memory. In *Papers on Psychoanalysis*. New Haven, CT: Yale University Press, 1980, pp. 148–173.

Winnicott, D. W. (1953). Transitional Objects and Transitional Phenomena—A Study of the First Not-Me Possession. *International Journal of Psychoanalysis*, 34: 89–97.

Winnicott, D. W. (1971). *Playing and Reality*. New York, NY: Routledge.

Chapter 13

Obituary

Hans W. Loewald M.D. (1906–1993)

T. Wayne Downey

Hans W. Loewald, a key figure in twentieth-century psychoanalysis, whose thought bridged philosophy and psychoanalysis, died of pneumonia in a state of quiet resolve, on Saturday, 9 January 1993, in Hamden, Connecticut. He was 86 years old. Hans was best known in the United States, where he had a long and fruitful career as an innovative psychoanalytic writer, educator and clinician.

Hans Loewald was born in the Alsace, then a part of Germany, in the town of Colmar, on 19 January 1906. Shortly after his birth his family moved to Berlin, where he grew up. He was raised fatherless. His father, a Jewish physician with an interest in dermatology and psychiatry, died shortly after his birth. Hans was reared by his mother and a favourite aunt in a complex and often difficult family situation. He spent a good part of his adolescence in quiet but determined rebellion against his autocratic German schoolmasters.

Hans eventually went on to matriculate at the Universities of Marburg and Freiburg. His attraction to the philosophical ideas of Martin Heidegger drew him to Freiburg, drawn to the philosophical ideas of Martin Heidegger, who became Hans's teacher and mentor. However, Heidegger's conversion to National Socialism led to Hans's disillusionment and very painful estrangement from him and ultimately to Hans's withdrawal from philosophy as an exclusive endeavour. Heideggers's embracing of Hitler (even to the extent of growing a moustache like Hitler's) introduced a vast contradiction between the purity of Heidegger's philosophical thinking and the corrupt ideals of his political life; a moral conflict which could never again sustain a relationship between Loewald and Heidegger.

Hans loved philosophical exercises and modes of thinking, but even before his break with Heidegger he had been wary of philosophy's tendencies towards exclusions, other worldliness, and a reason too abstracted from life. After leaving Freiburg, he travelled to Rome to become a physician and by this act to redress his philosophical imbalance with the immersion in human experience which medicine provided. While in Italy he married his first wife. He received a medical degree from the University of Rome in 1934 and moved to Padua, where he set up a private psychiatric practice. In 1939, with fascism growing in Italy, Hans went to Paris, where he made a desperate attempt to become a French citizen. He reasoned that with Colmar and the Alsace having reverted to France from Germany after the First World War, he should be eligible for French citizenship! After all, Paris was his favourite city; he dearly wanted to live there, and he favoured French cuisine. Fortunately for psychoanalysis in the United States, and finally, I think, fortunately for the ongoing development of Hans's creative energies

DOI: 10.4324/9781003328230-16

and satisfactions in life, his request was turned down. We can only wonder what kind of union might have been formed had Hans become a part of the French psychoanalytic movement!

Later, in 1939, Hans came to the United States with his young family, which now included his sons, Richard and Francis. After a brief stay with relatives in Cleveland and a year's employment at a state psychiatric hospital in Rhode Island, he settled in Baltimore, Maryland. There he worked in the adult and child psychiatric clinics of the University of Maryland School of Medicine. His experience with children in the clinics there contributed to the developmental dimension in his theorising which made his thinking different from that of many other analysts of adults. However, his own considerable grasp of his psychological origins, forever being retrieved, lost and reconstructed, was the most salient factor in establishing his developmental point of view.

In the early 1940s Hans entered psychoanalysis in search of understanding and remedies for a persistent malaise. His analyst was Lewis Hill. While Hans was quite comfortable with the Germanic rigour which stamped his thought, he was equally pleased with the rich emotional lineage of his 'Budapest connection'. With his wry sense of humour he would relate how his analyst, Hill, had been analysed by Clara Thompson, who had been analysed by Ferenczi! He cherished the 'Romany' emphasis upon spontaneity and a certain respect for the life of the affects which was part and parcel of this analytic pedigree. In a short time he became an analytic candidate, graduated, and joined the faculty of the Baltimore-Washington Institute. At the age of 45, in 1950, he published his seminal psychoanalytic work 'Ego and reality' in this journal. In the last passage of that paper, Hans wrote, better than I could summarise, what was to be the major premise underlying the continuing development of his psychoanalytic thought:

> it would seem that the more alive people are (though not necessarily more stable) the broader the range of ego-reality levels is. Perhaps the so-called fully developed, mature ego is not one that has become fixated at the presumably highest or latest stage of development, having left the others behind it, but is an ego that integrates its reality in such a way that the earlier and deeper levels of ego-reality integration remain alive as dynamic sources of higher organisation.
>
> (p. 20).[1]

In 1955, he came to New Haven to join the newly-founded Western New England Institute for Psychoanalysis as a Training and Supervising Analyst. He also joined the newly-constituted Education Committee of the Institute, which consisted of Erik Erikson, Alfred Gross, Robert Knight and William Pious. He was encouraged in this move by Theodore Lidz, an old friend and psychoanalytic colleague from Baltimore who had previously moved to Yale. Hans came with a new wife to start a new family and a new phase of his life as an analyst. He joined the faculty of the Yale University School of Medicine, where he later became a Clinical Professor of Psychiatry in the Department of Psychiatry and the Child Study Center. The bulk of Loewald's psychoanalytic contributions were written during his time in New Haven.

In terms of his intellectual heritage, we might say that Hans was born to philosophy, but grew into psychoanalysis. From an early age Hans was captivated by a love for the ideas of Nietzsche, Heidegger, and the poet Goethe. However, it was psychoanalysis that sparked his mind. We might also note that his early career as a philosopher lent his prose a sometimes dense style of philosophical phraseology, which could tempt readers and critics either to oversimplify and to sentimentalise his ideas or to reject them as inaccessible. And yet, having said this, it should be noted that there is often a poetic lilt and artistic emphasis in his writing. The four-part form of his paper on therapeutic action (1960) follows that of a string quartet, Hans's favourite form of music. In its world-view, his thought had much in common with the German and American transcendentalists such as Hegel and Emerson.

Loewald's model of mind shared their emphases on unity of all things in the midst of diverse polarities. It also shared much with them in his emphasis upon intuition (primary-process thought) as an indispensable complement to scientific thinking (secondary-process thought) as modes by which the world's realities may be best and most truly grasped and comprehended. He opposed closed systems of thought such as those he perceived in the linear hierarchical analytic model culminating in ego psychology and in the idealisation of an objective, rational science. By the same notion, his arguments were an attempt to counter the concept of the 'objective analyst' perched without persona behind the couch, providing only an abstracting and reflecting mirror for the analysand's thoughts. As defined by Loewald, the individual *qua* analyst might be potentially limited by time, place, culture or neurosis. However, by exercising intellectual, honest, compassion, and an openness to art, a life rich in creative instability and spiritual growth could be achieved and a life of neurotic rigidity or suppressed madness could in large part be avoided.

Loewald's many papers and monographs are characterised by his employment of an unusually close and faithful reading of the works of Freud. This was Loewald's intellectual point of departure for the development of his own revolutionary ideas about psychoanalysis and its therapeutic process. He attempted a fair scrutiny which encompassed Freud in all Freud's discoveries, truths, complexities, contradictions and incompletely-developed psychoanalytic observations. In this endeavour Loewald built upon Freud in quite novel ways. As he stated in his 1970 paper 'Psychoanalytic theory and psychoanalytic process', he 'reformulated' Freud.

> It seems to me that most of the views I have advanced are at least implicit in Freud's work and that of many other psychoanalysts. Perhaps my contribution consists mainly in making some things explicit and drawing some unfamiliar conclusions.
>
> (p. 299)

Loewald's reformulations of Freud have amounted to a radical rethinking of the nature of the individual. He attempted to revive Freud as the dynamic intellectual which he was. We can infer this from his prescient, dynamically-oriented translation 'Where id was, there ego shall become' ('W° Es war, soil Ich werden', Freud, 1933) in the place of Strachey's more static 'Where id was, there ego shall be'. In this conceptualisation (1970, p. 280), as the individual pursues his destiny he is both shaper and shaped by it. Within psychoanalytic theory Hans contributed many other reconceptualisations. His views on the psychological representations of instinct, the development of the ego, the often Interpsychic character of analytic change, the meaning of 'metapsychology' and the nature of love in the psychoanalytic setting are all ideas which have been marked out by many current analysts as unique and vital contributions to contemporary and future psychoanalysis.

Loewald's classic paper 'On the Therapeutic Action of Psychoanalysis' (1960) came out of the passion, ferment and freedom which was gathered up into his crisis of creativity in the 1950s. In it he set forth his ideas about the role which interactions with the environment play in the formation, development and vicissitudes of the psyche. He explored the connection between ego formation and object relations. He boldly stated that the therapeutic action of psychoanalysis is directly related to the 'resumption of ego development [which] is contingent upon the relationship with a new object, the analyst' (p. 221).

Here he introduced the concept that, in metaphorical terms, the action of psychoanalysis turns ghosts into ancestors. In his argument, he proceeds in typical fashion from Freud's image in Chapter 7 of *The Interpretation of Dreams* of the ghosts in the underworld of the *Odyssey*. These ghosts symbolise the indestructability of unconscious mental acts. Loewald builds the image into one in which the ghosts of the transference come to life, attracted by, and to, the presence of the analyst. They are then converted into ancestors as they are laid to rest by the work of the analyst—analysand dyad, their power transformed into a more vivid experience of current life. In Loewald's model such growth occurs in a *transindividual* field in which it is shared differentially by both parties. He draws by analogy on the woman's growth as mother even as she raises her child through successive stages of higher development.

Historically, Hans Loewald's death marks the waning of an era of psychoanalysis in which he, D. W. Winnicott, Marion Milner and Margaret Mahler, all explicitly or implicitly expanding upon Freud, explored a new theoretical realm beyond psychoanalysis's traditional endopsychic boundary. They all wrote about and lay claim to a common area of interest which Loewald came to term the 'interpsychic' or 'transindividual realm'; which Winnicott termed 'transitional'. It fell to him more than to the other members of this adventurous cadre to conceptualise it formally as the area of transmental functioning, and to establish this transindividual area's relationship to psychoanalysis proper. With particular dedication and clarity Hans described this special psychological space which individuals may enter, share, or emerge from depending upon their developmental level. It is a place where as a part of a developmental or analytic dyad they share, create, organise and differentiate in the context of their common yet separate experience.

What is true of Loewald's writing, that it is energetic without being polemical, and creative without being solipsistic or narcissistic, was also true of the way he conducted an analysis. He practised as he wrote, without preaching. As an analyst he showed a remarkable range in the depth and breadth of his knowledge, insight and emotion which he contributed to this joint analysand—analyst endeavour. As situations warranted, he could be as silent as the most abstinent 'classical' analyst. By the same token he could 'mix it up' and come to close quarters with his patient. He could react with passionate challenging, anger, or just plain irritation when some important existential analytic moment seemed in danger of being lost to the patient's anti-analytic crisis of pettifoggery or prevarication! In the analytic session or on paper, his words were to speak for themselves of the realities of the psychoanalytic and human conditions. Hans had perfect pitch and that blessed his listening to a patient, Louis Armstrong in the 1920s in Berlin, or cursed a faltering string quartet! When he left his analytic chair for vacations he loved to climb mountains, hike and travel. He travelled widely throughout Europe, across North America, and to his special places in Maine on the islands of Monhegan and Peaks.

In the main, Hans Loewald's psychoanalytic legacy is to be found in three works, one of which I have already cited: *Papers on Psychoanalysis* (1980), *Psychoanalysis and the History of the Individual* (1978) and *Sublimation* (1988).

In re-reading these texts, we garner a strong sense of the man, who in the midst of closeness and immediate presence always seemed to have one eye fixed upon the vague outlines of some far-off mountain; a man who lived, worked and laboured beyond the horizons of most minds. In his 1978 monograph on the history of the individual and in his 1988 work on sublimation, he approached from very different perspectives the question: how do we grow into and become part of our history? How do we unify competing tensions? How do we love, relate and continue to internalise creatively our experience while growing as individuals? Loewald was forever questing.

Hans's last five years, spent retired from the practice of psychoanalysis and in failing health, were a trial. Above all else, he loved, lived and breathed psychoanalysis. To be retired was almost beyond comprehension for him. He could not imagine being parted from psychoanalysis any more than he could accept separation from his loving and beloved family. In his last years awards and acknowledgements of his courageous ground-breaking achievements flowed from colleagues and organisations. He took quiet pride in them. He was pleased and briefly warmed by the recognition contained in *The Work of Hans Loewald,* edited by Gerald Fogel (Aronson, 1991), and in receiving the Mary S. Sigourney Award in 1991 and the Laughlin Award in 1992 from the American College of Psychoanalysis. He was predeceased by his son Richard. He is survived by his wife, Elizabeth L. Loewald, M.D., a son, Francis, and two daughters, Katherine and Caroline.

Hans Loewald might have become a philosopher-king in his own psychoanalytic fiefdom. Instead, he opted to translate psychoanalysis's metapsychological abstractions into a newer, more dynamic and humanistic syntax. As he restated it in his transcendant paradigm: 'where id was, there ego shall become'.

Note

1 All papers cited can be found in *Papers on Psychoanalysis*, Hans W. Loewald, M.D., New Haven: Yale University Press, 1980.

Index

Note: Page numbers followed by "n" denote endnotes.

Abraham, Karl 110
adolescence: drive to develop in 158–166; as vital stage of development 161
Adorno, T. W. 108–109, 111
Alexander, Franz 7, 10
American Ego Psychology 26, 71, 117
American independent tradition 10, 20
American psychoanalysis 3–10, 57, 61, 114; see also psychoanalysis
American Psychoanalytic Association 4, 14, 20, 25, 27, 29–30, 35n5, 44, 106n1
The Analysis of the Self (Kohut) 177
analyst as new object 8–9, 31
analysts 17–19, 105; classical 8, 89; émigré 6–10; European 6–10; Freudian 7; of the Hartmann Era 117; interpersonal 25; relational 9, 122n19
analytic objectivity 34
analytic primary maternal preoccupation 171, 175
the analytic third 180–182
Anzieu, Didier 134
archaic experience as source of aliveness and creativity 111, 116
archaic merger 154
Arendt, H. 66–68, 72, 75
Aristotle 66, 80
Armstrong, Richard 120n1
Aspects of Internalization (Schafer) 16
authenticity 83–87
autonomy 82, 129–130, 132, 135, 138, 150, 151

Baudry, Francis 10n4
Behrends, Rebecca 21
being: "not-yet"-the "something-more"- of 100–101; in the world 73–74, 77, 80–82, 106n2
Being and Time (Heidegger) 65–66, 70, 72–75, 77, 90, 99

Benedek, T. 139
Benhabib, Seyla 120n1
Bibring, G. 139
Binswanger, L. 98
biographical information 35n3
Black, Natasha 171–176
Blatt, Sidney 21
Bleuler, Eugen 3
body 90–91
Bohleber, Werner 120n1
Born to Run: A Hidden Tribe, Superathletes, and the Greatest Race the World Has Never Seen (McDougall) 49n10
Brenman, Margaret 15
Brenner, Charles 17, 27; *An Elementary Textbook of Psychoanalysis* 17; *The Mind in Conflict* 17; *Psychoanalysis: The Science of Mental Conflict* 17; *Psychoanalytic Technique and Psychic Conflict* 17
Brentano, Franz 65, 71; *On the Manifold Meaning of Being according to Aristotle* 65
Brill, Abraham Arden 3
Brody, R. 92n2
Bultmann, Rudolf 66
Burr, Harry Saxton 17

Cameron, Norman 18, 27
Castel, Pierrer-Henri 120n1
Chodorow, N. 20, 56
Civilization and its Discontents (Freud) 119
classical analysts 8, 89
Cohen, Donald 21
concepts of reality 116, 117
Concluding Unscientific Postscript to the Philosophical Fragments (Kierkegaard) 49n7, 49n16
Congress of the International Psychoanalytic Association (1957) 30
contemporary re-visioning 101–102

Cooper, A. M. 53, 55, 61, 62
COVID-19 pandemic 158, 163, 176
creativity 5, 7, 82, 118
critique of rationality 54, 111

death 82–83
deconstruction 77–79
de-differentiation 117
"depth psychology" 4, 6
desexualized Eros 82
Dews, Peter 120n1
Didion, Joan 152; *The Year of Magical Thinking* 152
differentiation 40; dedifferentiation 117; ego-object 115; ego/reality 54, 151; internal 155; non-differentiation 77, 113, 115; promoting 77; sexual 82; union in 155
Dilthey, Wilhelm 70
Dobyn, Stephen 21
Downey, T. Wayne 21
dramatic play 180–182
drive-conflict model of psychoanalysis 7
drive-defense ego-psychology 170, 177
drive to develop in adolescence and analysis 158–166
"dual unity" 115
dynamic fluidity 116

ego: intersubjective 60; organization 85, 131; primitive 115; psychology 26, 71, 117, 170, 177, 186; synthetic function of 54, 115, 119; unity of 116
"Ego and Reality" (Loewald) 54–55
ego-object differentiation 115
ego-object integration 117
ego/reality differentiation 54, 151
ego-reality integration 54, 114, 116–117, 119–120, 185
ego transformations 136, 151
An Elementary Textbook of Psychoanalysis (Brenner) 17
emigration, of European 6–10
émigré analysts 6–10
enacted dimension 180–182
enactive memory 181
engulfment 117
entangled: modes of time 98–99; transference and unthought new 99–100
Erikson, Erik 185
Eros 38, 115, 116, 152, 161, 168
European analysts 6–10
Exemplarist Moral Theory (Zagzebski) 49n16
Expression and the Inner (Finkelstein) 49n14

fantasy 21, 78, 105, 118, 120, 147, 148, 153–154, 156, 159–160, 175–176; significance of 58; unconscious 71, 76

fecundity of birth and symbolism 133
Ferenczi, Sandor 7
Fierman, L. 22n2
final dream 182
Finkelstein, David 49n14; *Expression and the Inner* 49n14
Fogel, Gerald 53, 56, 81, 142n1, 188
French, Thomas 9, 25
Freud, Sigmund 13, 32, 38, 71, 89, 111; a case of breastfeeding 136–142; *Civilization and its Discontents* 119; dialogue among Loewald, Heidegger and 75–91; *The Interpretation of Dreams* 13; "official" Oedipal theory 116; *Project for a Scientific Psychology* 17; reformulation of Freudian concepts 186; *Three Essays on the Theory of Sexuality* 133; *Totem and Taboo* 111
Freudian analysts 7
Friedman, Cryrus 11n5
Friedman, L. 53
Fromm-Reichmann, Frieda 9, 25
Fry, Northrop 17
The Fundamental Concepts of Metaphysics (Heidegger) 83
fusion: and merger 113; and non-differentiation 113

gender formation 129–142; a case of breastfeeding 136–142; case vignette of mother and son 134–136; places of gender interest in Loewald's writings 131–142; and "portraiture" 129
gender portraiture 129
ghosts and ancestors 30, 32, 34, 40–42, 47–49, 86, 138, 150, 155–156, 182, 187
Gill, Merton 15
"The Golden Age" of psychoanalysis 6
Goldstein, Kurt 63n1; *The Organism* 63n1
The Goshawk (White) 156
Gray, Paul 20
Greenberg, Jay 53
Gross, Alfred 13, 185

Hans W. Loewald Center 38–48
Hartmann, H. 16, 20, 32, 35n4
Heidegger, Martin 34, 53–62, 65–70, 72–73, 76–77, 82, 90, 96–97, 99, 110, 159, 184; on authenticity 83–87; Being and Time 72–75; *Being and Time* 65–66, 70, 72–75, 77, 90, 99; on the body 90–91; on death 82–83; dialogue among Freud, Loewald and 75–91; *The Fundamental Concepts of Metaphysics* 83; on time 87–90
Herder, Johann Gottfried 69
holding: Loewald on 178–180; Winnicott on 178–180
Holtzman, D. 139–140

Homer 102
Horney, Karen 7, 10, 10n3, 87
human environment 8
Hunt, Samuel 28
Hurwitz, M. 19
Husserl, Edmund 66–67, 72
"Hypnoid state, Repression, Abreaction, and Recollection" (Loewald) 58–59

illusion 79, 83, 141, 174
imagination 25, 39; empathic 97–98; limitations and conflicts of 105; rigidities and failures of 168
individuation processes 44–45, 55, 81, 153
"the inner future" 100–101
integration: ego-object integration 117; ego-reality 54, 114, 116–117, 119–120, 185; of libidinal and defensive forces 55; of polarities 34; psychic 122n22, 173
interactional processes 57, 60
internal differentiation 155
internalization 149–153
International Journal of Psychoanalysis 27, 31, 42
interpersonal analysts 25
The Interpretation of Dreams (Freud) 13
interpsychic 179; communication 179, 180; realm 179, 181
intersubjective ego 60

Jacobson, Edith 35n4
James, William 5
Jaspers, Karl 66
Jones, Ernest 3
Journal of the American Psychoanalytic Association 31
Jung, Carl 3

Kahr, Brett 10n4
Kaiser, Helmuth 18, 27
Kant, Immanuel 108
Katz, Gil 177–178
Kierkegaard, Søren 49n7, 83, 101; *Concluding Unscientific Postscript to the Philosophical Fragments* 49n7, 49n16
Klein, Melanie 7, 35n1, 71, 76; "Notes on Some Schizoid Mechanisms" 35n1
Knight, Robert 13, 15, 185
Knight Foundation 16
Kohut, Heinz: *The Analysis of the Self* 177
Korean War 13
Kris, Anton 8
Kris, Ernst 8, 35n4
Kris, Marianne 8
Kristeva, Julia 132, 134
Kulish, N. 139–140

language and development 75–77
Laplanche, Jean 134
Lear, Jonathan 106n1, 106n2; *Radical Hope* 106n2
Leavy, Stanley 20, 56, 70, 89
Levenson, Lawrence 21
Levinas, Emmanuel 104
Lidz, Theodore 13, 17–18, 35n2, 185
Loewald, Elizabeth Longshore 13
Loewald, Hans W.: and American psychoanalysis 3–10; on being lost 102–104; biographical information 35n3; characteristics of writing 61–62; concept of maturity 108–120; dialogue among Freud, Heidegger and 75–91; early papers 53–62; early stages and initial reception 25–31; "Ego and Reality" 54–55; and Heidegger 53–62; on holding 178–180; "Hypnoid state, Repression, Abreaction, and Recollection" 58–59; influences on Loewald's vision 55–58; and Martin Heidegger 65–69; obituary 184–188; "On the Therapeutic Action of Psychoanalysis" 25–34, 59–60; *Papers on Psychoanalysis* 46, 57, 145, 188; and philosophy 53–62; places of gender interest in writings 131–142; *Psychoanalysis and the History of the Individual* 188; *Psychoanalysis as an Art and the Fantasy Character of the Analytic Situation* 180; quiet revolutionary 91; and Sigmund Freud 71; "something more" 104–106; *Sublimation: Inquiries into Theoretical Psychoanalysis* 133, 140–141, 168–169, 188; "the paternal concept of reality" 114–115; "The Problem of Defense and the Neurotic Interpretation of Reality" 58; and the treatment of "Charlie" 177–178; and Winnicott 170–182; *The Work of Hans Loewald: Introduction and Commentary* 53, 188
Loewenstein, Rudolf 35n4
loss, and mourning 145–149

MacDonald, Helen 145–146
The Marriage of Figaro (Mozart) 108
maternal adoration 136
"maternal concept of reality" 115–117
maternal engulfment 117
maternal eroticism 132, 134, 139
maternal-infant matrix 132, 135, 159
maternal relationships 18
maternal reliance *see* maternal eroticism
mature object relations 154–156
maturity 108–120
McDougall, Christopher 49n10; *Born to Run: A Hidden Tribe, Superathletes, and the Greatest Race the World Has Never Seen* 49n10

McLaughlin, J. 10, 53
memory 38, 42, 46–47; enactive 181;
    microdynamics of 98–99, 106n10;
    representational 181; unconscious
    somatic 59
Menninger, Karl 14
Menninger, William 6
metapsychology 14–15, 17, 22, 62, 186
The Mind in Conflict (Brenner) 17
Minkowski, E. 98
Mitchell, S. A. 25, 34, 53, 110
Moscovitz, Seymour 15
mother-child unity 81, 87
"Motherhood Constellation" (Stern) 139
"mother-infant unity" 54–56, 59–60, 62, 81
mourning: differentiated union 154–156; loss
    145–149; mature object relations 154–156;
    mourning and internalization 149–153
Mozart, Wolfgang Amadeus 108; *The
    Marriage of Figaro* 108

natural environment as source of unity and
    at-oneness 140–141
Nazi movement 67
New Haven 12–22
new object: analyst as 8–9, 31; as
    re-connection with old objects 9, 60, 79
Nietzsche, Friedrich 83
non-differentiation 77, 113, 115
nonseparateness 113
"Notes on Some Schizoid Mechanisms"
    (Klein) 35n1

Obama, Barak 40
Oberndorf, Clarence 4
oceanic experiences 55, 115, 119, 122n14
"the oceanic feeling" 55, 115, 119, 122n14
Odyssey (Homer) 102
Oedipal Complex 55, 131, 137, 140; waning
    of 137
Ogden, T.H. 10
The Once and Future King (White) 148
*On the Manifold Meaning of Being according
    to Aristotle* (Brentano) 65
"On the Therapeutic Action of
    Psychoanalysis" (Loewald) 25–34, 59–60;
    annual meeting of American Psychoanalytic
    Association 29–30; Congress of the
    International Psychoanalytic Association
    30; early stages and initial reception
    25–31; influence of 31–32; preliminary
    drafts and sketches 26–27; prepublication
    presentations 27–31; Western New England
    Institute 30–31; Western New England
    Psychoanalytic Institute 27–29
The Organism (Goldstein) 63n1

organization: ego 85, 131; professional
    44–45; psychic 20, 59; unconscious 44–45;
    Zionist 14
Organization and Pathology of Thought
    (Rapaport) 17
"original unity" 77, 82, 91
orthodox religions 68

Papers on Psychoanalysis (Loewald) 46, 57,
    145, 188
paternal and maternal 29, 54, 117
"the paternal concept of reality" 114–115
Paul, Robert 120n1, 123n26
Peterson, Frederick 3
Petri, Elfride 66
Peyser, Ellen 53
Philebus (Plato) 115
philosophy 53–62
Pious, William 13, 185
Plato 68, 72, 115; *Philebus* 115; *The Republic*
    68
play, dramatic 180–182
Poland, W. 10
possibility of possibilities 97–98
potentialities 97–98
pre-Oedipal development 113
pre-Oedipal mother 117
pre-Oedipal turn 112–113, 116
Pribram, Karl 17
primary creativity 118
primary narcissism 54, 57, 76, 78, 82, 87
primitive bloodthirsty aggression 148
primitive ego 115
"*Primitive Emotional Development*"
    (Winnicott) 177
primitive oral sadism 153
primitive superego 173
"The Problem of Defense and the Neurotic
    Interpretation of Reality" (Loewald) 58
Project for a Scientific Psychology (Freud) 17
proto-objects 114, 151
psychic: integration 122n22, 173; organization
    20, 59; transformations of 132
psychoanalysis: in 1920s 5; in 1930s 5; in 1940s
    6; American 3–10; brief history, by decade
    3–6; challenge 10; drive-conflict model
    of 7; Hans Loewald 7–10; pre-Oedipal
    development 113; pre-Oedipal turn
    112–113, 116; in United States 3–6; WWII
    immigration of European analysts to the
    U.S. 6–10
*Psychoanalysis and the History of the
    Individual* (Loewald) 188
*Psychoanalysis as an Art and the Fantasy
    Character of the Analytic Situation*
    (Loewald) 180

Psychoanalysis: The Science of Mental Conflict
   (Brenner) 17
psychoanalytic metapsychology 62
Psychoanalytic Technique and Psychic Conflict
   (Brenner) 17
Psychoanalytic Terms and Concepts
   (Auchincloss and Samberg) 63n3
psychological growth and change 8, 30
psychology: American ego 26, 71;
   "depth psychology" 4, 6; drive-defense
   ego-psychology 170, 177; ego psychology
   26, 71, 117, 177, 186; metapsychology
   14–15, 17, 22, 62, 186

Radical Hope (Lear) 106n2
Rado, Sandor 7
Rapaport, David 10, 14, 15–16, 20, 21, 27–28,
   32, 62; *Organization and Pathology of
   Thought* 17
reception of/reactions to Loewald's papers
   3–10, 25–34
Redlich, Fritz 13
reformulation of Freudian concepts 186
regression in the service of the ego 87
relational analysis 9, 122n19
relational analysts 9, 122n19
religion and development 112, 121n13
representational memory 181
The Republic (Plato) 68
re-visioning 101–102
Richardson, W. 85
Romantic movement 68
Rothman, J. 92n2
Ryder, Norman 10n2

Safranski, R. 66–67, 92n1
Saketopoulou, A. 168
Schafer, Roy 16, 17, 21, 62; *Aspects of
   Internalization* 16
scientific objectivity 28
separation 44–45, 54, 87, 112, 115, 132–133,
   137–138, 140–141, 148, 150–151, 154–155
separation-individuation 114
sexual differentiation 82
Springsteen, Bruce 40
Stern, Daniel 139; "Motherhood
   Constellation" 139
Stern, S. 19
Strachey, J. 13, 18, 32
Strachey, Lytton 53
subjective objectivity 60
sublimation 21, 48n2, 82, 112, 121n6, 140–141,
   168–169
*Sublimation: Inquiries into Theoretical
   Psychoanalysis* (Loewald) 133, 140–141,
   168–169, 188

Sublimation Monograph (Loewald) 177
Sullivan, Harry Stack 13, 25
superego 45, 83, 85, 89–90, 100–101, 104, 133,
   150–151, 160, 171, 173
The Sword in the Stone (White) 148
symbiosis 113, 117
symbolism 148
synthetic function of ego 54, 115, 119

Teicholz, J. G. 53
therapeutic action 182
"The Use of the Object" (Winnicott) 10–11n4
third area of potential space 175
Thompson, Clara 9
Three Essays on the Theory of Sexuality
   (Freud) 133
time 87–90; entangled modes of 98–99;
   past-present-future 98–99
Totem and Taboo (Freud) 111
transference regression 175, 180
transformations of psychic 132
"true regression" 79, 85–86
The Truman Show (movie) 173–174
Tyson, Phyllis 53

unconscious: organization 44–45; somatic
   memory 59
undifferentiation 113
United States (US): psychoanalysis
   expanded in 3–6; "The Golden Age" of
   psychoanalysis 6; WWII immigration of
   European analysts to 6–10
unity 48–49n2; "dual unity" 115; of the
   ego 116; mother-child unity 81, 87;
   "mother-infant unity" 54–56, 59–60, 62, 81;
   natural environment as source of 140–141;
   "original unity" 77, 82, 91; structureless 117
unthought new 99–100

Valery, Paul 12
Vandevelde, P. 75

Waelder-Hall, Jenny 13
waning of the Oedipal complex 137
Weber, Max 111
Western New England Psychoanalytic
   Institute 27–31
Wexler, Henry 27–28
White, T. H. 145, 148, 156; *The Goshawk* 156;
   The Once and Future King 148; *The Sword in
   the Stone* 148
Whitebook, J. 53, 61
Windholz, Emanuel 29
Winnicott, D. W. 10, 170–182; on holding
   178–180; "living creatively" 118; "primary
   creativity" 118; primary maternal

preoccupation 147–148; *Sublimation Monograph* 177; "The Use of the Object" 10–11n4; third area of potential space 175
words as lived experience 99
The Work of Hans Loewald: Introduction and Commentary (Loewald) 53, 188
World War I 66, 72, 184

World War II 6, 67, 112, 157; immigration of European analysts to the U.S. 6–10

The Year of Magical Thinking (Didion) 152
Yovel, Yirmiyahu 109

Zagzebski, Linda 44, 49n16; *Exemplarist Moral Theory* 49n16

For Product Safety Concerns and Information please contact our EU
representative GPSR@taylorandfrancis.com
Taylor & Francis Verlag GmbH, Kaufingerstraße 24, 80331 München, Germany

www.ingramcontent.com/pod-product-compliance
Lightning Source LLC
Chambersburg PA
CBHW080132270326
41926CB00021B/4453